THE CRAWFORD COUNTY HISTORICAL SOCIETY

Takes Great Pride in Announcing the Publication of

"IN FRENCH CREEK VALLEY"

By JOHN EARLE REYNOLDS

❖

A dramatic and fascinating account of people and events in the years when Meadville was young. Contains many heretofore unpublished letters, much original material. The story of a community told by the third generation member of a family long important locally.

JOHN EARLE REYNOLDS

John Earle Reynolds is the son of William Reynolds (1820-1911), and the grandson of John Reynolds (1782-1871). The first John Reynolds came to Meadville in 1805 as a student in the Meadville Academy, later became a lawyer and was much interested in business and cultural development of this region.

William Reynolds was born in Meadville in 1820. He was graduated from Allegheny College in 1837, studied law and was admitted to the Bar in 1841. He was an important figure in the development of transportation, beginning with the formation of the Plank Road companies, later became active in the railroad field and was instrumental in bringing the first railroad to Meadville.

William Reynolds was intensely interested in anything having to do with Meadville history and began the collection of documents, old account books, maps, minutes of meetings and letters that has been continued by his son, John Earle Reynolds.

John Earle Reynolds, author of "IN FRENCH CREEK VALLEY," was graduated from Harvard University in 1888, and became a member of the Crawford County Bar. He has been mayor of Meadville three terms, president of the Merchants National Bank and Trust Company since 1916, and is an officer and director of many companies.

Mr. Reynolds' collection of source material on French Creek and Meadville is the finest in the world. Many of the documents and letters reproduced in his book are being printed for the first time.

"IN FRENCH CREEK VALLEY"

✢

George Washington traversing French Creek Valley from Venango on the Allegheny to the French fort at Lac Le Boeuf in 1753 and bearing important documents from Governor Dinwiddie of Virginia to the fort commandant, estimated the distance at 130 miles. Actually it is a little less than one hundred by the meanderings of the stream, fifty-four by highway, yet so important was the journey that one English historian has stated that young George Washington's mission altered the course of three empires and resulted in the formation of the United States.

It is of the development of this region that John Earle Reynolds writes in his long awaited book, "IN FRENCH CREEK VALLEY," now being published by the Crawford County Historical Society.

Fascinating and dramatic is the story of French Creek Valley. The present book gives many new facts culled from letters and diaries in the Reynolds' Collection, started by Mr. Reynolds' family before 1820 and considered today the finest collection of original material on French Creek.

Mr. Reynolds' authoritative, scholarly and intensely readable narrative takes one from the earliest days down to the period just before the Civil War. Its pages are filled with human interest anecdotes about people and events of the times when Meadville and the valley were young.

He tells of the flatboat or ark, "Ann Eliza," loaded and starting to the Ohio but 48 hours after her timbers had been growing trees along the banks of French Creek. He tells of the duel fought by Roger Alden and Alexander Foster, the daily life of the people, their schools and churches.

"IN FRENCH CREEK VALLEY" is the most important book about this region ever to be published. The Crawford County Historical Society is proud to have been selected as the publisher and to present to the public this pre-publication prospectus.

NOTE: John Earle Reynolds has assigned all profits to the Crawford County Historical Society.

"IN FRENCH CREEK VALLEY"

By JOHN EARLE REYNOLDS

❖

DETAILED TABLE OF CONTENTS

CHAPTER I—WASHINGTON'S JOURNEY, 1753—Washington's own story, Christopher Gist's observations—Venango—delays at Le Boeuf—results

CHAPTER II—A FRENCH HIGHWAY — early explorers — French forts — Waterford portage—Ft. Machault—English take over country

CHAPTER III—MEAD'S SETTLEMENT—David Mead's story—Indian troubles —Block house and stockade at Meadville—Troops at Venango and Waterford

CHAPTER IV—BUILDING A HOME—the first John Reynolds' account of pioneer life—Indians—wild animals—snakes—insects

CHAPTER V—RIVERS AND ROADS—the Venango Trail—French Creek an artery of transportation—difficulties—improvements

CHAPTER VI—"SENECA OIL."— Mound builders—Oil pits—oil as medicine—before the days of drilling—first petroleum to Europe

CHAPTER VII—FARM LIFE—the first John Reynolds' reminiscences of early days—tools and utensils—furniture and clothing

CHAPTER VIII—EARLY PROMOTION—Society for the Encouragement of Manufacture and Arts—some early businesses—improvement of stock

CHAPTER IX—"ANN ELIZA" AND TRADESMEN—boat building—navigation —stores—mills and manufacturers

CHAPTER X—HOLLAND LAND COMPANY—method of acquiring land— aims —"Prevention" clause—subsequent law-suits—Harm Jan Huidekoper

CHAPTER XI—ENTERPRISE BEGINS—influx of settlers—town surveyed— Meadville Academy—first newspaper—first bank

CHAPTER XII—LOCAL TALENT—music—culture—libraries—societies—the Thespians—dances

CHAPTER XIII—TIMOTHY ALDEN'S DREAM—founding of Allegheny College—Bentley Hall celebration—excellent library

THE DIAMOND IN 1840— Into Meadville about 1840 came Sherman Day, itinerant artist, author and historian. While here he secured stories from old residents, sold subscriptions to his forthcoming book. From the present site of the Library he sketched the Diamond, cut it in wood and published it in his "Historical Collections of Pennsylvania". This rare picture is reprinted in "In French Creek Valley".

"IN FRENCH CREEK VALLEY" — Continued

❖

CHAPTER XIV—THE ALLEGHENY MAGAZINE—Alden's literary publication—type of material—excerpts—failure

CHAPTER XV—WATER STREET—homes and businesses—taverns and inns—people and personalities—schools

CHAPTER XVI—VILLAGE LIFE—character of population—artisans—food—daily habits—social and civic life

CHAPTER XVII—FAMOUS VISITORS—Washington, Audubon—LaFayette—Zachery Taylor—James Buchanan

CHAPTER XVIII—TROOPS AND TRUMPETS—militia—the War of 1812—the Arsenal—Muster Day

CHAPTER XIX—POLITICAL BATTLES—the Aaron Burr conspiracy—Fourth of July Celebrations—party spirit—high feeling at the mobilization camp

CHAPTER XX—RELIGIOUS BUILDING—church services—the Brick Church—denominational buildings

CHAPTER XXI—GENERAL MEAD IN RETROSPECT—obituary in Alleghany Magazine, September, 1816—John Reynolds' recollections

CHAPTER XXII—DAVID DICK AN INVENTOR—careful student—the "hot air engine," forerunner of internal combustion motor—anti-friction press

CHAPTER XXIII—TURNPIKES AND TOLL GATES—early roads—the "plank road mania"

CHAPTER XXIV—CANAL DAYS — breaking ground for the canal — the French Creek feeder—canal and slack water navigation

CHAPTER XXI—THE FIRST STERN WHEELER—the Allegheny ascends the river to Franklin—the "Fulton of the West"

CHAPTER XXVI—THE ATLANTIC AND GREAT WESTERN — obstacles and difficulties—financing in Civil War years

CHAPTER XXVII—WASHINGTON'S LETTER—an unpublished letter to General James Ewing, December 1776—found in Meadville 161 years later—its travels

THE WASHINGTON LETTER

✧

Discovered last August in an old account book that had been in the possession of the Reynolds family for over 130 years, a letter from General George Washington to General James Ewing dated December 14, 1776, is published for the first time in "IN FRENCH CREEK VALLEY."

The letter had never been delivered. It contains orders to ascertain the disposition of the British forces and to learn if they were building ships. Written a few days before the Trenton campaign the letter throws new light on General Washington's courage in proceeding with less than complete information.

The document is historically priceless.

The story of the letter's coming to Meadville is the attempt of a son of Governor Thomas Mifflin to clear his father's name from charges of aiding the British. In an effort to locate a certain McGill, living near Meadville, the son came here and took desk space in the office of the first John Reynolds. In his haircloth trunk he had several account books, letters and other documents.

Shortly after young Mifflin's arrival here he died. It is not known whether he was able to contact McGill. John Reynolds, the first, acted as executor, stored the papers and books which were never claimed.

The story of the letter received amazing confirmation less than three weeks after it had been discovered when a gentleman named Nageotte told of a reported "lost" Washington letter. He was able to describe how a sudden British raid had prevented its delivery and how it was believed to have come into the hands of the Mifflins.

Historians consider it one of the most important bits of Washingtoniana to be unearthed in recent years.

GENERAL SUMMARY

❖

"IN FRENCH CREEK VALLEY" will have more than 450 pages and approximately 100 illustrations, many never before published. The regular first edition (pre-publication price $2.50) is bound in cloth. A de luxe edition limited to 200 copies numbered and autographed by the author, bound in leather with gold titles, is $12.50.

Every home in Meadville should have a copy of Mr. Reynolds' book. It will be an interesting and unusual gift for former residents of Crawford County and the French Creek Valley. Delightfully written, replete with anecdote and containing much information never before published, it is acclaimed by those who have read it in manuscript as the most important book ever to be published about this region.

The first edition will not be large and reservation orders will be filled in the order of their arrival.

Among the 100 illustrations are:

Map of French Creek

Plan of Forts Machault and Venango

Trail from Fort Pitt to Presque Isle

Survey of Mead Lands, 1794

General David Mead's House, Block House and Mill, unpublished sketch

Diagram of Mead's Stockade and State Block House

Sketch of Block House

French Road from LeBoeuf to Presque Isle

Dining Room in McHenry House

Harm Jan Huidekoper

Office of the Holland Land Company, Meadville

Captain Richard Patch's tavern. 1798

North Western Bank of Pennsylvania

Pomona Hall

Water Street and its Buildings, Meadville, about 1820

Augustus Colson's Store where Audubon had a studio

John Reynolds' House, Water Street

Pieter Huidekoper, unpublished portrait by Audubon, 1824

The Arsenal, Meadville

General John Dick

The Brick Church, 1820

David Dick's Anti-Friction Press

Gibson's Tavern

Plank Road, Water Street, Meadville

Locks and Slackwater Canal, crossed by the Aquaduct of the Beaver and Erie Canal

❖

CRAWFORD COUNTY HISTORICAL SOCIETY
P. O. BOX 386, MEADVILLE, PENNSYLVANIA

IN FRENCH CREEK VALLEY

WASHINGTON AT THE AGE OF TWENTY-FIVE

In French Creek Valley

John Earle Reynolds

HERITAGE BOOKS
2015

HERITAGE BOOKS
AN IMPRINT OF HERITAGE BOOKS, INC.

Books, CDs, and more—Worldwide

For our listing of thousands of titles see our website
at
www.HeritageBooks.com

A Facsimile Reprint
Published 2015 by
HERITAGE BOOKS, INC.
Publishing Division
5810 Ruatan Street
Berwyn Heights, Md. 20740

Copyright © 1938 John Earle Reynolds

Originally printed by
The Tribune Publishing Company
The Crawford County Historical Society
Meadville, Pennsylvania
1938

— Publisher's Notice —
In reprints such as this, it is often not possible to remove blemishes from the original. We feel the contents of this book warrant its reissue despite these blemishes and hope you will agree and read it with pleasure.

International Standard Book Numbers
Paperbound: 978-0-7884-1322-3
Clothbound: 978-0-7884-6178-1

To the Pioneers in French Creek Valley
This Book Is Dedicated.

CONTENTS

Chapter		Page
I	Washington's Journey, 1753	5
II	A French Highway	17
III	Mead's Settlement	31
IV	Building A Home	42
V	Rivers and Roads	53
VI	"Seneca Oil"	68
VII	Farm Life	76
VIII	Early Promotion	83
IX	"Ann Eliza" and Tradesmen	91
X	Holland Land Company	104
XI	Enterprises Begin	115
XII	Local Talent	129
XIII	Timothy Alden's Dream	139
XIV	The Alleghany Magazine	154
XV	Water Street	167
XVI	Village Life	184
XVII	Famous Visitors	195
XVIII	Troops and Trumpets	208
XIX	Political Battles	225
XX	Religious Building	235
XXI	General David Mead in Retrospect	244
XXII	David Dick, Inventor	251
XXIII	Turnpikes and Toll Gates	261
XXIV	Canal Days	271
XXV	The First Stern-Wheeler	286
XXVI	A Railroad At Last	297
XXVII	An Historic Letter	310
	Appendix	317
	Bibliography	345
	Index	349

ERRATA AND ADDENDA

Throughout, "stuff (q.v.)" should read "stuff (q.v., Vol. 1)".

Page 2 at "artificer" should read " ."dexterous or artful fellow"; "

Page 3 at "bail" should read ".. gain freedom pending "

Page 4 at "bearing tree" should read ".. line tree monument, not usually a corner..."

Page 7 at "boatswain, (etc)"; both clauses should read ". that enlisted member of a ship's company..."

Page 9 at "bung" should read "...after the barrels were drained "

Page 12 at "chew the fat" should read ". suet, just as we now chew ."

Page 14 at "codpiece" should read "...Navy enlisted dress..."

Page 18; The entry "cracker, corn cracker" is duplicated

Page 19 at "cupplate" should read "poured into a larger ."

Page 38 at "handguns" should read " ..cap and ball (q.v , Vol. 1) .."

Page 52 at "molasses, (etc)." should read ". and used beet sugar, ."

Page 56 at "out-lier, out lier" should read ". .early (perhaps), one whose home .." Also, "Palatinate, (etc)" should read ". .county, city, or territory which served..."

Page 57; The ship depicted was *Mauretania* (sister ship of *Lusitania*) which held the trans-Atlantic speed record for several years

Page 80; The entry "trick, turn(ing) tricks" is duplicated.

Page 87; The caption should read "Map of Ohio showing the several surveys from which most descriptions of land in *Ranges*, *Townships*, and *Sections* were derived "

Page 88; The caption should read "Map of early reservations of Ohio land by Congress, for bounty and settlement purposes; by some states for similar purposes; and by the *Ohio Company* for profit "

Page 89; The caption should read "A township is made up of 36 sections "

LIST OF ILLUSTRATIONS

	Page
Washington at the Age of Twenty-five From a miniature by J. DeMere	Frontispiece
Map of French Creek Land advertisement, 1848	3
French and English Forts at Venango, Pennsylvania Plan showing relative positions	7
Map of Washington's Journey, 1753 His route through French Creek Valley. Courtesy of the Honorable D. M. Larrabee	10
DeLery Map of the Ohio River, 1753 Engraved by Sieur de Lery, the Younger. Drawn by Sieur de Mandeville. Courtesy of Frontier Forts and Trails Survey, Pennsylvania Historical Commission	18
Father Bonnecamps Map, 1749, MS. de Celoron Expedition	20
Map at the time of English Occupation, 1760-1763 Courtesy of Frontier Forts and Trails Survey, Pennsylvania Historical Commission	28
Survey of Mead Lands, 1794	31
David Mead's House, Block House, and Mill From William Reynolds sketch	32
Robert Fitz Randolph, Pioneer Courtesy of Mrs. Jacob Heckman	32
Cornelius Van Horn, Pioneer	33
Diagram of David Mead Stockade and State Block House Courtesy of Mrs. Winthrop H. Perry	35
Block House Drawn by W. D. Craig	40
John Reynolds From portrait	42
French Road, between Le Boeuf and Presque Isle Courtesy of Frontier Forts and Trails Survey, Pennsylvania Historical Commission	54

Andrew Ellicott, Astronomer and Surveyor 55
    From crayon portrait
William Reynolds 68
Indian Pits 70
    From William Reynolds sketch
Indian Mound 71
    From William Reynolds sketch
Port of Meadville 95
    From bank note of the North Western Bank of Pennsylvania
First Bridge over French Creek, 1810 96
    From painting by A. G. Richmond, Esq., from William Reynolds sketch
Major Roger Alden.. 108
    Courtesy of Allegheny College
Harm Jan Huidekoper 108
    Courtesy of Mrs. Winthrop H. Perry
Roger Alden House............................ . 110
    From William Reynolds sketch
Office of the Holland Land Company, Water Street . .. 112
    From daguerreotype, courtesy of Mrs. Winthrop H. Perry
Perkins House 118
Subscription List for the Meadville Academy, 1804. 118
Thomas Atkinson, Editor 119
Richard Patch Tavern, 1798 120
    From portrait
Dr. Thomas Rustin Kennedy 121
North Western Bank of Pennsylvania 126
    From William Reynolds sketch
Judge Jesse Moore 132
    From portrait
Timothy Alden 140
    Courtesy of Allegheny College
Bentley Hall, Allegheny College 141
    Courtesy of Kurt C. Glaubach
Judge Henry Baldwin 160
    From portrait painted by James R. Lambdin
Judge Henry Shippen 162
    Courtesy of Mrs. Henry P. Kidder
Judge Alexander Addison.... 162

Water Street, Meadville, and its Buildings	168
From William Reynolds sketches	
Pomona Hall, Residence of H. J. Huidekoper.... ...	184
From daguerreotype, courtesy of Mrs. Winthrop H. Perry	
First Brick House, Meadville. Later the residence of A. C. Huidekoper	185
John Reynolds House, Water Street	193
From William Reynolds sketch	
Pieter Huidekoper	196
From Audubon portrait, courtesy of Mrs. Winthrop H. Perry	
Lafayette Signature	205
Courtesy of Allegheny College	
General John Dick....................	216
From portrait	
The Arsenal	216
Drawn by W. D. Craig, from William Reynolds sketch	
The Diamond, Meadville, 1840	222
From wood cut by Sherman Day	
Squire Samuel Lord	231
The Brick Church, Meadville, 1820	237
From William Reynolds sketch	
David Mead House	246
Courtesy of Miss Elizabeth Byllesby	
Seal of Meadville	250
David Dick	252
D. Dick's Anti-Friction Press	255
Medal Awarded D. Dick, London..	258
Courtesy of Mrs. Joseph McK. Speer	
Plank Road, Water Street, Meadville, 1856............	268
From daguerreotype	
Map of Canal Feeder, Meadville.... 272	272
Beaver and Erie Canal Aqueduct and Slackwater Locks	282
North Street Bridge over Canal, Meadville	283
Canal Measurements	284
From William Reynolds Diagram	
Canal Basin, Market Street, Meadville	284

Atlantic & Great Western Railway Depot, Meadville..... 306
    From William Reynolds sketch
McHenry House, Meadville 307
McHenry House Dining Room 308
    From lithograph
Washington Letter 314

PREFACE

In these pages no attempt has been made to write a formal history, but rather to sketch informally the story of the development of French Creek Valley. Incidents in the early exploration of northwestern Pennsylvania and in the settlement of the Valley have been retold, in so far as it was possible, in the words of those who experienced them.

Encouragement received from the late Harry Bosler, use of the written records of John and William Reynolds, manuscrips, maps, and pictures made available by many persons—all are gratefully acknowledged. Valuable suggestions were made by Dr. Russell J. Ferguson of the University of Pittsburgh; Miss Edith Rowley of Reis Library, Allegheny College, Miss Helen Dermott of the Meadville Public Library, and Miss Sara L. Miller of the Crawford County Historical Society, gave generously of their time to assist in research. To these and the following people the author proffers his sincere gratitude: Mrs. Winthrop H. Perry, for maps, portraits, manuscripts, and letters; the Honorable D. M. Larrabee, for his *Washington Journal*; A. G. Richmond, Esq., and Mr. W. D. Craig, for original pictures; Mr. William F. Mann and Mr. Donald H. Kent, of the Frontier Forts and Trails Survey of the Pennsylvania Historical Commission, for manuscripts, maps, and photographs; and

Mr. Kurt C. Glaubach, photographer, for expert services. And without the untiring and faithful assistance of Mr. James Ray Shryock in collecting data and handling details of printing, this story of French Creek Valley could never have been published.

The tale is written, and it is presented to the friends of French Creek Valley for whatever enjoyment they and their children may find in reading it, now and in the years to come.

J. E. R.

February 22, 1938.

IN FRENCH CREEK VALLEY
by
JOHN EARLE REYNOLDS

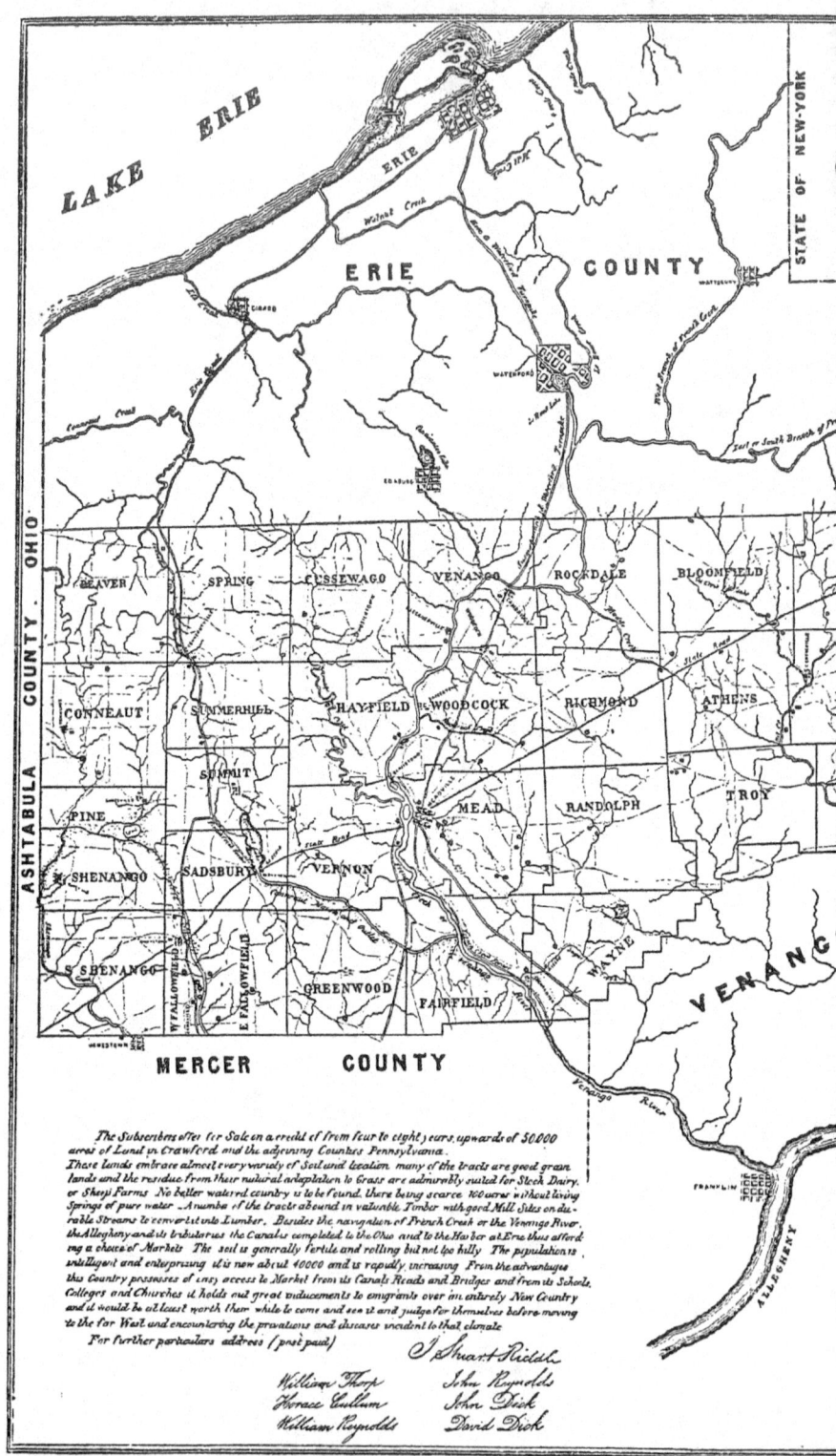

IN NORTHWESTERN PENNSYLVANIA

French Creek is a beautiful, transparent, rapid stream. For many miles from its confluence with the Alleghany, or the Hoheyu of the aborigines, it is little less, than one hundred feet, in width. Its ramifications are very numerous and overspread a large extent of territory abounding in good land and blessed with a salubrious climate. From the head of one of its principal forks, which is within the limits of the state of New York, to its termination, its general course, though, in some parts, extremely crooked, is not greatly different from that of a semi-circle. At certain seasons, its waters are navigable for boats, carrying 20 tons, to Waterford, fourteen miles from the borough of Erie; yet, for a few weeks, in the summer, it is, usually, impassable by any craft larger, than a canoe. The three considerable branches, commonly called the Forks, which unite, a few miles below Waterford, are susceptible of boat navigation. Washington in his Journal, calls Le Bœuf Creek the western fork, which is correct; but, besides this, there are three others, and these are now particularly designated by that name. In addition to many small streams, in all directions, proceeding northerly from the mouth of French Creek, its most noted contributory waters, all of which have mill privileges and the most of which are furnished with sawmills and gristmills, are Big Sugar Creek, Deer Creek, Little Sugar Creek, the outlet of Konneyaut, Kossewaugo, Woodcock, the outlet of Konneautte, Muddy Creek, and Le Bœuf Creek, on the banks of which, about a hundred perches above a small lake, Waterford is built, three or four miles above its union with French Creek. The most of these, as well as the Forks, before mentioned, have their rise in lakes, which are of different dimensions, but not exceeding four or five miles in length. Some of the rivulets, which are to find their way, along the channel of French Creek and on, to the gulf of Mexico, proceed from the lofty swell of land in the vicinity of lake Erie, and wind in such a manner as to interlock others, which descend into the great lake in their course for the gulf of Saint Lawrence.

From Franklin to Waterford, to pursue the publick road, the distance is fifty two miles; yet, to measure the meanders of French Creek and Le Bœuf, to the last named village, it is nearly one hundred miles. Washington thought it one hundred and thirty, at the time of his perilous descent.

     Timothy Alden,
     ABORIGINAL, NUM. VIIII,
     THE ALLEGHANY MAGAZINE,
     March, MDCCCXVII, 218.

CHAPTER I

WASHINGTON'S JOURNEY, 1753

Venango!

Those lights ahead were a cheering sight after a hard day's travel, for twilight came early in western Pennsylvania that fourth day of December in 1753—at last fire to dry rain-soaked clothes, hot food to warm tired bodies of twelve weary men. Those on horseback welcomed the thought of shelter for the night, as did the men who had walked twenty-two miles from Great Beaver Creek over sodden ground. Down one more steep hill and those glimmering lights below would mark the end of their nineteenth day on the northward journey through the wilderness. A few cabins where La Riviere aux Boeufs flowed into La Belle Riviere beneath heavily wooded mountainsides—that was Venango.[1]

In this forlorn settlement the four Indian escorts might find friends, but what reception would the white men have? Would the leader, who wore the uniform of a major of the Virginia Militia, a tall, wiry young man, be permitted to proceed with the message he carried to the fort in the north? Other men had failed in attempting to carry the demands of Virginia's Governor to the French Commandant. This fort was built in the

[1] Franklin, Venango County.

wild country west of the mountains, claimed as part of the Virginia Grant. With him on this mission, acting as companion and guide, was a man somewhat older, a fresh, rugged frontiersman, with natural dignity and experience.

That evening, Major George Washington, the leader, entered in his diary—[1]

arrived at Venango an old Indian Town at the mouth of French Creek and the Ohio.

So the name French Creek was recorded in history, while the stream flowed peacefully on its crooked way through the great forest which nature has spread over its lovely valley. This stream known to the Indians as In-nun-gah and Venango[2] was to the French La Riviere aux Boeufs. Abundance of buffaloes had ranged over the land which it drained; then too, one of its branches found its source in the little Lac La Boeufs just south of the divide separating the waters of the Ohio River from those of Lake Erie. It was at the fort built on the shore of this lake that Washington expected to meet the French Commandant.

Starting on this mission, Major Washington could little realize that it was the first incident in a series of events that would result in changing the map of the

---

[1] Don Marshall Larrabee, *The Journals of George Washington and His Guide, Christopher Gist, on the Mission to the French at Fort Le Boeuf in 1753* (1929), 30-32.

[2] See Appendix, 326—Aboriginal Num. VIIII, *Alleghany Magazine*.

world. It was in French Creek Valley that the historic stage was set for the drama which altered the destinies of three empires.

As the travelers entered Venango, they found the *fleur de lis* of France waving over the cabin of the Commandant, Jean Couer. He was a well-known frontier charac-

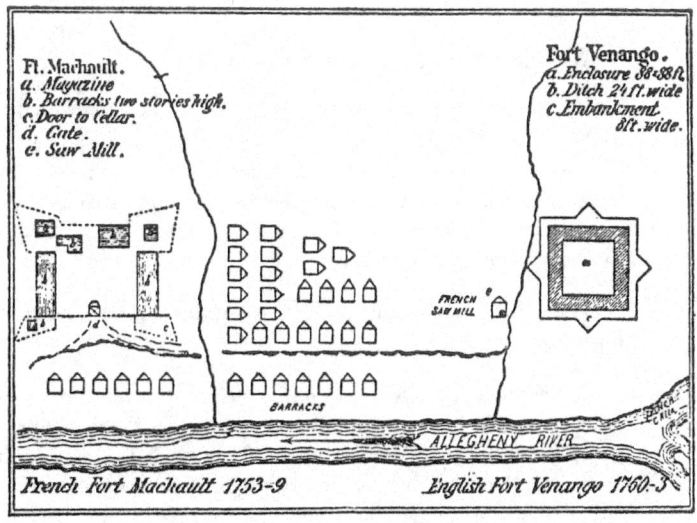

PLANS OF THE FRENCH AND ENGLISH FORTS.

ter, as was his father before him. Because of his knowledge of the country and his influence with the Indians, Jean Couer had been selected four years before by Celoron as the chief guide and interpreter for his expedition down the Ohio. When Celoron and his party arrived at Venango, they found an English trader, John Frazier, in a cabin used as a trading post. That Frazier was ordered out and his property confiscated is evidenced by a petition signed by him in 1763 and presented to the Pennsylvania Assembly asking for damages for losses sustained during the French and Indian War, 1749-1758, amounting to 2585 pounds, 12 shillings.[1]

Washington wrote of Jean Couer:

He invited us to sup with them, and treated us with the greatest complaisance.

The wine, as they dosed themselves pretty plentifully with it, soon banished the restraint which at first appeared in their conversation, and gave a license to their tongues to reveal their sentiments more freely.

The diary of Washington's companion, Christopher Gist, tells of the next day:

Wednesday, 5th. Rain all day. Our Indians were in council with the Delawares, who lived under the French colors, and ordered them to deliver up to the French the belt, with marks of the four towns, according to the desire of King Shingiss. . . So our Indians could not prevail with them to deliver their belt; but the Half-King did deliver his belt, as he had determined. Joncaire did everything he could to prevail on our Indians to stay behind us, and I took all care to have them along with us.

---

[1] George Croghan, Papers. Four items, including a map of Croghan's holdings in the vicinity of Pittsburgh in 1797. In the John E. Reynolds Collection, Meadville.

Washington reported:

6th. The half king came to my tent, quite sober, and insisted very much that I should stay and hear what he had to say to the French. . . . As I was desirous of knowing the issue of this, I agreed to stay; but sent our horses a little way up French Creek to raft over and encamp; which I knew would make it near night.

About ten o'clock, they met in council. The king spoke much the same as he had before done to the general, and offered the French speech belt which had before been demanded, with marks of four towns on it, which Monsieur Joncaire refused to receive, but desired him to carry it to the fort to the commander.

7th. Monsieur La Force, Commissary of the French stores, and three other soldiers, came over to accompany us up. We found it extremely difficult to get the Indians off to-day, as every stratagem had been used to prevent their going up with me. I had last night left John Davidson (the Indian interpreter) whom I brought with me from town, and strictly charged him not be out of their company, as I could not get them over to my tent; for they had some business with Kustologa, chiefly to know why he did not deliver up the French speech belt which he had in keeping: but I was obliged to send Mr. Gist over to-day to fetch them, which he did with great persuasion.

At twelve o'clock, we set out for the fort, and were prevented from arriving there until the eleventh by excessive rains, snows, and bad traveling through many mires and swamps; these we were obliged to pass to avoid the creek, which was impossable, either by fording or rafting, the water was so high and rapid.

We passed over much good land since we left Venango, and through several extensive and very rich meadows, one of which, I believe, was nearly four miles in length, and considerably wide in some places.

On this date, Gist wrote:

All encamped at Sugar Creek, five miles from Venango. The creek being very high, we were obliged to carry all our baggage over on trees, and swim our horses. The major and I went first over, with our boots on.

Saturday, 8th. We set out and traveled twenty-five miles to Cussewago, an old Indian town.[1]

Sunday, 9th. We set out, left one of our horses here that could travel no further. This day we traveled to the big crossing,[2] about fifteen miles, and encamped. Our Indians went out to look out logs to make a raft; but as the water was high, and there were other creeks to cross, we concluded to keep up this side the creek.

Monday, 10th. Set out, traveled about eight miles, and encamped. Our Indians killed a bear. Here we had a creek to cross, very deep; we got over on a tree, and got our goods over.

Tuesday, 11th. We set out, traveled about fifteen miles to the French fort, the sun being set. Our interpreter gave the commandant notice of our being over the creek; upon which he sent several officers to conduct us to the fort, and they received us with a great deal of complaisance.

Washington told of his reception at Fort Le Boeufs:

12th. I prepared early to wait upon the commander and

---

[1] Meadville—Chosen by Mead for his settlement because of the "rich meadows" mentioned by Washington.

[2] Gist probably used the term "big crossing" as it was used by early travelers to mark the crossing of a stream by large herds of buffaloes. The location of this place is in doubt, but undoubtedly it was between the Broadford Bridge and the first rapids below the "dead water" in French Creek, some distance north of the present village of Venango.

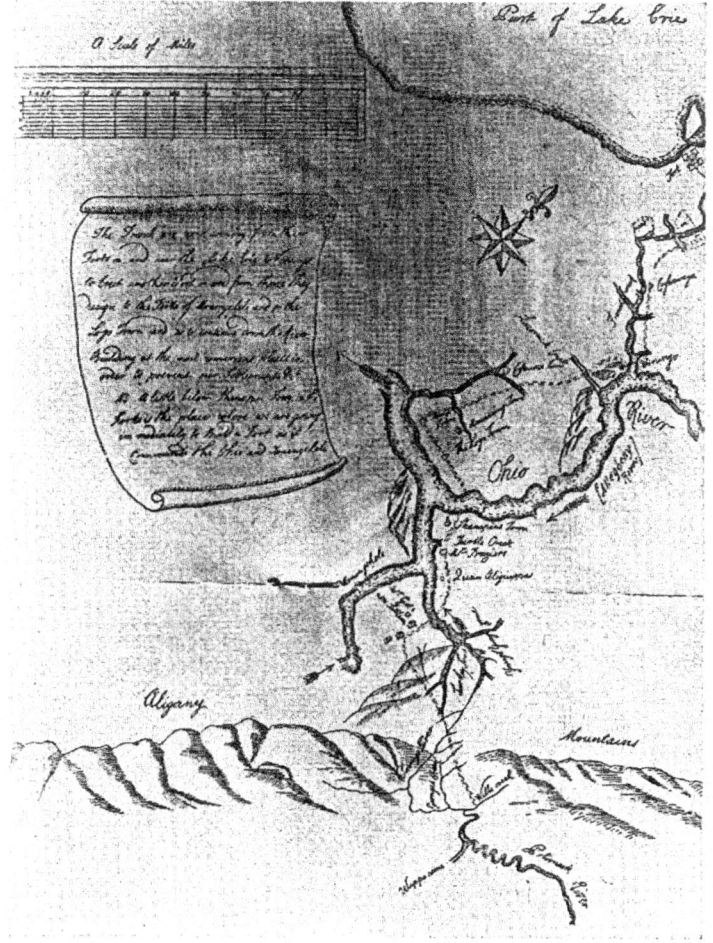

West Pennsylvania and Virginia, 1753. Showing Washington's route to Fort Le Boeuf. Original in the British Museum, London, England.

was received, and conducted to him by the second officer in command. I acquainted him with my business and offered my commission and letter: both of which he desired me to keep until the arrival of Monsieur Reparti, captain at the next fort, who was sent for and expected every hour.

This commander is a knight of the military order of St. Louis, and named Legardeur de St. Pierre. He is an elderly gentleman, and has much the air of a soldier. He was sent over to take the command, immediately upon the death of the late general, and arrived here about seven days before me.

At two o'clock, the gentleman who was sent for arrived, when I offered the letter &c. again, which they received,[1] and adjourned into a private apartment for the captain to translate, who understood a little English. After he had done it, the commander desired I would walk in and bring my interpreter to peruse and correct it; which I did.

13th. The chief officers retired to hold a council of war,

---

[1] Voyage to Canada, MS initialed "J. B. C." (Probably by M. Bonnefons who served under Captain Pouchot.)

1753. In November a messenger arrived in Quebec to the Governor-General sent by Captain St. Pierre commander at the fort of Presqu' Isle to say that he had had a visit from an English Officer bringing a summons with an injunction to the French to evacuate the fort and all neutral ground which was to be used only for commerce with the Indians. He had answered that he was on French territory and could not retire without orders from his general to whom he would transmit the news, also, that he had been extremely polite to the English Officer before sending him away.

Governor Duquesne learning that this was an order from the Governor of Virginia named (Dinwiddie). He was further informed that preparations were being made in English colonies to take the French under the pretext of protecting the rights of the Indians. The pretext was false as the French were friendly with the Indians, under the circumstances wishing to put themselves in a position to be able to meet force with force. In case of an attack they determined to send a strong detachment of troops and militia not only to Presqu'Isle but on the Belle and Ohio Rivers where they had learned that the Indians had established a fort.

Consequently they drew up a plan for opening the coming campaign.

which gave me an opportunity of taking the dimensions of the fort, and making what observations I could. . .

14th. As the snow increased very fast, and our horses daily became weaker, I sent them off unloaded, under the care of Barnaby Currin and two others, to make all convenient dispatch to Venango, and there to wait our arrival, if there was a prospect of the river's freezing; if not, then to continue down to Shanapin's town, at the forks of Ohio, and there to wait until we came to cross the Alleghany; intending myself to go down by water, as I had the offer of a canoe or two.

As I found many plots concerted to retard the Indians' business, and prevent their returning with me, I endeavored all that lay in my power to frustrate their schemes, and hurried them on to execute their intended design. . .

This evening, I received an answer to his honour the governor's letter, from the commandant.

15th. The commandant ordered a plentiful store of liquor, provision, &c. to be put on board our canoes, and appeared to be extremely complaisant, though he was exerting every artifice which he could invent to set our Indians at variance with us, to prevent their going until after our departure: presents, rewards, and everything which could be suggested by him or his officers. I can not say that ever in my life I suffered so much anxiety as I did in this affair. I saw that every stratagem, which the most fruitful brain could invent, was practiced to win the half king to their interest; and that leaving him there was giving them the opportunity they aimed at. I went to the half king and pressed him in the strongest terms to go; he told me that the commandant would not discharge him until the morning. I then went to the commandant, and desired him to do their business, and complained of ill treatment; for keeping them, as they were part of my company, was detaining me. This he promised not to do but to forward my journey as much as he could. He protested he did not keep them, but was ignorant of the cause of their stay; though I soon found it out. He had promised them a present of guns, &c. if they would wait until the morning. As I was very much pressed by the Indians to wait this day for them, I consented, on a promise that nothing should hinder them in the morning.

16th. The French were not slack in their inventions to keep the Indians this day also. But as they were obliged, according to promise, to give the present, they then endeavored to try the power of liquor, which I doubt not would have prevailed at any other time than this; but I urged and insisted with the king so closely upon his word, that he refrained, and set off with us as he had engaged.

We had a tedious and very fatiguing passage down the creek. Several times we had like to have been staved against the rocks; and many times were obliged all hands to get out and remain in the water half an hour or more, getting over the shoals. At one place, the ice had lodged, and made it impassable by water; we were, therefore, obliged to carry our canoe across the neck of land, a quarter of a mile over. We did not reach Venango until the 22d, where we met with our horses.

This creek is extremely crooked. I dare say the distance between the fort and Venango, can not be less than one hundred and thirty miles to follow the meanders.

Gist tells of the return trip to Venango in the diary[1] he left.

Sunday, 16th. We set out by water about sixteen miles, and encamped. Our Indians went before us, passed the little lake, and we did not come up with them that night.

Monday, 17th. We set out, came to our Indians' camp.

---
[1] Larrabee, *Fort Le Boeuf*, 39-40.

They were out hunting; they killed three bears. We stayed this day and

Tuesday, 18th. One of our Indians did not come to camp. So we finding the waters lower very fast, were obliged to go and leave our Indians.

Wednesday, 19th. We set out about seven or eight miles, and encamped, and the next day

Thursday, 20th. About twenty miles, where we were stopped by ice, and worked until night.

Friday, 21st. The ice was so hard we could not break our way through, but were obliged to haul our vessels across a point of land and put them in the creek again. The Indians and three French canoes overtook us here, and the people of one French canoe that was lost, with her cargo of powder and lead. This night we encamped about twenty miles above Venango.

Saturday, 22nd. Set out. The creek began to be very low, and we were forced to get out, to keep our canoe from oversetting, several times; the water freezing to our clothes; and we had the pleasure of seeing the French overset, and the brandy and wine floating in the creek, and run by them, and left them to shift for themselves. Came to Venango, and met with our people and horses.

Venturing forth into unknown wilderness the only inhabitants of which were none too friendly Indians, Washington for help and guidance took with him Christopher Gist, Barnaby Currin and John M'Quire, who lived by trading with the Indians, Henry Stewart and William Jenkins as servants, John Davidson, to act as interpreter with the French, and Jacob Van Braam, as Indian interpreter. Four Indian sachems for safe conduct through hostile territory were Tanacharisson, of whom he spoke as the Half King, White Thunder, Kakakee and Guiasuta The Hunter. Captain La Force and three French soldiers joined him at Venango without invitation.

Seldom those who labor to make such an undertaking possible realize that what they contribute toward its accomplishment is more than part of a day's occupation—in this, they aided in making history.

This is the story of the Washington expedition, that part of it which found action in French Creek Valley. The letter which Governor Dinwiddie gave Washington to deliver to the French Commandant at Fort Le Boeuf "complained[1] of the intrusion of French forces into the Ohio country, erecting forts and making settlements in the western parts of the colony of Virginia" and "inquired[1] by whose authority and instructions the French Commander-General had marched this force from Canada, and made this invasion." In reply the Chevalier de St. Pierre said he would transmit the letter to his general: "As to the summons[1] you send me to retire, I do not think myself obliged to obey it." To Major Washington, then a young man of twenty-one years, was entrusted the safe delivery of this letter and the return of the French answer. This he accomplished, traveling through practically unknown territory covered with virgin forest, the hunting ground of hostile Indians, in

[1] Larrabee, *Fort Le Boeuf*, 11.

bitter, stormy winter, enduring great physical suffering and mental anxiety. This journey was preliminary to the French and Indian War, being the first in the sequence of events which resulted in American Independence.

CHAPTER II

A FRENCH HIGHWAY

Approximately two and a half centuries before there were any settlers ensconced in their sturdy log cabins on the banks of French Creek, France projected her colonial aspirations into North America. James Cartier in 1534 sailed up the St. Lawrence, re-enforcing the French king's claim to that region. A company was formed for trading in furs in 1564, and Monsieur de Montr was appointed Viceroy of Acadia, later called Nova Scotia. The rights of this company were purchased by the Marchioness de Guerniville to whom King Henry IV ceded the sovereignty of New France from the St. Lawrence to Florida. Champlain accompanied the expedition sent out and became the first Governor of Quebec in 1606—fourteen years prior to the landing of the Pilgrims at Plymouth. Through the influence of Jesuit priests an association was formed for the establishment of a colony. The name was fixed as Montreal. The new colonists disembarked on May 16, 1642.

With the early French adventurers were large numbers of Jesuit priests filled with religious zeal for the conversion of the Indians. Their missionary journeys extended through the far region of the west, and their

IN FRENCH CREEK VALLEY

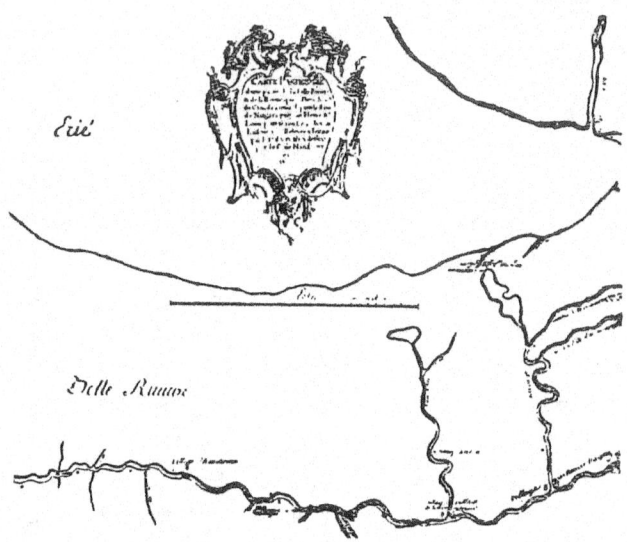

Portion of unpublished map of the Ohio River, de Lery Expedition, 1739, which traveled the route de Celoron followed ten years later.

discoveries incited others to exploration. Father Marquette founded a mission at Sault Ste. Marie in 1661. In 1673 he accompanied Joliet, who had been commissioned to explore the Mississippi River, up the Fox River and down the Wisconsin and Mississippi Rivers to Arkansas. He founded a mission at Kaskaskia and died upon his return on May 16, 1675. La Salle and Father Henopin discovered the Ohio River. From the

Great Lakes, they descended the Illinois and Mississippi Rivers, and named this land Louisiana. These early discoveries and the occupation of the land gave France a good claim to the vast region watered by the Mississippi and its tributaries. By the Treaty of Utrecht in 1713, however, France ceded Acadia and Newfoundland to England; and in 1745 the English forces captured Louisburg and the Island of Cape Briton.

Thus the one hundred and forty years since the founding of Quebec had wrought great changes. The Jesuits had extended their missions among the Indians and built strong bonds of friendship with many tribes. They had also been active, through the distribution of lavish presents by the French officers, in securing the good will of the savages occupying the discovered territory.

The English colonies, however, had made greater growth in population than the French and had extended their settlements into the provinces claimed by Canada. The French colonies were inconsiderable and few west of Montreal. Traders from Pennsylvania and Virginia filtered through the Cumberland Gap and other passes of the Allegheny Mountains, penetrating the region west of these mountains and along the Ohio River.

It is a surprising fact that, while the territory north of the St. Lawrence River and the Great Lakes was well known to the French as early as the middle of the 17th century, yet it was one hundred years later before the country lying between the Ohio River and Lake Erie was known to either the French or the English. The chief reason for this was that the region south of Lake Erie was claimed by the warlike Iroquois who always resisted the intrusion of white men, and because the northern route via the Ottawa River and the Great Lakes to the Mississippi Valley was shorter and less dangerous. An early map drawn in 1749 by Father Bonnecamps, a Jesuit priest with Celoron's expedition down the Ohio, shows the south shore of Lake Erie as "terra incognita," and names what we know as French Creek "La Riviere aux Boeufs."

Starting from Montreal the latter part of June in 1739 a detachment of officers, cadets, soldiers and Indians numbering four hundred and twenty two under the command of Baron de Longueuil[1] journeyed down the Ohio River to serve under the orders of M. de Bienville of Louisiana. A map in the Archives of the Dominion of Canada shows some knowledge of La Riviere aux Boeufs at that time. In the years that followed and as the number of English traders increased in the region between Lake Erie and the Ohio the French were prompted to take active measures to enforce their claim to this valuable territory. The early part of 1749 the Governor, Marquis de la Galissoniere, sent Captain Bienville de Celoron with a detachment of two hundred and seventy men, including among the officers de Con-

[1] C. B. Galbreath, *Expedition of Celoron to the Ohio Country in 1749* (Columbus, 1921), 46.

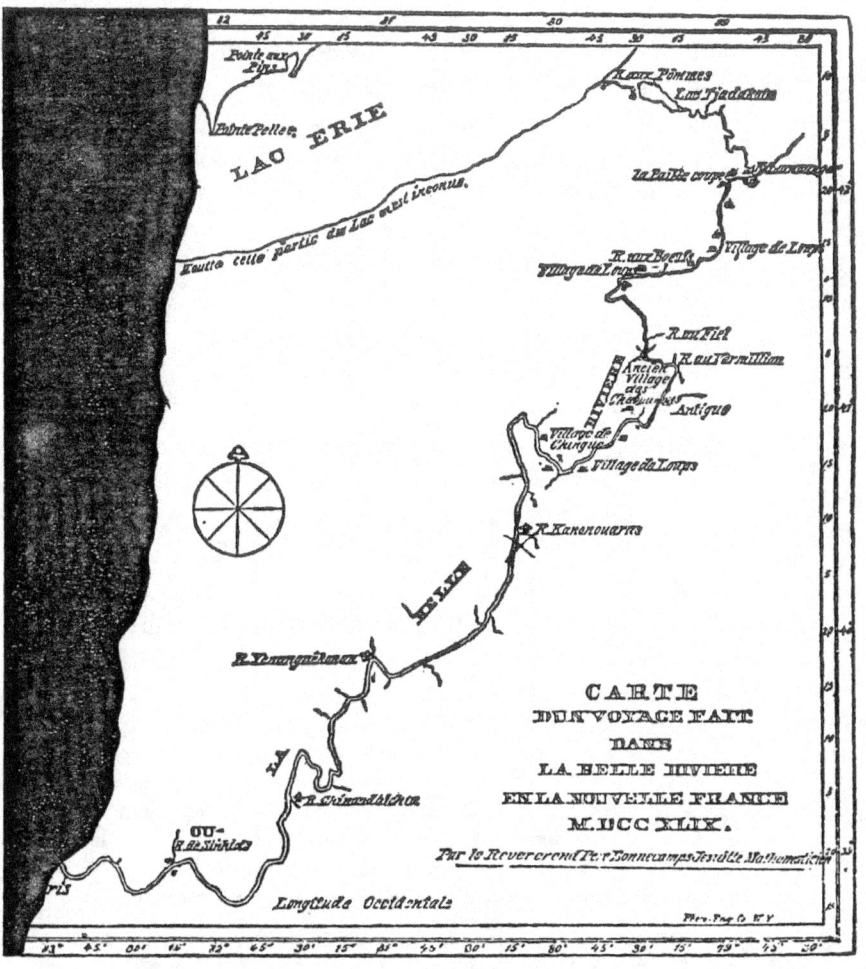

Father Bonnecamps' Map, de Celoron Expedition, 1749.

trecouer and Coulon de Villiers, with orders to descend the Ohio and formally take possession of all the lands drained by that river and its tributaries, and to make peace with the Indian tribes. From Lake Erie he crossed overland to Chautauqua Lake, down the Connewango to its confluence with the Ohio,[1] stopping at several places to bury lead plates on which the inscriptions set forth the claims of France to all the lands drained by the Ohio River. One of these plates was buried with formality on the east side of the Ohio near a huge rock on which there were rude Indian carvings some eight miles below the mouth of La Riviere aux Boeufs.

After these early invasions of western Pennsylvania no further steps were taken to enforce the French claims until 1752, when an expedition was sent out by the Governor of Canada to build forts on the shores of Lake Erie and the Ohio River. A deposition by Stephen Coffen,[2] a soldier with this expedition, taken before Sir William Johnson in 1754, tells in interesting detail how this was accomplished.

Stephen Coffen . . . deposed that he was taken a prisoner by the French and Indians of Canada at Menis, in the year 1747 . . . In September 1752 the Depon^t was in Quebec, and endeavouring to agree with some Indians, to convey him to his own Country New England, which the Indians acquainted the Govr of, who immediately ordered him to Goal, where he lay

[1] Warren, on the Allegheny River which the Indians called Ohio.
[2] John Romeyn Broadhead, *Documents Relating to the Colonial History of the State of New York* (Albany, 1855), VI, 835-837.

three Months; at the time of his Releasement the French were preparing for a March to Belle Riviere or Ohio, when he offered his services, but was rejected by the Govr General Le Cain . . . the Deponet applyed to Major Ramsey, for liberty to go with the army to Ohio, . . . he was Equipped as a Soldier, and sent with a Detachment of three hundred Men to Montreal, under the Command of Monsr Babeer, who sett off immediately with said Command, by Land and Ice, for Lake Erie; they in their way stopt a couple of days to refresh themselves at Cadaraghqui Fort; also at Taranto on the North side of Lake Ontario; then at Niagara Fort 15 days; from thence sett off by Water being April, and arrived at Chadakoin[1] on Lake Erie, where they were ordered to fell Timber, and prepare it for building a Fort there, . . . but Monsr Morang coming up with 500 Men and 20 Indians, put a stop to the erecting of a Fort at that place, by reason of his not liking the situation, and River of Chadakoins being too shallow to carry any craft with provisions ettc. to Belle River. The Deponent say, there arose a warm debate between Messrs Babeer and Morang thereon, . . . Morang . . . then ordered Monsr Mercie, who was both, Commissary and Engeneer to go along said Lake, and look for a good situation; which he found, and returned in three days, it being 15 Leagues to the S. W. of Chadakoin; they were then all ordered to repair thither; when they arrived, there were about 20 Indians fishing in the Lake, who immediately quit it on seeing the French; they fell to work and built a square Fort, of Chesnut Loggs squared, and lapt over each other to the height of 15 foot; it is about 120 feet square, a Loghouse in each square, a Gate to the Southward and another to the N. ward, not one port hole cut in any part of it; when finished

---

[1] Portland, Chautauqua County, New York.

they called it Fort la Briske Isle.[1] The Indians who came from Canada with them, returned very much out of Temper, owing as it was said among the Army to Morang's dogged behaviour and ill usage of them, . . . As soon as the Fort was finished, they marched Southward cutting a Waggon Road through a fine level Country, twenty one Miles to the River of Bœff.[2] (leaving Captn Deponteney with a hundred Men to garrison the Fort la Briske Isle) they fell to work cutting timber boards ettc for another Fort, while Monsr Morang ordered Monsr Bite with 50 Men to go to a place called by the Indians Ganagarah 'hare,[3] on the Banks of Belle Riviere, where the River O Bœff empties into it; in the mean time Morang had got large Boats or Battoes made to carry down the Baggage and provisions ettc to said place; Monsr Bite on coming to said Indian place, was asked what he wanted or intended; he upon answering, it was their Father the Govr of Canada's intention to Build a Trading house for their, and all their Brethren's conveniency, was told by the Indians that the Lands were theirs and they would not have them build upon it; the said Mr Bite returning, met two Englishmen Traders, with their horses and goods, whom they bound & brought prisoners to Morang, . . . the said Bite reported to Morang, the situation was good, but the wate[r] in the River O Bœff too low at that time to carry down any Craft with provisions ettc. . . The Deponent further saith, that about eight days before he left the Fort La Briske Isle, Chev: Le Crake arrived express from Canada, in a Birch Canoe, worked by 10 men, with orders . . . from the Governour Le Cain to Morang to make all the preparations possible again the spring of the year, to build then two Forts at Chadakoin, one of them by Lake Erie, the other at the end of the carrying

---

[1] Presque Isle.
[2] French Creek.
[3] Franklin.

place at Lake Chadakoin;[1] which carrying place is 15 miles from one Lake to the other; . . . when the Fort la Riviere O Bœff was finished (which is built of wood stokadoed Triangularwise, and has two Logg Houses in the inside) Monsr Morang ordered all the party to return to Canada, for the winter season, except three hundred men, which he kept to Garrison Both Forts, and prepare materials agst the spring for the building other Forts; he also sent Jean Coeur an Officer and Interpreter, to stay the winter among the Indians at Ohio, in order to prevail with them, not only to allow the building Forts on their Lands, but also persuade them if possible, to join the French interest against the English. The Deponent further saith, that on the 28th of October last, he set off for Canada under the command of Captn Deman, who had the command of 22 Battoes, with 20 Men in each Battoe, the remainder being 760 Men, followed in a few days, the 30th arrived at Chadakoin, where they staid four days, during which time Monsr Peon with 200 Men, cut a Waggon Road over the carrying place from Lake Erie to Lake Chadakoin, being 15 Miles, viewed the situation which proved to their liking, so sett off Novr 3^d for Niagare, where we arrived the 6th: . . . We left 50 Men here to build Battoes for the army again the spring, . . . then sett off for Canada; all hands being fatigued with Rowing all night, ordered to put ashore to breakfast within a mile of Oswego Garrison, at which time the Deponent saith, that he and a Frenchman slipt off, and got to the Fort, where they both were concealed, until the Army passed. . . .

Sworn before me this
10th day of January 1754.
      Wm Johnson

               his
Stephen + Coffen
      mark

---

[1] Chautauqua Lake.

IN FRENCH CREEK VALLEY

After the departure of Captain Deman, a detachment under the command of Captain Joncaire was sent to Venango to occupy the ground and build a fort. Captain Joncaire[1] was an old man whose romantic career was too picturesque to overlook. When a young boy he was captured by the Iroquois and afterward adopted by the tribe. He grew to manhood among them, acquiring their habits and mode of life. Later he became a most efficient and valuable agent of the Canadian Government in their negotiations with the Indians. "He[2] had the wit of a Frenchman and the eloquence of an Iroquois. He was by terms an embassador to the Iroquois, a mediator between tribes and a leader of their warriors on their forays." His many years among the tribes in the Ohio region rendered him a competent officer for the post at Venango. He took possession of the house of John Frazier, the English trader, while preparing to build the fort. Captain Joncaire was in command under the French flag on the evening of December 4, 1753, when Washington and his men arrived at Venango. During the winter of 1753-1754, the fort was completed and named Fort Machault[3] after a noted Parisian statesman

---

[1] Captain Joncaire, Jeancouer, and the Couer mentioned in the foregoing affidavit are evidently one individual. Old records show that there were almost as many ways of spelling a man's name as there were individuals who did not rejoice in sharing it with the person mentioned.

[2] *Discourse delivered before the New York Historical Society at their Anniversary Meeting 6th December 1811 by the Hon. DeWitt Clinton one of the Vice Presidents of the Society* (New York, 1812), 41.

[3] Elk Street in the City of Franklin passes through the former site of Fort Machault.

and financier. It was situated on the Ohio River some sixty rods south of French Creek, built of timber and earth, 175 feet in length and 75 feet in breadth, exclusive of bastions and mounted six swivel guns.

The answer of St. Pierre being unsatisfactory to Governor Dinwiddie, it was on the advice of Washington that the Governor ordered the completion of a fort at the forks of the Ohio River. The building of this fort was started and it was called Fort Trent in honor of the commanding officer, who was a brother-in-law of Colonel George Croghan. On the 24th of April, before the completion of the work, General Contrecour appeared with a force of about 1600 and some cannon, which he had embarked at Le Boeufs and Venango in a fleet of 80 bateaux and 300 canoes, floating down the river on the spring freshet. The small English force surrendered and were permitted to leave. General Contrecour immediately proceeded to complete the work of construction of the fort and named it Fort Duquesne after the Governor of Canada.

After two disastrous attempts to capture Fort Duquesne—that of General Braddock, 1755, and of Major Grant in September, 1758—in the early part of the latter year the English Army was assembled under Colonel Boquet for the third attempt. Washington led the advance and on November 25 arrived within sight of the Fort to find that the formidable bulwark had been abandoned. The victories of the English in Canada had cut off the re-enforcement of troops and the transport of military supplies. The force had been reduced to not more than 500 men. On the evening preceding, the commander had blown up the magazines and set fire to the fort. He then embarked his troops in bateaux and sailed down the Ohio. Thereafter, upon the ruin of Fort Duquesne, the English reconstructed a fort and named it Fort Pitt in honor of the Earl of Chatam.

The only important fort now remaining to the French in Pennsylvania was Fort Machault at Venango. The posts at Presque Isle and Le Boeufs had of late but little importance. A large force, about 1,000 French soldiers and 1,000 Indian allies, was assembled at Fort Machault in 1759 with the design of making an effort to recapture Fort Pitt, but the siege of Fort Niagara brought orders for the recall of all the troops and the evacuation of Machault. As there were no means of transporting the munitions and supplies, the former were destroyed and the latter distributed among their Indian allies. Thus ended the seven years of French occupancy of Western Pennsylvania.

In 1760, when the English prepared to take over the evacuated French forts from Fort Pitt to Presque Isle and by so doing make a new connection by which the important post of Detroit could be reached, we find

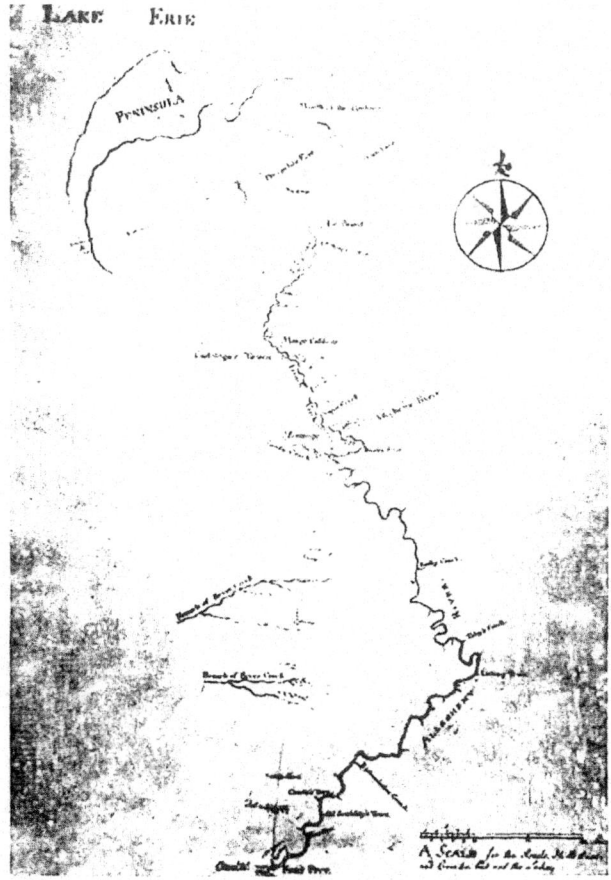

Trail from Fort Pitt to Presque Isle, English Occupation, 1760 to 1763.

from letters[1] between British officers that the burdens and hardships of the trail fell as heavily on the English as on their former antagonists, the French.

The English in 1760 constructed a fort known as Fort Venango on a site near the former French Fort Machault. This post, together with the posts at Le Boeufs and Presque Isle, were occupied by small English garrisons until these forts were destroyed during the period of Pontiac's War. The capture of Fort Venango well illustrates the Indian tactics. According to Dr. S. J. M. Eaton,[2] one of the early historians, the Indians were playing ball in the vicinity of the Fort and occasionally threw or knocked the ball over the Fort barricade into the enclosure. Obtaining permission to go inside for the ball, they rushed through the gate and, taking the garrison by complete surprise, murdered all and tortured the commanding officer, Lieutenant Gordon. The game was known as La Cross and originated with the Canadian Indians.

Notwithstanding all the effort made by the French to secure possession of that part of the Ohio Valley in which French Creek is situated, destiny seems to have planned otherwise, and eighteen years before the Declaration of Independence found all that region under the control of the English. The western boundaries in

---

[1] See Appendix, 317-321; three letters and Croghan's Journal.
[2] William H. Egle, *History of Pennsylvania* (Harrisburg, 1876), 1126.

most of the grants of lands from the British king to the Colonies were indefinite, and when the western line of William Penn's grant was definitely settled this fertile district lay comfortably within Pennsylvania.

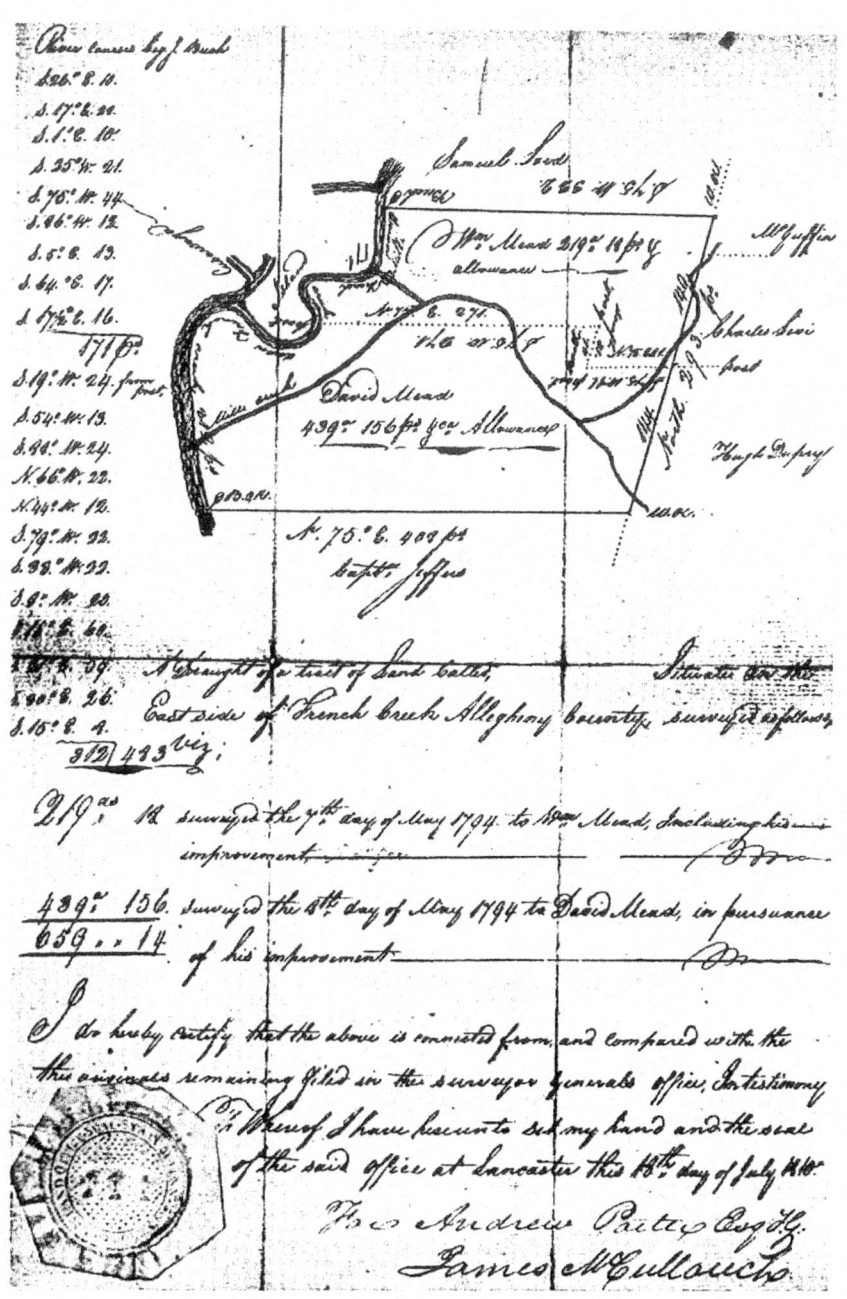

Survey of Mead Lands, at Cussewago, 1794, the Site of Meadville.

CHAPTER III
MEAD'S SETTLEMENT

The history of this new land is a story of danger, hardships, and struggles, and of slow growth and development. Thirty-five years after Washington's journey to Fort Le Boeuf, few changes had taken place in French Creek Valley. Except for occasional broad fertile "savannahs," most of the country was still densely covered with great forest trees through which the only trails were those made by Indians or wild animals, and travelers found these trails not only arduous but dangerous.

Though Fort Franklin had been built near the confluence of French Creek and the Allegheny River in 1790, several years were to pass before Mead's Settlement was accomplished. On a spring day, May 12, 1788, nine men who had traversed the Susquehanna Trail from Northumberland County to Fort Franklin and thence along the Venango Trail pitched camp on the bank of Mill Run not far from the place where it flowed into French Creek. There this hardy little group of pioneers made the first permanent settlement[1] in the region north of Pittsburgh and west of the Allegheny mountains. Let

[1] "June 22d (1794)—Marched at seven. The road and land from Franklin to Cussewaga excellent. Got to the settlement about three o'clock, where we found some people 'forted,' as it is called. This the only place where a settlement has been attempted this side of Pittsburgh." A Military Journal kept by Major Ebenezer Denny, 1781 to 1795, printed in *Memoirs of the Historical Society of Pennsylvania* (Philadelphia, 1860), VII, 382-409.

General David Mead, leader of the men and founder of Meadville, relate the events and trials of the early years of the settlement as he told it years later in a Circuit Court of the United States.[1]

In the Month of April 1788 I moved from the County of Northumberland thro' the Wilderness to Cussawaga,[2] now Meadville on French Creek, in Company with several Adventurers, and some hired Hands, to make a Settlement where we arrived in the Month of May, and I have made it my place of Residence ever since except when compelled to abandon it to seek safety from Indian Hostilities. The year 1789 I erected a Saw Mill, the first known West of Allegany River, & in 1790 I set a pair of Mill Stones running—connected with the Saw Mill which made very good meal.

Early in the Spring of 1791 our Settlement was alarmed by fears of Indian Hostilities from the Western Indians. We had kept up a friendly intercourse with the Senecas on Allegany River,[3] and with the Indian Village at the mouth of big Coniott Creek on Lake Erie. The Chiefs of the latter Village, more than once that Spring communicated to us the danger to which we were exposed of being cut off by the Western Indians, then at War with the United States. At length so great were our

---

[1] MS copy of testimony by General David Mead, in ejectment of the Holland Land Company, vs. Actual Settlers, was given to William Reynolds by Mrs. William Gill, a daughter of General Mead (Reynolds Collection)

In the Circuit Court of the United States for the District of Pennsylvania—Third Circuit—
Richard Smith an Alien Lessee of Harm Jan Huidekoper an Alien—
vs.
William Stiles with Notice to Robert Burns a Citizen of Pennsylvania Tenant in Possession
Ejectment as of— October Sessions 1802—

[2] See Appendix, 325—Aboriginal Num. VIII.
[3] See Appendix, 323—Aboriginal Num. VI.

Robert Fitz Randolph, Pioneer.

Old Mead Homestead house of 1795

General David Mead's First House, Block House, Grist and Saw Mills.

William Reynolds Sketch.

MEAD'S SETTLEMENT

apprehensions of Danger, that about the first of May, the entire Settlement broke up, and moved to Fort Franklin, at the mouth of French Creek, mostly on Rafts of Boards prepared for the purpose, escorted by "Half Town" and other Chiefs and Indians of the six Nations in Number I think between 20 & 30, some of the Settlers went off to the Settled Country, and others

Cornelius Van Horne, Pioneer.

(of which number was my Family) remained at Fort Franklin. In a few days after Cornelius Vanhorn, Thomas Ray & William Gregg and others returned to Cussawaga, without any Families in order to Plant Corn, (they began to Plough and to Plant about the middle of the Month) I also returned about this time to Cussawaga, accompanied by Captain Jeffers, then commanding officer at Fort Franklin, and three or four friendly Indians and several Indians, but being disappointed in finding Vanhorn, Ray and others we went and examined the field where they had been at work, and found some of their cloaths a Rifle Gun and their Dinners, but neither Man or Horse could be seen, we then returned to the Mills and near dusk in the Evening Cornelius Vanhorn came in with his Arms tied behind his Back, (I think with his own Plough lines) who informed us that he had been taken Prisoner by the hostile Indians, and in that Condition had escaped from them near the little Coniott Lake,[1] and from his information it was supposed that the other Men were killed. In June following Mr Ray returned by way of Detroit and Niagara, and gave us a more correct Statement, *viz*. That Gregg was killed near the spot where he was taken, and that the others had escaped. The same year my Father (Darius Mead) was missing, and it was afterwards discovered that he was taken Prisoner, about the first of August near Fort Franklin by the Indians and by them killed on Shenango.—In October having procured a Guard of Soldiers from Capt Jeffers and several hired Hands, I moved my Family back to the Mills at Cussawaga. But about Christmas Capt Jeffers sent an Express to me, informing of the Defeat of the Army under Genl St. Clair, and ordered the Soldiers I had to return immediately to the Garrison; this reduced my strength so much that I was again obliged to remove my Family back to Franklin. In the beginning of April 1792, there was not one Person resident in the Country, North, and West of the Rivers Ohio[2] and Allegany and Conewango Creek, within the State of Pennsylvania, except the remains of the Settlement that had been at my Mills, and these were then obtaining Shelter and Pro-

---

[1] See Appendix, 324—Aboriginal Num. VII.
[2] See Appendix, 322—Aboriginal Num. III.

tection at Fort Franklin. Fort Franklin then Commanded by Capt Cass, was the only regular Garrison in the Country. Some Block Houses were erected and Posts or Stations Established on the Allegany River near the Settlements on Allegany & Westmoreland Counties where spies and Scout in the Service of the United States & of this State & Detachments of Militia were stationed.

In the Spring of 1792, I procured from Capt Cass a Sergeant, Corporal, and twelve Men, and leaving my Family at the Fort I returned to Cussawaga. I also had permission to furnish and to Issue Rations to any number of Indians not exceeding Twenty, and to give to each of them a Shirt and a Pair of Leggins at the Public Expense. Issues were accordingly made during part of that Summer, to the Indians, and the Expense was defrayed by the Public. In the beginning of

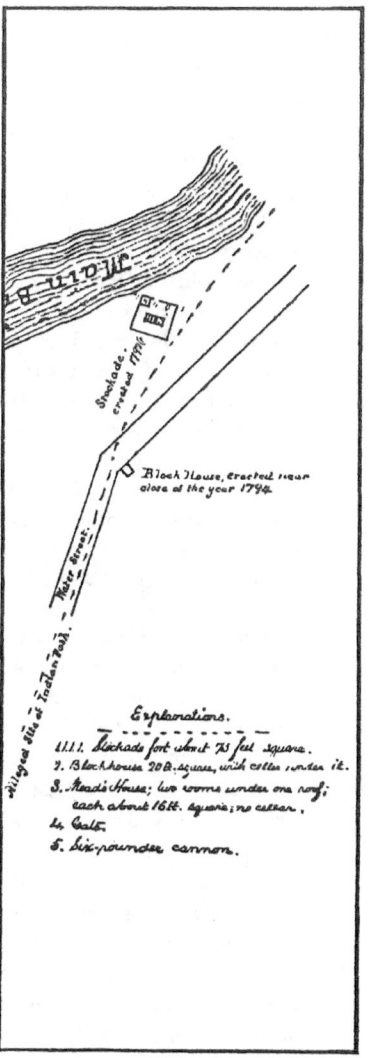

Location of Mead's Stockade and State Block House.

August I began to make a Stockade around my dwelling House near the Mills, and then ventured once more to remove my Family from Franklin. Sometime in November by application to Gen^1 Wayne, I procured a detachment consisting of a Subaltern & Thirty Men, and with their Aid completed the Stockade and erected a Block House, projecting over the Bank of French Creek in order to prevent the Enemy being concealed or having any Shelter under the Bank of the Creek either above or below our Fortification. The Protection, and assistance I thus received in the year 1792 alone enabled me to return to my Mills at that time, and was the cause of the Subsequent Security and increase of the Settlement. Under that Protection and by the Public supplies we acquired the Friendship and respect of the Indians who received the Rations from me, a Stockade and Block House, capable of being defended against Indians, was constructed and afforded us future Security, our danger was nevertheless great, the Enemy Indians had been recently victorious, and Murders and other depredations had been committed by them on the Frontiers of Allegheny and Westmoreland Counties, and even near to Pittsburgh as was generally understood, and as was reported in the Settlements on the Ohio below. In the Spring of 1793 the Detachment of Troops was recalled, but another detachment consisting of a Sargeant and Twelve Men was sent to us. Many Persons came out, chiefly from the West Branch of Susquehanna to look at the Country, and to make what were called Improvements in the Woods, some then remained and lived with us, and afterwards (when Peace was made with the Indians) settled Permanently. No actual Damage was sustained from Indians, by the Settlement or Travelers, but we still entertained apprehensions of danger, as we were 100 Miles advanced into the Country Claimed by the Indians, beyond the Frontier of the Westernmost Settlements of the State. We did not consider ourselves in safety & no person ventured to Reside out of the little Settlement at my Mills. In the latter part of the Summer we were very much alarmed in consequence of an Express being sent from Franklin to the Commanding Officer informing us of the failure of the Treaty under Gen^1 Lincoln at Detroit & other reports, & of his being appraised by Cornplanter, of the intention of the Western Indians to destroy the Settlements. In Consequence of this Intelligence almost all the People out looking at the Country fled, and the few Families that were with us moved away: I was determined, if possible to preserve the Settlement, and used all the address in my Power to induce the Inhabitants to remain. I was confident that we could defend ourselves for some time against a body of Indians and that we should be informed in time, for Escape, or defence, of their approach by the Indians of Cornplanters Town if it should happen. I did not succeed however in prevailing on any but those employed by me to continue. The Inhabitants when at work planting Corn &c. generally went in Parties and armed, and usually all returned at Night to Cussawaga. In the year 1794 our Settlement was considerably increased but several Murders, as we were informed were committed on the Allegany River, and in parts of the Country. Two Men of the Names of Wallace & Powers were killed, it was said on the Road about 20 Miles South of Fort Franklin; a Boat & a Canoe, was attacked by Indians, and some Persons killed and Wounded: a Soldier missing from the Garrison at Franklin, was found Dead and Scalped, near the Fort, all this was reported at the time. In August or September James Dixon, an Inhabitant, in our Settlement, was wounded in three parts of his Body having received four Shots from Indians & the fourth passed through his Hat, only a small distance from my Mills, near the Bank of French Creek, in the open day. On hearing the Shots of the Indians I ordered a number of Muskets, and small Arms to be discharged within the Pickets with a view to alarm the Scattering People. In a few minutes after Mʳ Dixon came within sight, & I ran out and led him in, very much covered with Blood from his Wounds. Before this time, and after the murder of Wallace and Power, an Express was sent to Pittsburgh, in order to obtain some aid and Protection from the Public Officers, and in consequence authority was given by the General Officers of the Militia to enroll a certain Number of Men for our defence, who were furnished with Arms, & received Pay and Rations.

Shortly after the attack on Mʳ Dixon, the Inhabitants Erected a new Block House, convenient to the old Block House & Stockade and mounted a six Pounder within the same.

In this year great apprehensions of danger were generally expressed by all People in the Country. None ventured to reside out of the Village, and when they worked out it was always in Parties, and generally Armed, some standing as Sentinels, or Patrolling, while others worked, at Night they all assembled within my House, the Block House adjoining or one or two other Houses, for mutual Protection and safety. In the year 1795 a great many adventurers came to Cussawaga, but not a Family ventured to settle West of French Creek that Summer.

In April or in May we had information that two Men of the Name of Rutledge were killed near Presque Isle. In June Findley & McCormick were killed near the mouth of Coniott Creek and were buried at Cussawᵃ and a Day or two after the Camp of William Power—Dep'ty-Sʳ (Surveyor) was broken up, and a Man of the name of Thompson taken Prisoner, and carried off to Detroit & there released, this last information is from the Statement of Thompson to me, immediately after his return from Captivity. The Inhabitants were again enrolled

MEAD'S SETTLEMENT 39

this Summer a Company Commanded by Cornelius Vanhorn was under Pay & Rations.

Altho Danger still existed, yet the Inhabitants, and other Persons at Cussawaga, felt more secure, at all events were encouraged by the confident hopes entertained generally that Peace would be made this Season, with the Indians by Gen[l] Wayne and all would be able to move out the next Spring to the Lands which they had selected for their Farms.

During the years 1792, 1793, 1794, and the greater part of the year 1795, I did consider it imprudent, for a single Family with Women and Children to attempt to make a Settlement and Residence in the Woods at a distance from a Plan of Defence, and it is a truth, that none did make the attempt West of French Creek during that Period, nor to any other place to remain Permanently until the Fall of 1795.

We who were settled in the Country were compelled to make the best of our situation, and it was naturally our Policy to induce as many as possible to remain. The enrollment of the Inhabitants of Cussawaga for Militia Duty was necessary for their safety, and the object of those who obtained the enrollment was not merely to pay and to feed those who were enrolled. The pay and Rations given I believe induced some to stay, who, otherwise would have abandoned the Country, their staying caused others to remain, and all felt a greater degree of Confidence and Security.

In the Summer of 1794, a Body of State Troops was stationed at Le Boeuf, now Waterford Commanded by Major Denny, in 1795 Gen[l] Irwin & Mr. A. Ellicott, laid out the Towns of Erie, Waterford, Warren and Franklin, & for their protection were attended by a Company of State Troops under Cap[t] Buchanon and some Troops of the United States. Co[l] Rochefontaine in the Service of the United States, accompanied by General Neville, Co[l] Neville Brigade Inspector, Major

Craig and others in order to lay out the Fort at Presque Isle; were escorted thro' Meadville by a Detachment of Cavalry in the Service of the United States.

General Mead's account of the early years of his settlement is ample testimony of the difficulties encountered and the fear engendered by Indian raids. Furthermore, his report explains fully the reasons for the slow and laborious growth of the pioneer country. This report is

Block House

a measure of Mead's moral and physical courage. His father Darius was one of the first men killed by the Indians. Of the nine adventurers who accompanied him, his brother Joseph Mead, Chrystopher Snyder, John Watson, Thomas Martin and Thomas Grant later returned to the east, while James Fitz Randolph, Cornelius Van Horn and his brother John remained with David to face adversity and the struggle for existence. It was the stamina and valor of these four remaining men which made possible the continuance of a permanent settlement on the banks of French Creek, and their presence there encouraged many to follow and join them in the succeeding years. The perpetuation of one's name by establishing a town at this date in the virgin part of the United States was no task for a dilettante.

CHAPTER IV
BUILDING A HOME

Because of a demonstration against Dissenters in July, 1793, William and Lydia Reynolds left their home in Birmingham, England, the following year. John, the eldest son, and his six sisters joined them at Lansingburgh, New York, in 1795. After two years there, John and his father journeyed to western Pennsylvania and became settlers. John was then sixteen years old. Eight strenuous years followed. Having been drilled in the classics by his maternal grandfather, Joshua Thomas, pastor of the Baptist Church in Leominster, Herefordshire, John went to Meadville to continue his education at the new Academy, earning his way by chopping wood and carrying a chain for Colonel Marlin, surveyor for the Holland Land Company. In the office of the prothonotary, Dr. T. R. Kennedy, he was a clerk and studied law, being admitted to practice in 1810. During 1809 he was principal of the Academy; afterward he had a school of his own. Dr. Kennedy died in 1813 and John was co-executor with Henry Baldwin. The following year he married Andrew Ellicott's daughter, Jane Judith, the widow of Dr. Kennedy. He was a director and later the receiver for the North Western Bank of Pennsylvania, first treasurer of Allegheny College, real estate agent for Philadelphia firms, a member of the

John Reynolds.

committee for building the Meadville Church, the first Library, and active in most of the public improvements. He was Burgess of Meadville for two terms.

It would be difficult to find a more illuminating description of conditions and the early settlers of this region than is pictured by John Reynolds[1] in telling of his own experiences.

In August 1797, 5 of us in comp^y left Fort Pitt, as Pitts^h was then called and with 2½ days riding reached F^t Franklin. On crossing the All^y at Pitts^h one log house was on the bank, the residence of Mr Robinson, Father of the late Genl Wm Robinson, the only house on this side of the river in what is now All^y city. A few settlers had pitched their tents, miles asunder, between Pit. & Franklin.

Fort Franklin had a few soldiers under the Commandant, Capt. Fowler, an aged officer, he had been in British and afterward Continental service; The Holl^d Land Co^y had opened an office, of which Alex. McDowel was incumbent, under the gen^l Agent Maj. R. Alden whose office & residence were in Meadville (then better known by its primitive name Cussewago).

In Franklin were 3 small stores in small log buildings on the bank of F. Creek, also two public houses. A few single men in addition, comprised the am^t of its population. The mercantile profits were derived chiefly from the Indian trade, peltries being the chief export. Transportation was by keel boat or canoe, and the supply of provisions was brought from the older settlements up the Monongahela & around Pitts^h.

Our object was settlement under contract with the Holl^d L^d

---

[1] John Reynolds MS: Reminiscences of the Olden Time, *Meadville Daily Republican*, 1867 (Reynolds Collection)

Co^y to whose Agent we had letters. Col. McDowel the next day rode out a few miles with us & put us on a narrow road newly opened by the Holl^d L^d Co^y to the forks of Oil Creek. We found Johnathan Titus (then a young man) who had the previous spring settled on the tract where he afterwards lived and died, in a log cabin, which he was preparing to live in. The same evening we rode to the place where that day had been raised the frame of the first saw mill erected on the little or eastern branch of the stream, and where next summer the Comp^y added a grist mill. Here we were introduced by letter given by M^r McDowel, to Samuel Kerr, Surveyor & sub agent for the Comp^y to shew lands &c. No land had been taken up between Franklin & Oil Creek 18 miles and as we crossed the valley of Cherrytree run, my Father decided to locate there, accordingly Mr Kerr went with us & shewed us the corners & lines of 4 tracts at Cherrytree run. We returned to Franklin & contracted with the Agent for the settlement of three tracts, to receive a gratuity of 100 acres from each and a young man of our comp^y contracted to settle the 4th tract. On the 30th Augt 97 myself, my Father & James Maddock, who accompanied us from N. Y., left Franklin with a horse load of Provision, tools & blankets, for the purpose of making settlement in the land whereon Cherrytree village now is. We arrived in the evening of a sultry day at the head of a spring of good water on the eastern side of Cherrytree run, where my Brother Joshua now resides, an hour or two before sunset (I will promise that neither of us had ever handled an axe for felling trees or chopping). It was a transition from Birmingham, Engl^d to the solitude of the wilderness, with no experience of a woodman's life. We cut four stakes with a fork at the top, on these we laid poles which we covered with bushes, & set some round on three sides. We kindled a fire with the aid of a gun, (no friction match in that day) and cooked our supper. A hot day was succeeded by thunder & heavy rain; soon after we lay down, the water flooded our beds, & we had the alternative of lying, sitting or standing during a night of rain, without shelter. The next day we cut small logs and built our house to the eaves, say 3 sides about 10 feet square, the 4th side open to the fire w^h was outside. We then cut a tree & attempted to make clap boards to roof our cabin, the tree wo^d have made better mould board for ploughs than shingles. To add to our troubles our hands blistered. The following day my Father went 8 miles to the Holl^d L^d Co^y mill & Mr Kerr kindly sent a man to come & make clapboards & roof our cabin, and now we had a *Home*.

The nights soon became cold, and we built a wooden chimney in the open side & chunked the spaces between the logs of the cabin with moss, we gathered from old trees. This was my dwelling the ensuing 13½ months—a room 10 feet square 6 feet story, split oak puncheons the floor—no nail used in its whole construction. It was my kitchen, Parlor & chamber. All the bread I ate I baked in the ashes, & washed & mended my shirt.

Thus the first settlement was commenced between Franklin & Titusville, except that the previous Spring John Morrison (the old Court crier) had cleared about ¼ of an acre in the bottom a little below where Richd Irwin saw mill is built & had planted a few hills of corn & then abandoned it.

The last 16 weeks I was the sole occupant of the cabin; my Father went to Whitesborough near Utica, to meet my mother who with the children had remained with friends in Brooklyn. She met him there, & thence by waggon to wood creek; by boat thence by way of Oneida Lake, Oswego river & Lake Ontario to Fort George, by waggon to Fort Erie, by boat to Presque Isle and by waggon to Fort Franklin. Thus by necessary delays occasioned by sickness & difficulty in means of transportation, what is now a 24 hours journey was then protracted to more than 4 times that number of days; well to my great joy they arrived at home on the 18th October; my Father had left me 4th July—those weary intervening weeks how had I lived? I had no neighbor between me & Franklin 12 miles, or Jon. Titus 6 miles, except two or three in Oil Creek valley to whom I had no path. No person to speak to, except an occasional call of a traveler, or an Indian hunter. I wo^d gladly have dispensed with visits from the latter; on one fine afternoon I was hoeing corn when an Indian came to me and asked for bread & bacon, pointing toward my cabin, s^d the squaw sh^d help me to hoe corn until sunset—he spoke in broken English & by signs. I co^d not spare any & refused. He looked sullen & left me, walking in the direction of my cabin. I thought it best to follow lest he might steal my provisions &c., he was a very ill looking man. I found a company of 14 of both sexes, being two men, old Snip & Jim Thickleg, & children. They had made a fire near my cabin & the squaws had a kettle on, for cooking. I was again importuned for bacon, which I refused. The two men were of bad repute, had been suspected of the murder of a white man the preceeding year on the All^y river. They departed near sunset; that was to me a dreary night, I knew they were not far distant, that the temptation was strong, to murder a Boy of 16 take his blankets and provisions, burn him and his cabin together & have none to witness against them at man's tribunal, but God restrained them and protected me. I had the companionship of wolves around me every night, I sometimes saw them sulking before it was dark. I had one visit from a Panther, but the rattling tenor of the vengeful snake was my habitual dread, knowing that if bitten, a dreadful death wo^d be inevitable as no human help was near.

The fall and winter of 1798, 9 we had in close proximity several Indian camps, they supplied us with meat; in that day

BUILDING A HOME

they overspread this region. It was their favorite hunting land on every little stream they made their encampment, and hunted & trapped through autumn & winter; in the spring they returned to their towns and through the summer scattered along the river fishing and watching deerlicks, while the squaws raised a little corn & some vegetables, dressing deer skins and made moccasins; all manual labour was performed by their women, such as making their winter camp, cutting & carrying fuel &c.

The warriors having been but recently chastised by Wayne; and enforced to make peace; were taciturn & sullen, especially the older men, who had been in many a foray on the frontier.

In witnessing the occupancy by the white man of what had been from time immemorial the choice hunting land of the tribe, they could not at all times restrain their malevolent feelings, could ill brook the sure result, of the conversion of their hunting ground into the peaceful farms of their ancient foes. The charms of war and hunting, are rarely dissolved when they mingle with the memories of youth.

About the 10th day of December, two genteel, well educated young Englishmen, visited my Father; one, Th^s Wedgwood, was of the family celebrated as manufacturers of the ware called by their name, the other, John Dadford was educated a civil engineer. They were smitten with the mania for possessing land in America. Of our confined quarters we gave them the occupancy of one half. They rode two fine blooded horses, one of which soon became food for the wolves; the survivor, Mr. Titus wintered without shelter on cornstalks and turnips, with a little half ripe corn; our own horse he wintered in like manner.

They remained with us near three months, when they commenced settlement on two tracts of land, two miles eastward from us. Toward spring we assisted them in building a cabin larger and better than our own. They made small clearing around it, but in May, abandoned it in disgust, & returned,—Wedgwood to New York, where he died of yellow fever in the fall of 1798 & Dadford to tell his friends in England of a terrible night's experience in America, which was this wise;

The 3rd day after their arrival, they returned to Franklin for provisions, blankets, &c; the weather was extremely cold, and the snow deep; French Creek was a third on each side frozen, & running ice in the centre. On their return with loaded horses next day, Dadford was taken over by canoe; Wedgwood was to drive the horses off the ice into the water, and Dadford to catch them at the other shore. Then Wedgwood was to be taken over, and all proceed homeward. The horses were fractious, and Wedgwood slipped off the ice into the creek, and then returned for the night, and lodged in Franklin. Dadford pushed homeward with the loaded horses; at 7 miles he reached the "two mile run"; it was night, the horses would not go on the ice; he had no alternative but to take off the loads and remain with them, or walk the additional five miles through snow knee deep. He tried the latter, but in the first mile he was convinced that to save his life he must return and avail himself of the blankets. He had shoes on, but one of them he lost in the snow. With feet well nigh frozen, he got back to the horses, wrapped himself in blankets, and sat with his back against a tree, expecting to die with cold before morning. He said he amused himself with the surprise of his friend, when on his return next day he would see him sitting a frozen corpse. About midnight wolves came toward him with their fearful howl. He bethought him, of a camp kettle and frying pan, which he hastily seized, & rattled with effect, affrighting the wolves, as they had affrighted him. The agitation of fright caused his blood to circulate more briskly, and perhaps saved his life. He was able in the morning to get on one

BUILDING A HOME

of the horses, but on arriving at the cabin, he could not alight. My father lifted him off & carried him in.

* * * * *

Settlers came in, few in the first years, but increasing annually in number, as facilities of roads & subsistence increased.

Ancient forest during untold centuries had overshadowed the hills & valleys of this region. Beauty and variety marked the plants that grew & flowered beneath the leafy canopy of the gigantic trees.

Game abounded. Deer were numerous & valuable, they supplied the larder of the settler, and venison then was much finer than in these latter years we see it. They had fine pasturage in summer & acorns, chestnuts & beechnuts in autumn, and were not subject to constant alarm from hunters & dogs, hence the carcase was well covered with fat.

Elk were rarely seen—I remember one to have been killed by an Indian near the mouth of Oil Creek. I saw the tracks of 3 in the winter of 1797-8, from some unexplained cause they were rarely seen in this region. Black squirrels were numerous, but no gray ones were seen until some years after settlement began.

Turkies were abundant, and grew large. I killed one that weighed 22^{lb} but I heard of some 10 or 12^{lb} heavier, these were males, and in the spring of the year the woods resounded with the cry of the Gobblers.[1]

Pheasants[2] enlivened the forest with their peculiar drumming; the Partridge, or quail, was not seen or heard until fields of grain were here, to give them sustenance. Pigeons in autumn and spring covered the country when nuts were plentiful. The Conneaut and Pymatuning marshes were favorite roosting places. In the evening they filled the sensible horizon,

---

[1] See Appendix, 326, description of a turkey hunt.
[2] Grouse.

and the sound of their myriad wings resembled distant thunder, as they came fluttering and covering the trees and bushes, many of which were broken with their weight. In the morning they took their flight in like manner, spreading over the land, until neither beach nut or acorn remained.

Of noxious animals, the wolf was the most numerous & destructive. Their lugubrious howl and peculiar cry of the pack, was the nightly serenade to the early settlers. Calves and swine, required watchful care & especially nightly protection.

Bears were also numerous and troublesome, hogs of large size they wo^d seize & drag away. The flesh of a fat bear, was prized by the early settlers; they sometimes weighed 400 and even 500 lb^s, and yielded a large quantity of oil, which in those days was valued in the culinary department of the housewife. Panthers were few & shy, seldom seen.

The wild cat or Lynx was sometimes bold & threatening, in close quarters it was a ferocious & dangerous animal.

Of the fur bearing animals—the Beaver was most valuable. They inhabited the Conneaut & Pymatuning Marshes in numbers and were found along the smaller class of creeks wherever the convenience of sites & timber for the formation of their dams were found. As late as 1807 I saw recent work done by them on the "little Broken Straw" creek. Some 30 years ago I saw the skin of one brought into Franklin, it was supposed to be the last inhabitant of the county, was trapped on Sandy Creek. They soon migrate when man disturbs their solitude.

The next animal of value for its fur, which inhabited our creeks, was the Otter. They were numerous, but have become nearly extinct. Otter slides were seen on the clay banks of our creeks until late years. The mink fur next in value was also found in the neighborhood of brooks.

The red & gray Fox & the Raccoon were found every where. The raccoon was very destructive to the corn fields of early times. The most dreaded, because the most dangerous nuisance of the first years of settlement was the Rattlesnake. They were numerous along the creek vallies & the adjoining high lands. Many were of immense size, having attained their maximum growth, as the Indians seldom or never killed them. Very few persons were bitten by them. I remember but 5, two of whom died. But hairbreadth escapes were many. In 1798 the Blacksmith employed by the Holl^d Ld Comp^y when building their Grist mill on Oil Creek, made his lodging in his shop, it being open & cool. One morning opening his eyes, a large rattlesnake was quietly in coil, within a few inches of his face. He remembered being partially awake some time before, and by moonlight saw what he supposed to be his bl^k silk handkerchief, which had been his nightcap, he quietly slept again until daylight revealed the proximity of his dangerous companion. Needless to say his shop was no longer his lodging place. Gen^1 John Dick remembers, with myself, the finding of a hen's nest in a hollow stump, by some school boys, on the lot now the residence of Alfred Huidekoper, Esq. They were about to make a prize of the eggs when a sudden motion revealed a rattlesnake snugly coiled around the nest.

The gnat was the most troublesome pest to the early settlers; so small as to be almost invisible, yet so tormenting by their sting as to render it impossible during morning and evening hours, or cloudy days, in the summer, to do any such work as hoeing, weeding, &c., without smoke, movable with the person. Vain were the attempts to sleep, unless the entrance of the cabin had the customary protection of a smouldering fire of chips. The exposed skin of a person (if stationary) would instantly appear black, and the pain was of minute sparks of fire.

These insects were troublesome to horses and cattle; but their chief plague was the large horse fly, which drove them in from the woods every clear day about 8 or 9 o'clock. Exposed horses died under the infliction, by pain and loss of blood. We made fires of rotten wood & chips, and the cattle would run in as the morning advanced, and hold their head & neck in the smoke, with a self protecting instinct.

CHAPTER V

RIVERS AND ROADS

Since communication and transportation are so essential to the development of a region, it may be that the lack of roads and tardy development of river communication were responsible, at least in part, for the relatively slow growth of the population in northwestern Pennsylvania. Prior to the coming of the French only the trails used by the native Indians served as channels for communication.

How or by whom the original trails were made through this part of the country by those who early explored it is still conjecture. Perhaps it may never be known—not that it matters much. But it is of interest to note that they more frequently followed the water courses where possible, taking advantage of easy grades and of the lesser elevation at a "divide" which separated the sources of streams. Between the Great Lakes and the Ohio River were several trails over which travel was possible and laborious. Of these the trail from Presque Isle on Lake Erie to Logstown at the forks of the Ohio was of greatest importance to the new English Colonies. This fact was recognized by New France when she planned to build a chain of forts to support her claim to the land between the Great Lakes and the Ohio River.

Washington and Christopher Gist have given the earliest records of this trail in their journals of that epoch-making journey to Fort Le Boeuf which resulted in saving this territory to an English-speaking people. Today there is nothing to mark the Venango Trail, but early records and maps indicate that it paralleled the banks of French Creek. From Venango on the Ohio northward, it followed the east bank through the Indian village of Cussewago, on and up over the "Big Crossing," continuing on the west side to the source, Lac Le Boeuf. From there was a fourteen-mile portage over the divide to Presque Isle. To the time of American Independence this trail was used in making the difficult passage between the St. Lawrence valley and that of the Ohio by the Indians, and also by French, English, and American colonists. For many years afterward it continued to be the shortest route between the two regions.

Making its source in six glacial lakelets, French Creek flows southward as a tributary to the Allegheny River. Before the last ice cap receded, geologists think that the middle branch of the Allegheny River then used French Creek Valley to flow northwest and empty into Lake Erie near Conneaut Harbor. Nothing was done about improved roads from that time until 1753 when the French cut a road over the fourteen miles between Le Boeuf and Presque Isle, this construction consisting principally in cutting down enough trees—leaving the stumps—and underbrush to let military supply wagons

Road Built by the French before 1760, from Le Boeuf to Presque Isle, as it appeared in 1937.

Andrew Ellicott, Astronomer. Surveyor General under Washington.

pass, and in building a few bridges. If at this time the building of any other road west of the mountains had been started, there is no record of its completion.

Over this road down to Le Boeuf moved all the military supplies for the erection of the French forts south and west, there to be loaded in boats and sent on the flood waters of French Creek to their destination. The troops of General Contracour used this route in starting out upon the campaign in which Fort Trent was captured and which upon its completion was renamed Fort Duquesne. During the several years following, close communication was maintained between Presque Isle and Fort Duquesne, dispatches, men, and supplies being transported over the road and river between the two forts.

At the termination of the French and Indian War, the posts along the Venango Trail were occupied by the British and communication was constant between them. In writing to General Monckton from Presque Isle in August, 1760, Colonel Boquet enclosed a rough draft of this wild territory, outlining the route from Fort Pitt to Presque Isle between Custologa's town and Fort Le Boeuf on the west side of French Creek; while in another letter he gives the position of his command, which was composed of "Royal Americans and Virginia Militia," as near the Mingo town on Beef River, stating that he had marched 104 miles from Fort Pitt and that he was yet 30 miles distant from Presque Isle. This would indicate his position as being at Cussewago. This use of the name "Beef River" undoubtedly arises from confusion with "La Riviere aux Boeufs," the original French designation for the stream. It occurs in another letter[1] which he wrote to General Monckton, March 20, 1761, from Fort Pitt:

... *Beef River* would be one of the best communications if cleaned of Trees and Logs, They are so entangled & heaped in some narrow Places & the Channel so deep there, that it would require a great number of hands to do it effectually, as it continues from Place to Place for about 50 miles, And unless the Trees hanging in the water on both sides are cut down, They will be daily falling in & form new obstructions; which makes me think that the best way for this year will be to open only Beaver dams, & a narrow channel for one Batteau; ...

As to the Carrying Place,[2] The French had two Waggon Roads, The old one pretty hilly, 15 miles long which they intend to abandon, the Bridges being all to Pieces; The other more level and three miles shorter is cleared of Trees but full of bushes grown since, ...

Three decades passed before the state took formal steps to solve the problem of communication in the region of French Creek Valley. In a Military Journal[3] kept by Major Ebenezer Denny an entry describes the condition of the portage road in 1793.

October 18th.—Set out with twelve men, accompanied by

---

[1] *Collections of the Massachusetts Historical Society, The Aspinwall Papers* (Boston, 1871), Fourth Series, IX, 396.
[2] Portage from Presque Isle to Le Boeuf.
[3] *Memoirs of the Historical Society of Pennsylvania* (Philadelphia, 1860), VII, 382-409.

Mr. Ellicott, on a visit to Presqu'Isle. Went by what is called the grubbed road. It seems that the French had opened the Indian path from Presqu'Isle to Le Boeuf, and wagoned considerably upon it, they found that it was some miles about, and that they had commenced the road upon a wrong plan; that it would take more labor to keep it in repair than would open one upon a straight line, notwithstanding, near five miles was a crossway'd, and no road can be had from the lake to French creek with less. However, the direct course was found, and they began with cutting it out forty feet in width, which was pursued from the ford on Mill creek all the way to Le Boeuf. They also erected several large bridges, thirty, forty, fifty feet in length, across hollow ways and deep runs, overlaid with purcheons about eighteen feet long. But there does not appear to have been any cross-way done. Though it will certainly want as much as the old road, yet there has been a vast deal of digging. The course being straight, the way unavoidably led up and down every little precipice that presented, but all these were leveled; every point and sidling ground was made easy, and is still so. But the bridging has decayed and fallen down in the centre. But what appears the most extraordinary is the grubbing. The country through is covered with a vast deal of heavy timber, notwithstanding every tree, from one end to the other, has been taken up by the roots and rolled out. However, it does not appear that ever they made use of this road; for when the trees were taken up the holes were yet so deep as to make it bad for horses. No doubt the road was intended for a grand way. It is now grown up with small wood, but the largest to be seen does not exceed six inches. It is supposed that eight men could cut out a mile in a day. After that there must be a cross-way for four or five miles, and some of the old bridges repaired, the root holes filled; in places ditching would be very serviceable. The distance is between ten and twelve miles. We left Le Boeuf about eight o'clock and were at Presqu'Isle about two. Spent the afternoon along the lake and looking around the old fort...

19th.—Left Presqu'Isle about seven o'clock. Returning by the old cart road. Got back to Le Boeuf about two o'clock. The old road appears now to be dryer than the grubbed one. Indeed in many places where the cross-waying is, the ground does not appear to want it. The country upon both roads is wet; will make fine grazing farm...

In April of 1793 Governor Thomas Mifflin wrote to General William Irvine[1] and Andrew Ellicott about the laying out of a town at Presqu'Isle which had been authorized by the Legislature, and in closing mentioned that he would include the name of Mr. John Wilkins, Jr., in the commission for laying out the road but the road was of secondary importance. The road was planned from Reading to Presqu'Isle.

His work of laying out the city of Washington, D. C., having progressed to a point where he could leave it in charge of his brothers and assistants, Major Ellicott, one of the few scientific men of that time and an astronomer of note, left Philadelphia and arrived in Pittsburgh by the thirtieth of May. With him were his son Andrew, seventeen, and Enoch Lewis, the latter not deterred by the warning the Major had given that th

... proposed expedition[2] would not be accomplished without

---

[1] Thomas Mifflin to William Irvine and Andrew Ellicott, April, 1793, Irvine Papers. (In Library of the Historical Society of Pennsylvania, Philadelphia.)

[2] Memoir of Enoch Lewis, quoted in Catharine Van Cortlandt Mathews, *Andrew Ellicott His Life and Letters* (New York, 1908), 108.

privation and exposure, and that the hardships incident to a long journey in the wilderness far beyond the limits of the white settlements, and the risk of sickness with such miserable attendance as a camp could supply, ought not to be encountered without due consideration, and that the dangers arising from the revengeful feelings of the Indians with whom a fierce war had been recently waged, and whose peaceful dispositions could not be relied on, were not to be disregarded.

This advice had been gained in the hard school of experience while in 1784, with David Rittenhouse and other commissioners, they had completed the unfinished Mason and Dixon boundary between Pennsylvania and Virginia. The following year a letter from his friend David Rittenhouse informed him that he had been appointed one of the commissioners to run the Western Boundary of the State of Pennsylvania, which was completed the same year.

Already the road from Reading to Pittsburgh had many travelers to the frontier and beyond, but from the latter place to Presqu'Isle there was only an Indian trail overland to Venango following French Creek up to Lac Le Boeuf and a long portage to Lake Erie. The appointment of a commission to survey and build a road in the western frontier emphasizes the importance attached at this time to the opening of this territory to settlers by both the State and the Federal Governments.

Early in June, 1793, Ellicott sent off the surveyors to measure the road from Pittsburgh to Venango. He is mentioned by Captain Denny as being at Le Boeuf the following month, but little was accomplished that season owing to the "hostile disposition" of the Indians, who asserted that the lands surveyed had not been legally purchased from them. Andrew Ellicott in a series of letters wrote to Governor Mifflin and others of the progress, trials, and obstacles of projecting the surveys and roads. As a result Governor Mifflin wrote to President Jefferson that "a firm hand will better make the Indians behave than a seeming deference."

May 24, 1794, Governor Mifflin[1] wrote from Philadelphia to Commissioners William Irvine, Andrew Ellicott, and Albert Gallatin:

> The enclosed copy of a letter from the Secretary of War, ... will show you that it is the particular request of the President of the United States, that the survey and the establishment of the town at Presqu'-isle, should for the present be suspended. Though I have reason to lament that this interposition was not made at an earlier period, a sincere desire ... to avoid the imputation of extending the sphere of the Indian hostilities, commands on my part a prompt and willing acquiescence. ...

A letter[2] written to Captain Denny from Fort Franklin on June 14, 1794, is apprehensive of trouble.

Sir/

From the best information which can be collected respecting the present disposition of the six nations there is reason to

---
[1] Irvine Papers (in Historical Society of Pennsylvania, Philadelphia), XII, 48.
[2] Mathews, *Ellicott*, 113.

apprehend that owing to British influence they are meditating an attack upon this place—On which account considering the weak state and great importance of this post both to the United States and State of Pennsylvania it appears necessary for your detachment to remain at this place until the arrival of Capt. Obeal who has been sent for by Gen. Wilkins and myself— It must be evident that if we should proceed to Lebeuf and the Indians to obtain possession of this post that our retreat would be cut off and the inhabitants of Cussawago left to the mercy of the savages.

      I am Sir
        with great esteem
         and regard
           AND ELLICOTT.

And to General Israel Chapin:[1]

      FORT LE BEUFF, June 25th 1794.

Dear Sir/

. . . I shall have no objection to an interview with the Chiefs of the six nations and hearing their complaints if any— Capt Obeal is mistaken about his warrior being lost below Venango— he is now at that place and has been constantly treated with respect by the white people— In a drunken frolic an Indian was killed by one Robinson at that Post and they in return have killed five for him. . . I shall be glad to see you, my old friend. I am with much esteem

        Your real Friend
          A. ELLICOTT.

To Governor Mifflin[1] from Le Boeuf, June 29th:

Sir,

 In my last Letter . . . I mentioned that you might expect to

---

[1] Ibid., 114.

hear from me both from Fort Franklin and Le Boeuf, but . . . no opportunity occured of writing from the first. On my arrival there the place appeared to be in such a defenceless Situation, that . . . we remained there some time and employed the troops in rendering it more tenable. . . The Garrison at present consists of twenty-five men, . . . double that number would not be more than sufficient, considering the Importance of the Safety of the Settlements on French Creek. At Fort Franklin Gen¹ Wilkins and myself wrote to the Corn-planter[1] to attend there that we might have an opportunity of explaining to him the nature of our business. . . After repairing Fort Franklin we proceeded to this place, and are now beginning to strengthen the works here so as to render it 'a safe deposit for military and other Stores. . . .

I am your Real Friend
A. ELLICOTT.

Again to the Governor:[2]

LE BOEUF Oc^t. 1st, 1794.

Sir/

We have been for some days past anxiously waiting to hear the result of the pending treaty with the Six Nations at Buffaloe Creek. . . Capt Denny takes the same precaution as if the Fort was actually blockaded which confinement is very disagreeable to the detachment and has soured the minds of some of the Officers and the men generally who have heretofore been used to frontier scouting. They have manifested a desire to see the Lake but this being denied them (perhaps with propriety) has contributed considerably to increase their dissatisfaction. . .

---

[1] Cornplanter (Captain O'Bail) the half-breed Seneca chief, son of John O'Bail, an Indian trader, was born in 1732. An enemy of the Americans during the frontier warfare of western New York, he later became their friend.

[2] Mathews, *Ellicott*, 117-118.

If any encouragement had been given or countenance shown by the Commandant I am confident that at least thirty houses would have been erected at this place this season which would have added considerably to the importance of this part of the State and been a centre round which settlements would shortly have been made. But without encouragement and notwithstanding the risk, one house is commenced, two others up to the square, and about 400 logs ready for building on lots which have been applied for.

It appears to me it would be highly advantageous to the State to have a Town laid out on the Public reservation at Venango and the lots disposed of in the same manner as the Legislature intended those at Presqu'Isle. Every person acquainted with the geography of this State must not only be sensible of the importance of the following situations, Viz. Venango, Mouth of the Conowango River, le Boeuf, and Presqu'Isle, but also of the propriety of some encouragement to such adventurers as may settle at those places, for by a generous conduct emigrations from the State down the Ohio may be greatly checked and a very valuable part of the commonwealth put in a fair way of being peopled.

You need be under no apprehension of this post being surprized. The Vigilance of Capt. Denny will be found superior to any attempt of that kind.

In my last communication I mentioned the advantage which would result to the Public by having the Presqu'Isle road opened and put in order this fall by the detachment stationed at this place. The necessity of this measure appears to be daily increasing, and if gone into it will give the men an opportunity of seeing the Lake which was a leading motive with many of them for entering into the service. If they only see Presqu'Isle and the south side of Lake Erie I can answer for their becoming adventurers as soon as it can be done with safety.

A. ELLICOTT.

In Major Ellicott's opinion, the keeping open of the Venango Trail was vital to development of the western country.

> LE BOEUF, Oct 1st 1794 at 5 OClock[1]
> in the Morning.

MY DEAR SALLY

We are yet stationed at this place, but will shortly have to leave it and return home,—not by the command of Capt. Cornplanter, Wood-Bug, Dogs-about-the-fire, hot-Bread, hot-Ashes, Big-Boil-of a Kettle, Broken-Twig, Standing-Stone, flying-Cloud, Bears-Oil, Mud-eater, Big-fish-carrier, Old-Turkey, The-Terrepin, Snake, He-cant-find-it, the-stringer-of-***ts, Twenty-Canoes, or any other two-legged King of this country; but by the command of a much more powerful Monarch, who is now making a most violent attack upon my fingers, and toes; that is Capt. or King Frost.

We are all in a fine state of health, but almost naked for the want of cloaths. As yet we have been able to keep ourselves moderately warm with Blankets, and Bear-Skins. As to women, we know nothing about them except by recollection,— we have not seen one of any color for near four months. without joaking I expect we shall *certainly* receive orders to return in less than two weeks, if not, I shall *certainly* set out on the fifteenth of this month . . . for about three months past we have scarcely been out of sight of the Fort. From this circumstance my DEAR, you suppose that we are in danger, but that is not the case, we are not in danger near the Fort, and for fear of danger never leave it— There has not been an Indian seen within twenty miles of this place for almost three months, which is the only reason we have to suppose them not friendly— we amuse ourselves with playing Checkerds,

---

[1] Mathews, *Ellicott*, 118-119.

or what is an infinitely more intricate, and noble game Chess, which is played on the same board, with Kings, Queens, Bishops, Knights, Castles, and Pawns,—I have with my own hands, with my Pen-Knife made three complete sets, each consisting of thirty two pieces, and one half set couriously wrought in bone.

There is some discontent among the Troops, and too much sparing among the Officers— . . .

       I am my Dr Sally
         your Loving
          Husband.

Commissioners Irvine and Ellicott wrote to Governor Mifflin from Franklin in January, 1795, relative to continuing the survey at Presqu'Isle. In a letter dated at Philadelphia, April 18th, the Governor wrote to the President of the United States enclosing a copy of "An Act[1] to provide for the laying out and establishing towns and out-lots within the several tracts of land heretofore reserved for public use Situated respectively at Presqu' isle on Lake Erie, at the mouth of French Creek,[2] at the mouth of Conewango Creek,[3] and at Fort Le Boeuf."[4] Owing to the difficulty in enlisting sufficient Militia for protection and laborers, it was June before the work actually started at Venango and July when they reached Lake Erie. Ellicott wrote his wife in September men-

---

[1] Governor Mifflin to the President of the United States, April 18, 1795, Irvine Papers.
[2] Franklin.
[3] Warren.
[4] Waterford.

tioning "our Surgeon" Dr. Thomas R. Kennedy,[1] who later married their daughter Jane Judith and resided in Meadville. And the middle of that month Lieutenant Colonel Stephen Rochefontaine, in command at Presqu' Isle, sent the commissioners a copy of the treaty with the Indians.[2]

In the fall the commissioners wrote to the Governor.[3]

Pittsburgh, October 27th 1795
Your letter of the 25th of September met us at Franklin on our return from Cuniwango—Exploring ground for a road from Reading to Presqu'isle, having been charg [paper torn here] by your commission of long standing, but could not be entered on sooner, we thought we could not spend a few days better than in examining the ground from Le Boeuff to the Allegheny River accordingly we not only explored but actually cut a way commonly called a Bridle road or path directly on the rout or course to Reading . . . We arrived at this place on the 23rd instant, after having completed all business assigned to us, the time may seem long, but the work was great . . . a considerable time must unavoidably elapse before fair copies of the plans of all the towns can be prepared for you.

Few moderns in riding over hard surfaced roads

[1] November 4, 1795, the schooner "White Fish" built at Presque Isle by Dr. T. R. Kennedy, surgeon with the command of Captain Drury, and a young man of the camp, arrived at Philadelphia with the builder on board. Having been carried around Niagara Falls and over the portage between the Oswego and Mohawk Rivers, this was the first vessel to demonstrate that transportation could be established between Lake Erie and the Hudson River.

[2] Step. Rochefontaine to The Hon. Commissioners of Pennsylvania, September 18, 1795, Irvine Papers.

[3] William Irvine and Andrew Ellicott to Governor Mifflin, October 27, 1795, Irvine Papers.

think of the obstacles and dangers encountered by those hardy men when attempting to first lay them out through wild lands. The hazardous services of those men may be forgotten, but their work lives on.

CHAPTER VI

"SENECA OIL"

A shroud of mystery surrounds the first inhabitants of this region—a shroud which may never be lifted. There is abundant evidence that it was at one time occupied by a race of men very different in habits and civilization from the Indians, who were in possession when the white men first saw it. The mythical Alleghees perhaps drove out the Mound Builders, to be conquered in turn by the invasion of the western tribes, which afterward made the confederation known as the Six Nations. The latter exterminated the Eries, or Cats as the French called them, and the Kahkaws. But students of past records believe that a race possessing intelligence superior to the Indians, who inhabited the district when La Salle discovered the Ohio, built the mounds scattered over the middle west extending into Pennsylvania and western New York. It may be possible that the people who built the mysterious pits in the southeast corner of Crawford County and strange earthworks near the Pymatuning Reservoir and up through French Creek Valley belonged to this race.

In 1880 Alfred Huidekoper, T. R. Kennedy, Arthur C. Huidekoper, and William Reynolds visited some of the mounds in this vicinity, and a record[1] was kept by

[1] William Reynolds (Reynolds Collection)

William Reynolds.

the author's father. William Reynolds, the youngest of the children of John Reynolds and Jane Judith (Ellicott) Kennedy, was born in Meadville April 25, 1820, and in the 91 years which followed he was a leader, accomplishing much for his community. Graduating from Allegheny College in 1837, he was admitted to the bar of Crawford County in '41, and in '43 Jefferson College gave him the Degree of A. M. Like his father he was identified with many early enterprises and carried on a large land business. He was among those who planned and built the plank roads, also one of the incorporators of the Merchants National Bank and the Meadville Water Company, and president of the Meadville Library, Art and Historical Association, and the Meadville Gas and Water Company. Many years of his life were identified with railroads; he was largely instrumental in the building of the Atlantic and Great Western and was its first president. Also like his father, he did much to preserve records of northwestern Pennsylvania and the community in which he lived.

Passing through Shermansville the first point explored was on the land of Mr. G. Haven in Pine Township and very near the west line of Sadsbury Township. On the south side of the public road immediately and some 200 feet distant from the residence of Mr. Odell in an old clearing are a series of small pits about 15 feet apart. These excavations as now seen are nine in number forming irregularly three sides of a parallagram. About midway on the fourth side is a pit upon the margin of which is the stump of a tree of some 18 inches in diameter which evidently grew since the digging of the pit. These excavations are from 18 inches to 2 feet in depth and from 2 to 3 feet in diameter.

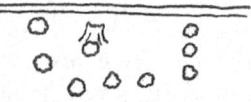

Upon removing the earth from the bottom to the depth of a foot small pieces of charcoal and brick red earth and stones bore evidence of fire, rendering it probable that they had been used for cooking purposes or for lodge fires.

After a careful examination of these the party left north on the road laid on the line of Pine and Sadsbury to the farm of Samuel Gehr about one-half mile from the Odell house. Here the road cuts through a circular earthen embankment 200 feet in diameter north and south and 243 feet east and west. The embankment and ditch from which the earth was excavated are very distinct. Outside of the enclosure on the eastern side 14 pits similar to those on the Haven land were counted. There appeared to be no regularity in location, and the number may have been much larger than we found. On digging the earth from the bottom the same evidences of fire were discovered—charcoal and burned earth.

About 80 rods east of this enclosure or fortification the party were shown a tumulus or supulcral mound in the midst of the native forest—30 feet in its greatest and 25 feet in its lesser diameter and about 5 or 6 feet in height. Trees of 18 inches diameter were growing on this mound. An excavation made some years ago by a son of Mr. Gehr in the centre of the mound disclosed human bones at a depth of 3 feet.

Further north one and one-half miles on the farm of R. Bishop west of the road the party visited two similar circular embankments each of near 100 feet in diameter. The latter are in a field which has been cultivated for many years and the plow has left very slight traces of the works which a few more years will entirely obliterate.

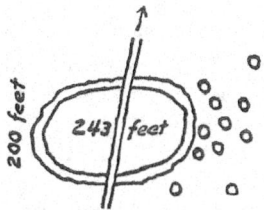

On bottom lands of French Creek there were other mounds; one just south of Meadville measured 100 feet in length, 25 feet in width, and was 8 feet high. Nearby a smaller one was 50 feet long and 3 feet high, from which were taken several skeletons and some implements. These were leveled and the Erie Railroad tracks cross the place where they were. There was another mound on land owned by Cornelius Van Horn across the Creek.

In writing of his visit to the pits near Titusville, William Reynolds quoted a part of an address delivered in 1843 by William H. Davis:

A short distance below the village of Titusville, and on the west side of Oil Creek, there are perhaps about *two thousand* pits, scattered over a level plain not exceeding five hundred acres. Some of them are very close together; as close as the vats in a tan yard, which they somewhat resemble, each being seven or eight feet long, four wide and six feet deep. These pits had nearly all been filled; some of them entirely so by vegetable deposit, perhaps the accumulation of ages. The mounds raised at the sides of the pits by the excavation of the earth from it are distinctly visible. Close upon the margin of them on the very mounds of the earth excavated are trees whose size indicates an age of two or three hundred years.

The early settlers first discovered the pits from the regularity of size. They were induced to open them and found that each pit was walled with logs regularly cut and halved at the ends so that they could lie close together. It was found that the water rose in the bottom of these pits and in a few days would be covered with oil to the depth of a third or half inch.

Of the many pits[1] that were cleaned out at this time and later, all were found to have been built and walled in like manner. Their probable purpose was for skimming what the first settlers knew as Seneca Oil. The Indians had no traditions about them and there are no records to show that they had been constructed by the French during their occupation. The size of the trees growing upon the mounds of earth would indicate that these pits antedated both French and Indians of the eighteenth century.

Like those who built these pits, the early settlers recognized the value of the oil which collected in them.

Nath[l] Carey was the first settler in the valley of oil creek,[1] he learned from the Indians that the oil flowed from a spring on the margin of the creek. they were not willing to take him

---

[1] John Reynolds to L. McKnight, January 9, 1860 (Reynolds Collection) See Appendix.

to the place, he feigned sickness & a desire to bathe in the spring—and by offer of money induced an Indian to take him from Franklin in a canoe to the spring. He soon afterwards took possession & settled the tract this must have been 1796 or 7. He made a business of gathering the oil—and peddling it over the state, as a valuable medicine. His handbill sheets recommending its use as an universal panacea for the ills that flesh is heir to—wo^d well compare with the quack bills of the present day He was well known thro' the State in his day, The tract has been known of late days as the Clapp farm. on it were many ancient marks of digging apparently to find the source of the oil, but at so remote a period, that neither the French or Indians had any traditionary history reaching so far in the misty past.

Hamilton McClintock settled in the spring of ,97 the tract adjoining Carey, who was his Brother-in-law, he discovered a spring in the centre of the creek, which he surrounded with a rough wall of stone, plastered with mud above the water mark, the oil accumulated on the surface of the water, & thus he collected 8 or 10 barrels during the summer season. I saw him thus gathering it with a piece of blanket. he told me that before he discovered the spring, he gathered 18 gall^{ns} by shovelling the gravel on the margin of the creek, into a canoe, then pouring in water & skimming off the oil—but he found it laborious & tedious, and soon discovered the spring.

The first record of the administration of an estate, that of General William Wilson, found within the Counties of Crawford or Venango, was discovered in a day book[1] kept at his store in the trading post at Fort Franklin, 1792-7. Under the date of November, 1797, appears this item: "3 kegs of Seneca oil $50 per keg." It is

[1] (Reynolds Collection)

IN FRENCH CREEK VALLEY

probable that this oil was gathered from the springs of either Nathaniel Carey or Hamilton McClintock, and this the earliest quotation of price for petroleum recorded in this country.

At a later date citizens of Meadville became interested in oil, as is evidenced by the writings of William Reynolds.[1]

When a small boy I rode on horseback with my father to his old pioneer home in Cherrytree, Venango County. On return we visited the farm of Mr. McClintock and in a canoe went to the oil spring in the creek and saw the process of collecting the oil. The oil was from time to time gathered from the surface of the water, spreading blankets and wringing out the oil.

Other small springs were afterwards utilized to a limited extent. In the vicinity of Titusville many ancient excavations proved more extensive production in a remote time.

In 1854 Messrs. Eveleth and Bissell of New York secured the right to a spring near Titusville. Prof. Sillimon, Jr. made a favorable analysis of the oil. Nothing further was done until Dec. 1857 when Messrs. Bowditch and Drake of New Haven commenced further explorations. Mr. Drake completed his arrangements for drilling the rock substrata in the winter of 1858-9 and on Aug. 26, 1859 oil was reached at a depth of 71 feet—the oil rising to within two feet of the surface. A small pump gave 400 gallons per day—a larger pump increased the production to 1000 barrels.

Continuing with reference to the mode of sending oil to the outside market:

[1] Early History of the Petroleum Industry, 1905 (Reynolds Collection)

"SENECA OIL" 75

The only means of transportation was by boat on Oil Creek and the Allegheny or by wagon to Shaws Landing on the canal five miles south of Meadville, to the Erie & Pittsburgh R. R. at Linesville or to Erie.

This account extends only to 1861, with an estimated daily of 1200 to 1400 barrells per day.

The first shipment of oil to Europe was twelve barrells to James McHenry by myself and Mr. Jas. Shryock in Jany. 1861 —samples from which were distributed to members of the board of trade in London and to chemical experts at Paris.

Mentioning the first oil for export to Europe, William Reynolds states:

In my correspondence with Mr. James McHenry our European Agent I had represented the importance of this traffic to the Atlantic & Great Western Railroad enterprise. Mr. McHenry writes—"Please send me large sample of oil in its various states and all information you can give me."

In compliance with this request Mr. James Shryock requestde his brother Mr. George Shryock to visit the Oil Creek wells and send twelve barrels of selected oil to Mr. McHenry at Liverpool. This consignment was carried by wagon to the terminus of the A. & G. W. R. R. at Jamestown, N. Y.

From Paris McHenry wrote on June 18, 1861:

The examination of the oil shows a splendid result for the purpose of the fabrication of gas . . . The Gas Company considers it *better* than any thing they know of for the fabrication, and all depends on the cost of oil placed in New York or London. . .

If the oil comes cheap the trade will be fabulous not only on the whole continent—Italy, Spain, England. . .

I consider the oil springs very greatly more valuable than any assistance you may get for the completion of your road.

CHAPTER VII

FARM LIFE

The farming[1] of Western Penn^a was without skill science or neatness. To clear and cultivate a farm in this region was to the first settlers an arduous undertaking. It required strong hands, stout hearts, & a willing mind. Many privations must be suffered. The settler must enter the forest, fell the trees, chop, roll and burn the logs, and grub the undergrowth. Early and late must be his working hours, giving scant time to eat his frugal meal.

Trees that wo^d die by girdling were permitted to stand until a more convenient time for removal, hence growing crops were frequently injured by the fall of the tree or its decaying branches during the wind storms of summer.

Exhaustion of the fertilizing elements in the soil was the effect of ceaseless culture without manure, which was permitted to accumulate in the barnyard, until it became a question of economy whether to remove the barn or the manure. I remember a notable instance of a farmer who had so great an accumulation, that he became weary of making paths through the piles to reach his stable door, and at a safe distance built a new barn, removed the old one (which was log) and taking advantage of a spell of dry weather, put fire to and consumed the manure heap.

The plough of those days was a rude instrument, wooden mould board with wrought iron share and coulter, which rarely turned a furrow neatly. Every few days a visit to the

---

[1] John Reynolds, MS (Reynolds Collection) *Reminiscences of the Olden Times,* Meadville *Daily Republican,* June and July, 1867 (in the *Tribune-Republican* file, Meadville)

blacksmith was necessary to sharpen the share and coulter, and blacksmiths were few and far between, and oftimes without coal; a serious disappointment to the poor wight who had carried the irons on his shoulders a half dozen miles. The harrow was oftimes a fork cut out of a tree with wooden teeth: Iron was dear and blacksmiths few.

The sickle & scythe reaped our grain and mowed the meadows. All mowing was done with the scythe having a natural crooked stick for its sneth (a hundred acres sometimes walked over to find one suitable). A few old men may remember in the days of their youth, the hilarity of the harvest fields, especially, when the maidens came with the ev^g refreshment, and all sat under the pleasant shade to partake, a half hour quickly passed when with revived energies the sickle was plied until sunset. Tho' hard labour, and homely fare, were the general experience of those days, yet there were compensations, vigorous health, & slow but sure advance in personal and neighborhood prosperity.

Threshing machines were unknown, & fanning mills very rare, the flail & a sheet were the instruments for threshing & winnowing the grain. Waggons were seldom seen in the new settlement, sleds with wooden soles were in general use for gathering harvest & going to mill &c. Horses were few in number and not much used except for the saddle. In the condition of the roads & newly cleared fields, oxen were preferable for draught and much easier provided with forage and shelter.

Before meadows co^d be made, the settler had difficulty in wintering his oxen & cow. He went with his axe morning and ev^g to the forest & cut down maple or linden trees, the small extremities of the branches, were eaten, this was called "browsing his cattle," which with little grain kept them in good condition. In the summer the woods afforded excellent pasture, the Pea vine entwined and covered the herbage, with its delicate tendrills & tiny pods, which with the wild bean supplied the cattle with nutriment of remarkably fattening qualities but swine and cattle soon destroyed those nutritious plants and reduced the wood pasture to the barren waste we now in summer see.

But the range was so extensive that much time was lost in hunting the cows. A good bell was a necessary appendage. One morning I went into a neighbor's house; he was eating a late breakfast, having just returned from hunting his cow which had lost her bell. Much of the family comfort was dependent on her milk and she had been absent a day or two. The good wife that morning turned over for another nap, after her husband early left the cabin. She dreamed "that she took her babe in her arms, and went along a path in the woods which led over a burnt ridge, half a mile distant; that a short distance to the left, as she stood on said ridge, she saw a high stump, to which she went, and found the bell. The cow had rubbed her neck on the rough wood and broken the bell strap." She awoke with the excitement and arose; the vividness of the dream in all its parts, impressing her as with reality; she took her babe realized all the circumstances of the dream, and brought home the bell, to the joy of her household.

The mystery of the dream I submit as one of the phenomena pertaining to mental philosophy.

In that day throughout the country simplicity and economy were almost universal with families. How did our Grandmothers kindle their fires? The tinder box was in every kitchen, a circular tin box with close fitting movable cover, half burnt linen, called tinder was kept in it, which received a spark, struck from flint & steel, and by the application of a brimstone match fire was obtained.

The pitch pine knot, the sheet iron lamp with its linen wick fed with kitchen grease and the tallow candle were the lights of those early nights.

The kitchen fireplace of wide dimensions, with crane and pothooks. The long spit on brackets, before the fireplace, on which our ancestors roasted their turkies, beef &c. and which were rotated by chimney Jack (a wheel in the chimney turned by smoke) a turn spit dog, or by hand. For this the large reflecting tin kitchen was substituted many years later. An outdoor clay oven was the convenience for baking. With the bright pewter, which in plates & dishes, had taken the place of the wooden trencher, the thrifty housewife made a fine display, shelf above shelf.

The pleasant hum of the spinning wheel which in the evenings of our boyhood so often lulled us to sleep. The click of the reel, and the rasping sound of the cards forming the wool into rolls, to be spun upon the large wheel were heard in the family circle. Every farm had its half acre of flax growing, in the beginning of the century. Every wife and daughter made fine linen and sold it, and exchanged with the merchant. With their needles they made themselves coverings of linen and woolen; and arrayed neatly in short gown & petticoat, she needed not furbelows and flounce to set off her personal charms, "She looked well to the ways of her household and ate not the bread of idleness."

Woman had her full share in the privations and discomforts of life, as also in the labours incident to the beginning of a home in this desolate region. No wonder that on her first introduction to the log cabin in the forest, her heart sank within her; and when her child asked, "Mother, is this home?" she replied by a gush of tears, unable otherwise to answer. All the sweet memories of friends far distant, of church associations, of the thousand nameless comforts of former home ties, would, in contrast make the present moment inexpressibly painful. But soon bright visions of the future dispelled the melancholy of the present. It was cheering to stand at the head of the opening vista, and in sublime faith, see future generations, filling the wide waste with happy homes, and thus in the all wise arrangements of Providence, to have part in the beginning of so glorious a development: extending and increasing until the final consummation; this was especially conciliatory to the christian matron: and soon the disappearance of the forest, the influx of population, and the renewal of the amenities and pleasures of society, with increasing comforts from year to year, with church & school privileges, made amends for all past privations.

Society gradually assumed a state of progressive improvement, kindness & hospitality were the rule; whenever in journeying night came on the traveler, the first cabin door was open to him, and a table spread with such as they had, generally wheat or corn bread, mush & milk & vegetables & a scant supply of meat. Milk the substitute for tea or coffee, was the daily fare.

Bedding was scarce and it was the general custom with the settler who expected not to be home at night, to hoppas his blanket on his back, and make his bed on the floor with his feet to the fire & a chairback for his pillow: if uncertain of shelter; he made provision for a lodging in the woods, by having with him flint & steel & a piece of dry punk to kindle his fire, and also a piece of bread to satisfy his hunger. What a blessing the friction match wo^d have been in those days.

One room & one bed was the extent of home comfort possessed by the majority of first settlers—a large proportion of whom were young persons setting out in marriage life without much means. And it was not unusual, when a well known neighbor called for a night's lodging, for the good wife to make the bed on the floor, and the husband take the middle, wife & neighbor one on each side. I have myself thus slept in a neighbor's cabin. Sometimes a Religious or social party wo^d collect together to spend an ev^g not expecting to return to their homes until the morrow. When at bed time the woman wo^d collect all the bedding, and spread it from side to side of the floor, a man & his wife w^d then take the centre & the men & women range themselves right & left. A very aged man (Wm Connelly)[1] yet lives in Franklin in whose house I remember to have been one of 12 or 14 thus comfortably lodged.

The conventional customs of those first years wo^d be intolerable now: they were a necessity then—and withal there was no lack of modesty with the females; in such cases there was not much disrobing, and the males retired while the females lay down.

We had no school except in the county seat until the 3^d or 4th year of this century. Occasionally a miss^y passed thro' the principal settlements & at some convenient place wo^d preach a sermon to the few families that could be collected.

Life was not without its compensations: privations & dangers equally shared, drew heart to heart; and family to family in mutual attraction. It was pleasant in those years to alternate family visits, and partake of such cheer as Esau found for his Father "Isaac."

The evening of such visits passed pleasantly, at the blazing hearth, around which we gathered & listened to the tales of earlier years, when French & Indian war desolated the frontier; and fearful whoop, gave signal of death, by fire & torture to many a happy family; or more recent when England's king, with the same cruel auxilaries, enacted similar tragedies within his revolted colonies. Old men co^d tell what they saw and knew in the progressive years of both wars, the zest of

---

[1] One of the original directors of the North Western Bank of Pennsylvania.

personal narrative giving minutiae of incident; in the sudden surprise & hairbreadth escape; as also the chivalrous deeds of frontier men & women of those days, by the transfer from the mouth of the witness who saw and acted.

CHAPTER VIII

EARLY PROMOTION

Many of the pioneers belonged to families of the men who were active in the creating of the American Republic. Their self-reliance and independence are picturesquely reflected in the first efforts and important improvements which marked the growth of the little village of Meadville. The leaders possessed a progressive spirit and culture which distinguished it among the other frontier settlements. The establishment of the seat of justice brought to it men of learning, making contact with neighboring settlements and the busy world outside of the community.

Difficulty in securing the necessities of life and the distance which the few luxuries must be brought inspired the citizens to combine in seeking to remedy this condition. This was the chief factor which led to the organization of The Meadville Society for the Encouragement of Domestic Manufactures and the Useful Arts, which early in 1807 was holding monthly meetings. The association was a forerunner of the modern Chamber of Commerce. New York, Charleston, South Carolina, New Haven, and Philadelphia were the only cities in the United States at that time which had boards of trade or societies for the encouragement of trade.

Meadville was the pioneer in this movement in western Pennsylvania.

THE MESSENGER.[1]

THURSDAY-MORNING, FEBRUARY 5. (1807)

The monthly meeting of *The Meadville Society for the encouragement of Domestic Manufactures, and the useful Arts*, will be held at the court house on Thursday evening next. By order of the society.

T. ATKINSON, *Secretary*.

ADDRESS

OF "THE MEADVILLE SOCIETY FOR THE ENCOURAGEMENT OF DOMESTIC MANUFACTURES AND THE USEFUL ARTS," TO THEIR FELLOW CITIZENS OF THE WESTERN COUNTRY.

Fellow Citizens,

A FEW persons, sensible of the wants and the privations of our infant settlement, and of the many embarrassments arising from the scarcity of money, the langour of improvement, and the stationary condition of our agriculture, have associated ourselves under the name of "The Meadville Society for the encouragement of Domestic Manufactures and the useful Arts," for obviating their wants and embarrassments, to the extent of our resources and example. No citizen of this territory can be so blind as not to see, nor so stupid as not to feel

---

[1] *The Crawford Weekly Messenger*, Meadville (For story of beginning of this newspaper, see Chapter XI)

the evils by which we are afflicted and the burdens under which we groan:— So obvious are these truths that we hear you all complain, while hitherto a single effort has not been made to discover the cause or apply the remedy. However, faithful to the cause in which we have embarked, and regardless of the impediments that may be thrown in our way by the few who live upon our dependent condition, we tell you the cause of this condition, and the means we propose to alleviate, if not remedy it; and call upon you earnestly to succour our efforts with all your energies; in mercy to yourselves.

The scarcity of money has become a standing theme of complaint, as if it alone were the cause, and not the effect, of our condition. In vain would we possess money, if industry and public spirit be wanting; for it is upon the internal industry and improvement of the country, that our wealth and independence must rest, and not upon any casual influx of specie. All the little money that occasionally comes in to our country, after a short lived tour is at length sent from it to procure those articles of use and necessity, which we can not dispense with. Why then does this happen? You need only look to yourselves for an answer. The want of manufacturing establishments must always keep us moneyless and dependant; and in a territory so extensive as ours, it is melancholy to relate, that except the manufacture of whisky, a few hats, a little course linnen and leather, we are entirely without manufactures.— All our hard and iron ware, paper, cloathing, such as is manufactured of cotton, wool, flax also, in a great measure—the manufactures of hemp, oil, beer, porter, with numbers of other articles, which the compass of this paper will not admit us to enumerate, are imported. Amongst these, those articles of pressing necessity must be procured, and all our resources exhausted, to attain them. Remotely situated from a market for our produce and bulky materials, the price of carriage would diminish the value of labour, and create a competition which we could not withstand, if even we were in a situation to attempt it; while the small return from such a source would not half equal the expences we are subject to for imported goods and wares. Here, then, the ballance would still continue against us, which preying on our lands like a cancer on the human body, would finally corrode them out of our possession. But, perhaps, the scarcety of specie here is not alone occasioned by supineness and want of industry in this quarter. It may be in part occasioned by a correspondent diminution of it throughout the United States. The last annual report of the secretary of the treasury of the United States, exhibits a balance of seven million of dollars against the United States, in the course of the trade for the last year. If then the goods imported into the United States, exceed in value the goods exported from thence, seven million of dollars, this sum must be transmitted in specie, or remain a lien on our commerce. The consequence plainly is that the wants of the country, in the articles of manufacture and use, exceed our surplus produce to that amount; and shews plainly that we can not independently exist, but are indebted to other countries for the necessaries and luxuries we use or waste, to that amount.— This balance proportionably effects us, and while it does, it forcibly points out to us an excitement to manufacturing, or a correspondent abandonment of the use of such imported articles.

The circumstances of Europe for a number of years past, ought to impress us deeply with this sentiment, as it is the workshop to which we all look to satisfy the wants of necessity, and gratify that of luxury.—the conflicts of ambition, of rivalship or of interest that exists there, render external commerce precarious, and enhance the price of articles by embarrassing the means of importing them— The peril of the risque when search and inequitous captures are to be encounted, raises the premium of insurance, which in the end is added to the goods— Who must pay this advance price? not the merchant who even lays *his centage* on this very enhancement; but the farmer and mechanic who eventually consume— Yes they must as long as a fatal negligence, and insensibility to all our resources and a distrust in our own means and energies, exist. If we import more than we expect, we must run in debt—our capital must daily diminish and depreciate, and our boasted independence will be sacrificed to this criminal and commercial dependence. If then, we desire as a nation to be independent, and as individuals to be comfortable and unimbarrassed, we must turn to our own use the materials which nature has so abundantly spread before us. To diminish our imports, we must either retrench our expences or manufacture for ourselves— But as it is not easy to suppress habits which our conveniences have created, we ought rather to cherish them when we can do it in a way that will increase the wealth and establish the independence of our country. Having the means in our power, it is only necessary that we begin to use them. Our lands are fertile, they are capable of producing all the articles of necessity and many of those of luxury; and as our bulky materials will not bear a distant transportation, let our energies be directed to the culture and establishment of those manufactures and arts, which would otherwise render such transportation necessary.

The wheat, flour and liquors, which when exported would bear no proportion to the necessaries we would require in exchange, might, if manufactures be encouraged and promoted, be expended at home in their support. This produce so applied, would equal our wants, keep specie in the country, and wear away in time, our dependent situation.

Impressed with these sentiments, and wishing to propagate

them for the good of our country, this society has been established. It will impart counsel and give aid in proportion to its resources, to every undertaking that may promote manufactures, and those arts which are useful. Money will be loaned, as soon as our funds will admit of such accommodation to those who will establish an oil mill, fulling mill, spinning and carding machines, a brewery, and every other manufacturing establishment of use, upon reasonable security— Any individual friendly to such an institution, can become a member of it, upon going through the formality of an election, and contributing his specified proportion to the creating of a fund.

Thus then, to alleviate the condition of our country, and render ourselves and fellow citizens more independent and respectable, we have embarked in our undertaking which we flatter ourselves will succeed and be useful; and in this short outline have succinctly explained our motives and objects.— If our fellow citizens will only look into their condition, they will see their wants— If they look to their resources, they will see their remedy— The object of every individual must be his own happiness, and the first step towards it, is to endeavor to be independent. The resources of the country furnish the means, and we doubt not, that the citizens, in weighing these considerations, will apply the remedy.

R. ALDEN, { *President of the board of Directors.*

Henry Phillips, *Secretary.*

That these meetings bore fruit, other than talk, is attested by advertisements which later appeared in the *Crawford Messenger*:

Notice,

IS HEREBY GIVEN, that a liberal advance will be made in money by "The Meadville society for the encouragement of domestic Manufactures," to any person who will undertake the establishment of a fulling mill, at any place within the distance of ten miles from this town, during the approaching summer.— Further particulars may be had on making application to R. Alden, president of the board of directors.

By order of the board.

H. PHILLIPS, *Sec'ry.*

April 9, 1807.

150 Head of Sheep.

WANTED to purchase by the Meadville Society for the encouragement of Domestic Manufactures, one hundred and fifty head of young healthy sheep of a good growth, in flece, to be delivered at Meadville on or about the 1st day of May next, for which a reasonable price will be paid in cash. Enquire of

DAVID MEAD, *President.*

S. Torbett, *Secretary.*

Printers Pittsburg, and Mr. Snowden of Greensburg, will confer a favor by giving the above a few insertions in their respective papers.

Jan. 21, 1808.

> Flax Wanted,
> FOR which cash will be given by the Meadville Society for the encouragement of Domestic Manufactures—apply to David Mead, esq.
> By order of the society,
> SAMUEL TORBETT, *Sec'ry*.
> Feb. 2, 1809.

The inconvenience of being without and the difficulties of transporting those things which were needed for actual living were responsible for starting the pioneer to make his own tools and materials. Other persons were willing to pay, so he began by making what they would buy, and manufacturing had a small beginning. Vision, enterprise, and public spirit abetted by education and intelligence supplied the incentive, and industry produced accomplishment—and a thriving village.

CHAPTER IX

"ANN ELIZA" AND TRADESMEN

Despite the many adverse conditions and obstacles confronting the pioneers in early Meadville, there were positive attractions which induced settlers to migrate to the region. The fertility of the soil in the immediate vicinity and the possibilities of a commercial or industrial nature served as a magnet to settlers. Activities in the purchase and sale of lands[1] and the industrial developments immediately after the turn of the century are evidence of the possibilities offered by the Valley.

It was after Charles II had granted the governor of Connecticut "all the land the width of the state, from the western boundary thereof through to the Pacific ocean" that he gave William Penn a grant for the lands which eventually comprised Pennsylvania. Among those who acquired title to land in the Wyoming Valley from Penn were nine men, Cornelius Van Horn, David, John, and Joseph Mead, Christopher Snyder, James Fitz Randolph, Thomas Grant, John Watson, and Thomas Martin, who were driven out by the Connecticut claimants and forced to seek elsewhere for some place to build homes. In Colonel Washington's report to Governor Dinwiddie mention was made of flat lands along the banks

[1] See Appendix, 329, "To all those who may be desirous of Emigrating to the Western Country:"

of French Creek—this was known to some of these nine men who joined together at Sunbury, Westmoreland County, and set out for the wilderness which David and John Mead had visited the summer before. On reaching the Allegheny River, they followed it down to Fort Franklin and after a short rest proceeded up French Creek in canoes to a place where Mill Run emptied into it. That night of May 12, 1788, they slept under a large wild cherry tree in one of the "extensive and very rich meadows" mentioned by Washington.

After a day spent exploring the surrounding country they crossed the creek near the mouth of the Cussewago to one of six islands formed by the changing channel of the stream. This island, the largest of the group, had been partially cleared. It had been used by the Indians for growing corn on account of the richness of the soil, but by whom and when this clearing was made the Indians did not know for the trees were gone when they came to this region. The other islands were thickly covered with huge old trees, water maples, walnut, butternut, and sycamores. The great branches of these trees hung far out over the water, while underbrush, the smaller crab apple and thorn, with the grape vines swinging from the larger trees, made an enchanted jungle of eerie beauty. Winding between and dividing these islands, the deep shady channels were the haunt of bass, salmon, and pike beneath the smooth surface of the water.

It was in this long abandoned field, covered with tall

wild grass, that David Mead with a plow, and Cornelius Van Horn riding one of the four horses pulling it, broke the ground to plant corn. The entire crop of this planting, eight or ten acres in extent, was destroyed the following month by a freshet which swept over the island, after which the work of putting in another crop had to be done. From this second planting, they obtained enough corn to carry the new settlement through the first winter.

A little way up stream beyond where Mill Run empties into it, the main channel of French Creek swerved east circling the lower end of the largest island to resume its northerly course. It was on the bank of this river bend that the Public Dock of the Port of Meadville was built in later years and the road running past it named Dock Street. Here travelers by water landed and took passage, cargoes of freight and merchandise from down the river were unloaded and the flatboats and keelboats reloaded for the return trip. The settlers gathered at the wharf to learn the latest news of the outside world from the boatmen. The shipping of the community centered at this point.

In selling lots on the south side of Dock Street, David Mead in November, 1797, made this restriction: "It is further covenented and agreed to and by the contracting parties to these presents that all the ground between the front of lots and French Creek to remain an open and public highway forever," and Dock Street was laid out to be 70 feet in width. In planning this open space along the water front, General Mead could not foresee that at the time when the railroad was built across the islands a new channel would be cut for French Creek on the west side of the railroad tracks diverting most of the water from the old channel. With the growth of the town and the laying out of new streets, eventually this part of the old channel and part of the island would be filled in to the street level and made into Mead Park and old Dock Street changed into Mead Avenue.

A short distance up stream from the Public Dock was the Ship Yard on the east bank where John Mattocks and Noah Town built keelboats and flatboats or arks. These boats were built bottom up on the bank of the Creek and, when ready for launching, word was sent through the village. In the evening the citizens assembled and the boat slid sideways down the bank until its edge was in the water, then by the man power of the settlement using pikepoles turned over and the launching completed.

The editorial column of the *Messenger,* December 4, 1828, announced:

> Cleared from (the port of) Meadville, the fast floating boat, 'THE ANN ELIZA.'
>
> All the materials of which this boat was built were growing on the banks of French creek on the 27th ult. On the 28th she was launched, and piloted to this place before

"ANN ELIZA" AND TRADESMEN

sunset, by her expert builders, Messrs. *Mattocks* and *Town*. Her cargo consisted, among other things, of 300 reams of crown, medium and royal *patent Straw Paper*, with patent book and pasteboards; and left this place early on the 30th ult. for Pittsburg, with about 20 passengers on board.

Keelboat at Port of Meadville, 1814. View from Chestnut Street west of River Street looking south toward Dock Street (now Mead Avenue). Reprint from bank note of North Western Bank of Pennsylvania.

All the work of constructing the *Ann Eliza* was done by hand. Today we think the so-called "machine age" has given us speed!

Among the items of news printed March 21, 1810,[1] was one marked:

> *State Legislature*—The committee on domestic manufactures, have reported a bill, granting a loan of money to Thomas Collins, to enable him to carry on his salt works in Butler county.
>
> A bill has likewise been reported, authorizing the governor to incorporate a company, to build a bridge over French creek at Meadville.

---

[1] *Crawford Weekly Messenger.*

IN FRENCH CREEK VALLEY

From Pittsburgh north the only means of crossing the Allegheny River and its tributary waters was by ford or ferry. To enter Meadville, travelers on the road which was later the Mercer Turnpike ferried across French Creek just below Mill Run. On the sixth of February, 1809, the overloaded ferry boat upset in midstream when Joseph Andrews and two others together with a team were drowned. Here the following year Dr. Thomas R. Kennedy built a covered bridge, lumber for the siding having been cut in New York State at his Connewango Mills and rafted down the Allegheny to Franklin by Joseph Dickson. From there it was brought to Meadville up the Creek by keelboat. The bridge being a private enterprise, toll was collected at the tollhouse on the west end; this continued over a period of years until a free bridge was built a short distance up the creek at the foot of Dock Street in 1828.

In 22 years after the first settlers came to the French Creek Valley, it presented a changed appearance, which was especially noticeable in Meadville. Clearings had encroached upon the forests, the trees that had been cut down had been used to build houses and buildings, more new roads gave access to nearby settlements and distant towns. By 1810 Crawford County boasted of 6,150 inhabitants and the County Seat had a population of 300, who listed among their possessions 2,142 horses, 5,389 cows, 4,120 sheep, 934 spinning wheels, and 313

First Bridge over French Creek, Built by Dr. T. R. Kennedy, 1810.
Foot of Mercer Street, Meadville.

looms. From the latter were produced in this year 53,-330 yards of linen cloth, 16,818 yards of woolen cloth, 3,212 yards of cotton cloth, making a total of 73,399 yards—averaging 12 yards per person.

They also found time to boil down sufficient sap from maple trees to make 70,000 pounds of maple sugar, and send to outside markets whiskey, black salts, lumber and staves for making pipe, which went as far down the river as New Orleans.

Truly, General Mead was the First Citizen in his own settlement—first to come; first to plow and plant; first in defense; his the first saw mill and grist mill; first to plan and plot the town; and first to make whiskey in his own still. Throughout his life he was a leader. Others were quick to follow his example by engaging in trades to make those things for which there was the greatest demand.

Few of these found it necessary to advertise their wares in the local press, but some found it profitable.

SAMUEL MOORE,[1]
SADDLER:
RESPECTFULLY informs his friends and the public in general that he continues to carry on the saddling business in its different branches, next door to Mr. Gibson's tavern—Gentlemen and ladies saddles of any description will be finished at the shortest notice and on very moderate terms.
Meadville, January 2nd, 1805.

[1] *Crawford Weekly Messenger.*

Wanted,

A boy between 12 and 15 years of age, by the subscriber, as an apprentice to the saddle business.

S. MOORE.

January 2nd, 1805.

Business was of sufficient volume to require assistants to the proprietor.

JOHN ROBERTSON,[1]
SHOEMAKER,

RESPECTFULLY informs his friends and the public in general, that he has lately removed to his new house on the southeast corner of the public square, Meadville, where he proposes carrying on the above business in all its branches. By having lately received a large assortment of handsome leather, he is enabled to furnish his friends with boots and shoes of every description on the most moderate terms and at the shortest notice.

Wanted

ONE or TWO boys, from fourteen to fifteen years of age as apprentices to the above business.

June 5, 1805.

---

[1] *Crawford Weekly Messenger.*

"ANN ELIZA" AND TRADESMEN

Nice Boots are a great support to slim Legs.[1]
M'MANNANY, STEEL & DEMPSEY,
Boots & Shoemakers.

BEG leave to inform their friends and the public in general, that they have commenced a Boot and Shoe Manufactory in the house opposite to Mr. Henry Richards tavern, Meadville, where they intend to carry on their business to the greatest perfection—Strangers, travelers and others, can be furnished with either boots or shoes at the shortest notice and on very reasonable terms—Strict attention will be paid to the newest fashions.

June 12, 1806.

Like most of his fellow townsmen, Eliphalet Betts found time to give his support to many enterprises for public benefit while carrying on his trade in his house on Water Street. William Reynolds said: "In his shop was made my first suit of tailor made clothes." Across the street his brother Ebenezer manufactured nails in a shop near the Creek, "cut from the iron bar by a foot treadle and headed separately in a vise by hammer."

Wanted,[1]
TWO OR THREE
Journeyman Taylors—A steady board and generous wages will be given, by
E. BETTS.
Meadville, April 17th, 1806.

[1] *Crawford Weekly Messenger.*

The number of trades[1] was much larger than at present. Every mechanic had his own shop with indentured apprentices & journeymen. He was his own master accountable only to his patrons.

Machinery was unknown, and each trade comprised the manufacture of all its several departments.

The tanner filled his vats with hides to remain for many months, and converted them into leather by laborious hand process.

The shoemaker made the entire shoe or boot—making his lasts, cutting the pegs, preparing the bristles and making the waxed end and the shoestring.

The smith like his prototype vulcan of old forged heavy, or more delicate work from the iron or steel bar.

The cabinetmaker, purchased his lumber in the rough and completed his work by hand: sawing, plaining, carving—sawing his veneers, making his varnish and completing work which calls forth admiration at the present day.

The carpenter hewed his timber, dressed the lumber and completed the entire building by hand. He was a skilled workman as is shown in the few old mantles of colonial type in some of the old houses yet remaining of that day.

Nail Manufactory.[2]

SAMUEL TORBETT RESPECTFULLY informs his friends and the public in general, that he has commenced the manufacturing of nails in the town of Meadville, and proposes keeping on hand a constant supply of nails of every

---

[1] William Reynolds, The Old Town, 1906 (Reynolds Collection)
[2] *Crawford Weekly Messenger.*

description, which he will despose of at the most reduced prices for CASH ONLY.
August 14, 1806.

A Wheelright[1]
WANTED.
ONE who can work at the above business & likewise at the making of chairs, will meet with constant employment and very liberal terms by the subscriber near Meadville
ALBERT HAINS.
Feb. 26, 1807.

Even with the liberal inducements offered, it was not easy to secure persons who were willing to undertake new ventures in manufacturing and it was a number of years later before Meadville had a fulling mill. The following year one was built farther down the stream.

FULLING MILL[1]
JAMES ADAMS, clothier, respectfully informs the public, that he has erected a fulling mill on French Creek three miles below Martin's ferry in Venango county, where he intends carrying on the fulling business in all its various branches, and flatters himself, from his long experience in the said business, to satisfy those who may please to favor him with their custom— Persons sending cloth, are requested to accompany it with written directions, in order to prevent mistakes.
September 8th, 1808.

---

[1] *Crawford Weekly Messenger.*

On June 25th, 1807, David Gurnfay announced the opening of his shop as watchmaker and silversmith.

> Green hides wanted,[1]
> FOR which cash will be given at the tanyard of the subscriber, Meadville.
> JAMES WHITE.
> Feb. 18, 1808.

(The rectangular form of eight or ten of Tanner White's vats, although filled and refilled many times, still show in the front lawn of the author near The Terrace.)

The following year the Society for Domestic Manufactures advertised for flax and

> WHITEOAK [1]
> Staves and Heading
> WANTED to contract immediately for a quantity of PIPE, HOGSHEADS, and BARREL STAVES, and HEADING—Apply to Thomas R. Kennedy, esq. or
> SAMUEL B. MAGAW.
> Meadville, Feb. 28, 1809.

In 1819, Samuel Magaw built a paper mill on Woodcock Creek. He was the inventor of straw paper. On her first trip "The Ann Eliza" carried straw paper from his mill.

John Brooks was a wheelright and manufactured spinning wheels at his home on the southeast corner of

[1] *Crawford Weekly Messenger.*

Walnut Street and the Public Square, for which he needed two or three more apprentices.

One man at least had a monopoly in his trade, for all "the tomb stones[1] were the work of John Birth, an English stonecutter, who lived in a small one-story brick house on the west side of Market Street. In my childhood I have often seen him sawing stone in front of his home. He perpetuated the memory of many of his contemporaries, but no stone designates his grave, no one lives to tell his history."

---

[1] William Reynolds, Reminiscences of Early Citizens, 1900 (Reynolds Collection)

CHAPTER X

HOLLAND LAND COMPANY

That the action of a group of men in Holland was to vitally affect the development of the Valley could scarcely be imagined by the earliest settlers there. The difficulties and hardships of those first years so discouraged some of them that they left for the east never to return. The courage and steadfast purpose of those who remained formed the firm foundation upon which was built the prosperity of the generations which followed.

Business men of Europe had been watching the thirteen United States in America since their Declaration of Independence and saw there increasing opportunities for profit. Encouraged by successful investments in bonds of the young country, bankers in Holland sought other channels for adding to their wealth. Those most interested sent Theophile Cazenove[1] to America in 1789 to report upon the prospects of venturing into the purchase of wild lands. This resulted in the title of large tracts of land in New York State and Pennsylvania passing into foreign hands. The group of Amsterdam bankers which became the Holland Land Company made in 1793 a contract through Honorable James Wilson for the "purchase[2] of 499,660 acres of land situate on

[1] Paul Demund Evans, *The Holland Land Company* (Buffalo, 1924), 4.
[2] Alfred Huidekoper, Holland Land Company, 2.

French Creek and between French Creek and the River Allegheny in the State of Pennsylvania. . . . The price to be paid for the land (499,660 acres) was to be three shillings four pence per acre, the six per cent of allowance for roads not to be included in the estimate; . . ." They also hoped to develop a sugar industry using sap from maple trees.

An Act of Assembly[1] passed the 11th day of February A. D. 1789 recited "That whereas the empowering of aliens to purchase and hold land within this Commonwealth would have a tendency to promote the public benefit, not only by introducing large sums of money into this state, but also by inducing such aliens as may have acquired property, to following their interest, and become useful citizens: Be it therefore enacted that, until the first day of January A. D. 1792, it shall and may be lawful for every foreigner or foreigners, . . . to purchase lands tenements and Hereditaments within this Commonwealth and to have and to hold the same to them, their heirs and assigns for ever as fully to all intents and purposes as any natural born subject or subjects may or can do."

The Act of Assembly of the 3rd of April, 1792, under which the Holland Company purchase was made, "recited in its preamble that the most valuable lands within the purchase made from the Indians in the year 1768 had already been taken up and that settlers were discouraged from purchasing the remaining inferior lands. . . ."

In regard[1] to these latter lands the Act of Assembly con-

---
[1] Huidekoper, Holland, 4-6.

tinued the following important proviso, viz: "That no warrant or survey to be issued or made in pursuance of this act for lands lying north and west of the Rivers Ohio and Allegheny and Conewango Creek shall vest any title in or to the lands therein mentioned, unless the grantee has prior to the date of said warrant, made, or caused to be made or shall within two years next after the date of the same, make or cause to be made an actual settlement thereon, by clearing, fencing and cultivating at least two acres for every hundred acres contained in one survey erecting thereon a messuage for the habitation of man and residing or causing a family to reside thereon for the space of five years next following his first settling of the same, if he or she shall so long live; and in default of such actual settlement and residence it shall be lawful to and for this commonwealth to issue new warrants to other actual settlers . . . Provided always, Nevertheless, That if any such actual settler or any grantee in any such original or succeeding warrant, shall by force of arms of enemies of the United States, be prevented from making such actual settlement or be driven therefrom, and shall persist in his endeavor to make such actual settlement as aforesaid, then in either case, he and his heirs shall be entitled, to have and to hold the said lands, in the same manner as if the actual settlement had been made and continued.

The State law provided for the taking up of land under the system of warrants and patents. In making the purchase of land in western Pennsylvania for the Holland Company, Cazenove paid little attention to the provision for settlement—the placing of a settler upon every one of the 400 acre tracts within a two-year period. This proved to be next to impossible when trying to

secure settlers, and especially in keeping them there
after they were on the land. There were many other contributory causes for this besides the hardships and the
laborious clearing of heavily wooded land. David Mead
has vividly described the hostilities of the Indians
which forced men to leave their homes for places of
safety. Men who left to bring back their families often
found their cabins in the possession of intruders upon
their return.

The prevention clause[1] in the act of Assembly of 1792 was
productive of much dissension in the first years of the century.
The opinion was industriously circulated by Deputy Surveyors,
and other interested persons, that every tract of 400 acres
without settlement commenced and continued, was open to the
entry and occupancy of the first bonifide settler, without regard to previous warrant. Settlers who had entered into contract with the several Land Companies to fulfil the terms of
settlement for a part of the land, were disposed to claim the
whole, under the plea that the companies had incured forfeiture of the land, and therefore the contract was obtained by
misrepresentation and was void.

The warrantee was thus brought into conflict with the intruder upon his land. The latter relying upon the legal correctness of the opinion so universally promulgated, took possession of the first and best vacant tract he could find, built
his cabin, and commenced to clear and cultivate his farm:
thus speedily the country was filled with a population known
as "actual settlers."

---

[1] J. Reynolds, *Reminiscences of the Olden Times,* Meadville *Daily Republican,* 1867.

Cazenove in the summer of 1795 sent Major Roger Alden[1] to succeed Judah Colt as agent for the Holland Land Company, with Mead's Settlement as his headquarters. Major Alden during the Revolution was with the platoon that fired the first shot at Lexington, had served as aide-de-camp to General Benedict Arnold and to General Parsons, and was among the last at the surrender at Yorktown. Afterward he was a deputy secretary to Congress and the principal clerk in the Department of State.

When Alden arrived at his post he found few settlers and those were gathered near the protecting guns of Fort Franklin and Fort Le Boeuf—Indians objected to white men preempting their lands. In 1796 he was authorized to offer a gratuity of 100 acres out of every tract of 400 acres to settlers who would agree to fulfill the conditions which were necessary to secure patents for the tracts. He also provided warehouses stocked with provisions and farming implements which could be had on credit by the settlers.

Other difficulties developed the outgrowth of legal restrictions and increased as time went on. Men who agreed to bring in settlers were unable to complete their contracts. As interest in land speculation grew, other persons, to further their desires for profit, resorted to politics; new laws produced complications, and titles were clouded by court decisions.

[1] Evans, *Holland*, 112.

Major Roger Alden, Agent of the
Holland Land Company, 1795-1804.

Harm Jan Huidekoper, Agent of the
Holland Land Company, 1804-1836.

William Morris accompanied Roger Alden when he went west to assume the agency for the Holland Land Company. In the winter of 1795-6 many of the tracts called for by the Company warrants were taken up by actual settlers. The Legislature had refused to grant an extension of time for fulfilling the settlement terms, and in the spring as further inducement to settlers Alden began opening up roads, building mills, and clearing the channel of Cussewago Creek. Competition for settlers was keen, and the terms offered by agent Alden were less liberal than those presented by rival land holders. Late in 1799 he reported one settler on each of 530 tracts, which was about half the number to which the Holland Land Company claimed title. After securing a settler it was difficult to keep him and get the land cleared. As reported at the close of 1804, not more than 400 tracts were occupied for the Company, and some of those did not comply with the law for occupancy and clearing.

Without adequate means to facilitate work the partially cleared lands produced poor crops for the new settlers. Few could meet the payments stipulated in the Company contracts. The situation grew daily more complicated for Alden. Suits of ejectment to clear the land of intruders and perfect the Company's title; difficulties in collections; his account for provisions and implements nearly $40,000 by 1799—with debts outstanding approximating $25,000, and half of that uncollectable

110 IN FRENCH CREEK VALLEY

—accountings which were unsatisfactory to the Holland Land office in Philadelphia—all these things led the Company to send Harm Jan Huidekoper out to inspect the agency at Meadville in 1802.

Roger Alden on coming to Mead's soon made his presence felt in the settlement by his initiative, vision, and activity in affairs for its improvement. He contributed generously to new undertakings, presiding at meetings, and giving abundantly of his time and energy. With Dr. T. R. Kennedy in 1795 he purchased the David Mead holdings in the landed interests of the town, revising the plan and selling lots. In 1800 he built a story and a half cottage on Second Street[1] on the square originally planned for a public park at the northeast corner of Walnut Street, planting six sycamore trees in front, three of which survived to be cut down at the age of 106 years. The following year he married the daughter of Mrs. Wahab, Eliza Craven. It was under these sycamores that his wife's friend, Rebecca Colhoun of Carlisle, Pennsylvania, was married to H. J. Huidekoper in 1806.

Roger Alden's House on Second Street.

There was excitement in the village when Roger Alden and Alexander Foster were the principals in a duel on

[1] Market Street.

the east bank of French Creek some distance below the town. Alden's second was Dr. Kennedy and Foster's, Dr. Griffith of Erie. The choice of professional men for seconds showed forethought for Alden was brought back in a canoe with a leg broken, and he limped through the balance of his life. He was a member of the Legislature and elected to Congress for two terms. Financial reverses came and in 1825 he was appointed Quartermaster at West Point. His household effects were shipped east over the new Erie Canal, and he followed after the citizens had given him a large farewell banquet at the Gibson Tavern.

On arriving in America from Holland in 1796, young Harm Jan Huidekoper sailed four days up the Hudson to Albany, drove three more to Utica, and then on to Oldenbarneveldt[1] to present his letters of introduction to Gerret Boon and Colonel Mappa. It was some years later that he became a clerk in the office[2] of the latter, which was the beginning of his connection with the Holland Land Company. 1802 found him the bookkeeper of Paul Busti, General Agent for the Company at Philadelphia, and it was in July of that year that he made his first visit to Meadville, he and his traveling companion Jabez Colt, Crawford County Agent for the Pennsylvania Population Company,[3] making the journey on horseback.

[1] Trenton, New York.
[2] At Trenton.
[3] An association of capitalists who organized in 1792 to acquire lands under the act of that year.

The Holland Land Company accepted Roger Alden's resignation in 1804. Bringing with him Pieter, a brother lately arrived from Holland, the first day of the new year found energetic J. H. Huidekoper installed in Meadville as agent for Northwestern Pennsylvania in Alden's stead. Confronting him was a task which required ability and skill not only in accounting but in dealing with his fellow men. In the years that followed he was successful in handling the affairs of his Company and brought order where there had been none.

Cazenove had bought a large number of shares in the Pennsylvania Population Company in 1793 for the Holland Land Company and both companies had lands west of the Allegheny River. The Holland Land Company sold their interest to Griffith and Wallace in 1810, but retained a mortgage upon the lands and certain control over management of the agency. The purchasers were never able to fulfill their contract, for while large sales were made many of those contracts were afterwards canceled as it was impossible to collect the money due, and later they found it to their advantage to have Harm Jan Huidekoper in full charge of their lands.

Jared Shattuck and Gad Peck in the summer of 1815 purchased 90,000 acres from Griffith and Wallace for approximately $60,000, but owing to losses in their maritime enterprises in the east and their inability to

Office of the Holland Land Company on Water Street.

HOLLAND LAND COMPANY   113

collect from resales their purchase was canceled. Peck moved on to Ohio while Shattuck remained in Meadville.

In 1816 Judge Griffith's interests were transferred to Messrs. Wurtz, and two years later the partnership of Wallace and Wurtz was dissolved, Wallace taking over the Wurtz interest. John B. Wallace found the debt of $310,000 difficult to reduce and brought his family from Philadelphia to Meadville in 1823. Then after five more years of struggle he made an assignment of his property. In 1836 it was arranged that Huidekoper and his sons should pay the Holland Land Company $178,400 for their rights and assume the settlement with Wallace. This covered lands in Erie, Crawford, Warren, and Venango Counties.

Harm Jan Huidekoper was a valuable citizen and did much for Meadville during his long life. Capable and farseeing, he acquired about thirty acres south of the town and in 1806 built Pomona Hall, his residence, with an office for the Holland Land Company just north of it. Across from the foot of Dock Street and just below the place where the Cussewago empties into French Creek, he built in 1818 a grist and saw mill with a vision of sending flour to the east over the Erie Canal. He was one of the group who built the Brick Church and later was instrumental in the forming of the Unitarian Church.

Through years of disputes and legal difficulties the

Holland Land Company continued to be an important factor for increasing the settlement of French Creek Valley. While complications of various natures multiplied and were in time eradicated, it is possible that with these conditions existing the settlement of the Valley may have been retarded for many years. Notwithstanding the Holland Land Company was a means by which the entire young nation was made aware of the great value of the State of Pennsylvania.

CHAPTER XI

ENTERPRISES BEGIN

The crushing defeat of the western Indians by General Wayne brought security to this frontier and many people came over the mountains to settle and build new homes. Before 1793 David Mead had laid out the nucleus of Meadville and sold a few lots. The year before when Arthur and Patrick McGill adventured up French Creek, they in passing stopped to greet those at Mead's settlement who had left Northumberland County before them. Three miles farther they found the Dicksons living on a little flat bordered by an alluring glen on the west bank at Magoffins Falls. Above this on the opposite side where Woodcock Creek empties into the larger stream a vista of rare beauty opened before them.

The banks[1] of French Creek were fringed to the water's edge with evergreen bushes and trees, while ranged along on the higher bank was a row of stately pines beautiful in their majesty as the cedars of Lebanon. In rear of the pines half a mile in extent was a very gently undulating plain on which grew great old oak trees with spreading tops, the rare old oak that tells of Centuries, a variety that now seems to be extinct. They grew with ample space between without underbrush or obstruction to the view, to the limits of this wonderful park. Around the outer semi-circle of the park there arose a little

---
[1] Captain A. McGill, *The McGills* (St. Paul, 1910), 94-95.

plateau, not ten feet in elevation, and from its base flowed springs of pure cool soft water, which fed a circlet of mighty elms, unrivaled in size and beauty . . . there were hundreds of these great trees with wide spreading branches supplementing in grandeur the great oaks they encircled. Beneath these grew hazel bushes, blackberry and raspberry bushes, hawthorn and crabapple trees and many varieties of beautiful shrubs and plants, while near the northern extremity there was a veritable orchard of wild plums bearing a great variety of large red and yellow fruit. The ground rose from the river margin in regular successive plateaus of easy grade covered with the finest timber of the most valuable and useful kind. The view was enchanting and they moored the canoe to the bank to make further explorations. Here they were met by John Fredebaugh, who had located a claim that took in Woodcock Creek and joined on the north the land that had attracted their attention. His land . . . was naturally alluvial and very rich . . . a forest of white walnut (butternut) with here and there a great sycamore towering above and extending its weird white arms over the umbrageous growth beneath. The wild grape vine interlaced the trees and hung in festoons from the branches, forming arborial recesses of rare and inviting beauty.

And there were groups of great hickory trees, their thick trunks rough with shaggy bark, the tips of their strong flexible branches laden with autumn-ripened sweet nuts for squirrels. Here birds of bright plumage made summer glorious with their resonate song. Woodcock and grouse too were plentiful.

No landscape gardener ever planned on so elaborate a scale. Could this be the work of chance, or had some fabled genie touched this jungle with his magic transforming it into this lovely glen? For centuries this identical spot had been the playground at the back door of the "long house" of the Six Nations. This was not the work of chance or enchantment. He who had planned and watched over the valley through eons of time surely had a definite purpose in making these acres so enchanting—only future events would disclose his object. The McGills looked no further for land on which to settle; this charming woodland gave them all that could be desired.

Of the pioneers who settled outside of Mead's village the Gill, Dickson, Frazier, Dunham, Le Fevre and Peiffer names were among those who chose lands north of it; to the west, Cotton, Beatty, Espy and Work; and south, Power, Cochran, May, King, Nelson, Porter, Heydrick, Van Horn, Wright, Herrington, Buchanan and Randolph; while east were Compton, Williamson, Guy and Ellis.

It was in the fall of 1794 that William Dick went down to Pittsburgh to bring back his family. They traveled by keelboat up the Allegheny River to Venango, arriving there in December, continuing to Cussewago on horseback through deep snow and driving storm, Mrs. Dick carrying her infant son John in her arms, her elder boy George walking. David Mead cleared out a small log building inside his stockade which was used as a storehouse, and in this the Dick family lived that first winter.

Among the residents of the village at the close of 1795 were many whose names were afterward identified with enterprises which helped the development and public interest of town and country—John Brooks, Henry Reichard, Jacob Rasor, John Davis, Dr. Thomas R. Kennedy, Major Roger Alden, Colonel Joseph Hackney, Henry Marley, Captain Richard Patch, and James Harrington. Before the close of the century may be added to these the names of James Gibson, Samuel Torbett, John Carver, William Clark, Henry Hurst, William McArthur, David Compton, Patrick Davis, Alexander Buchanan, Reverend Joseph Stockton, and James Herriott.

A survey was made of the town in 1795 by David Mead with Dr. T. R. Kennedy and Major Roger Alden. Mead eventually sold most of his holdings to them. That year the first school was opened by Jannet Finney in a log house on Second Street. The year before William Gill had homesteaded a tract of land north of Meadville and built a cabin. In the fall he went to Pittsburgh for his family, but owing to bad weather delayed his return until spring, when he brought his family to occupy their new home. Going to his cabin he found Jannet Finney in possession, who, with a rifle in hand, warned him off the property, saying that he had abandoned it and it now belonged to her by continuous occupancy. Her statement backed up by the rifle was convincing, so he settled further up French Creek. Jannet Finney became

Perkins House. Across Chestnut Street from the Patch Tavern.

Whereas the Legislature of the Commonwealth of Pennsylvania have passed
[...] one of four Thousand Dollars is secured and subscribed within four Mr.
Mead, Frederick Haymaker and James Gibson, Trustees for the Corp[oration]
[...] respective Names, at the time, and in the manner following, Viz[.]
day of [June] in the year 1804 and the remaining third part on the first
[...] demanded by the said Trustees and if the subscriptions exceed the [...]
[...] the said Law — as Witness our hands in the year 1800.

Date	Subscribers Names and Sums Subscribed
April 20th	David Mead Five hundred Dollars 500
April 21	Roger Alden Seven hundred & [fifty] dollars
April 21	M. Kennedy Five hundred Dollars
April 21	Roger Alden [...] for John [...] five hundred dollars
April 21	Cornelius Vanhorn Two hundred Do[llars]
April 21	Robert Fitz Randolph [...]
April 21	M. James Fitz Randolph Seventy five Dol[lars]
April 21	James Gibson Seventy Dol[lars]
April 21	Joseph [Hackney] Seventy five
April 21	Henry Tschirz one hundred & [Five]
April 21	William B Foster One Hundred Dolla[rs]
April 21	James Hamilton Seventy five Dollars
April 21	Edward Work Fifty Dollars 50
April 21	Jn° Davis one hundred & fifty
April 21	Geo McGunnegle Twenty five
21	[Patrick] Davis [...] one hundred Dollars
April 21	John McGunnegle Fifty D[ollars]
April 1 21	James [Myres] Sixty Dolla[rs]
April 21	John Patterson Thirty D[ollars]

$4470 Subscribed April 21 and 22, 1800

...tees of the County of Crawford at Meadville on the Condition that the
...we and each of us respectively do hereby promise to pay to David
...purposes in the said Act expressed, such sum of money as is assessed to
...day of June in the year 1803. One other third part of such sum on the first
...with Interest annually from the first day of June 1800, with security
...shall be appropriated for the support of the Academy to be established
...to our Signatures

Subscribers Names   and Sums Subscribed

	Subscriber	Amount
21	William Harriot fifty dollars	50
21	James ~~Fine fifty Dollars~~	
20"	Richard Bean fifteen Dollars	15
21"	Wm McGredy Sixty dolars	60
25"	William ——— one hund'd Dollars	100
"	John Cutler fifty dollars	50
2 16	Henry Baldwin fifty Dollars	50
"	James McDill Twenty Dollars	20
"	William Hope twenty Dollars	20
22	Wm Moore Sixty Dollars	60
"	Chambers Foster Thirty Dollars	30
"	Squire Chamberlain	60
"	Paid William ———	
"	William Gill	10
22"	William ——— Davis fifty dollars	50
22th	Arch'd Davison fifty Doll's	50
	——— ——— Seventy five Dollars	75
	David Compton & forty	40
	Henry Reichard Seventy five	75

To secure County Seat and erect Academy.

Thomas Atkinson, First Burgess of Meadville, who began publishing the *Crawford Weekly Messenger*, 1805.

ENTERPRISES BEGIN 119

the second wife of David Mead, and their grandson, William Gill, inherited the land which had occasioned a difference of opinion between his grandparents.

No longer needed for defense, Mead's block house was converted by him into a school in the winter of 1798-99 and presided over by an Irishman named Kelly. The increasing interest in land speculation in the east during the closing years of the century was reflected in the west by an influx of immigrants along the northern tributaries of the Ohio. By the beginning of the 19th century the population had increased to 2,346, which included 166 souls in Mead's growing town.

Richard Patch, at that time a resident of Meadville, was a veteran boatman of the Ohio River and its tributaries. In early April, 1800, Captain Patch embarked at Pittsburgh for Meadville in a keelboat. The cargo consisted of general merchandise for the frontier and mail for the settlers living as far north as Erie. His crew had little difficulty in poling the craft up the Allegheny River to Fort Franklin, and from there up French Creek made flush by the spring rains. All the news of the old world together with the gossip from the eastern part of the new Republic which had found its way as far west as the forks of the Ohio, was eagerly told by the crew to the citizens. Lengthening shadows of evening crept across the Creek as the boat reached a point where the dividing channel formed many islands. The pilot steered into the eastern or main channel under overhanging branches of giant sycamore trees and made secure at the public dock at the Port of Meadville.[1] The Captain brought important news to his fellow townsmen —the recent action of the Pennsylvania Assembly which created six new counties, Crawford, Erie, Warren, Beaver, Butler, and Mercer, from what had been up to this time the northern part of Allegheny County.

In planning to build his mills Roger Alden found the best site for a dam on French Creek was on land owned by Patrick McGill. Saw and grist mills being a necessity McGill sold two hundred acres to Alden in 1802 and the settlement which grew near them was known as Alden's Mills.[2] Between the two villages there was keen rivalry over the location of the new county seat. By the conditions imposed by the legislature it was necessary to raise the sum of $4,000 for a Seminary of Learning to obtain this desirable honor which would bring fame, together with many eminent jurists and attorneys to the successful town. This sum must be raised within four months! With pride and profit at stake, energy supplied action. In two days, April 21 and 22, the citizens subscribed $4,470 and settled the question. The Meadville Academy was erected in the summer of 1805, a one-story building in which there were two rooms.

---

[1] Mead Park, on Dock Street, later renamed Mead Avenue.
[2] Saegertown.

Tavern of Captain Richard Patch, built of shale rock, 1798.

Dr. Thomas Rustin Kennedy, Military Surgeon, Son of Washington's Surgeon General Samuel Kennedy. French Creek Valley's first doctor.

In the *Messenger* of August 7, the citizens read:

MEADVILLE ACADEMY.

THE Trustees of the Meadville Academy inform the public with pleasure, that they have completed their building and are now opening a Public School under the care and direction of the Rev. Joseph Stockton; in which will be taught, with the greatest care and attention, the English Language gramatically, together with writing and arithmetic—also, the Latin and Greek Languages, the different branches of the Mathematics; and those parts of Natural and Moral Science, which are usually taught in such institutions.

For the encouragement of parents and guardians, who may be desirous to give their children an accademic education, the price of tuition will be reduced to twenty five shillings the quarter, more than one third less than is usual throughout the state.

By order of the Trustees,
TH. R. KENNEDY, *Clk*.

N. B. Good boarding, and other accommodations, may be had on reasonable terms.

The Reverend Mr. Stockton, a learned man with high ideals and ambition, started the school on a long, successful career. Pupils in the upper grades were augmented with others for all the lower ones, and the school was soon crowded to capacity. Contributors to the institution felt that their children should have preference over those of non-contributors, so when they could not be admitted they established another school across the Creek.

At this time there were no improvements, forest trees

covered most of the village, and stumps were still to be taken out of the roadways. Houses were built of logs, General Mead's new one being the first of partial frame construction. With the influx of new citizens it was not long before improvements were started.

Among the men in Meadville at this time were Thomas Atkinson and W. Brendle, whose combined efforts brought forth the first issue of a newspaper, *The Crawford Weekly Messenger*,[1] on Wednesday, January 2, 1805. It was printed in a log building on the north side of Center Street,[2] east of the corner of Water Street, on a press which had been used many years before by Benjamin Franklin. There is a legend that some of the Continental money had been printed on this press. This partnership continued until July, and after that the paper was conducted by T. Atkinson until sold to Joseph C. G. Kennedy in 1834.

The editorial in the first issue sets forth the objects of the publication:

... it introduces the READER into the theatre of the world and shows him the great actors on the stage of TIME; while it leads him into the cabinet ... the field ... the senate ... the courts of justice ... the circles of the busy and the learned ... it promotes in a very important degree, the grand interest of

---

[1] *The Crawford Weekly Messenger*, published 1805-1831, at Meadville. Complete file in Meadville Library, Art and Historical Association.

[2] After Atkinson built a house on the northeast corner of the Public Square and Cherry Alley, the paper was published there.

Trade, Commerce, Agriculture . . . of *Literature* . . . and almost everything that adorns and dignifies mankind.

This paragraph follows the editorial:

In order that further means may be adopted to facilitate the distribution of The Messenger, and to give patronizers an opportunity of coming forward to throw in their *mite*, the editors propose suspending the publication of the second number until Wednesday the 16th inst.

Heading the editorial column of the next issue:

We lament our inability to lay before our readers the details of foreign and legislative news of the latest dates, on account of the delay of the post . . . the mail has not arrived, though it is nearly thirty hours after the fixed and usual time of arrival at this place.

IN submitting to the public the *second* number of *The Messenger*, we should consider ourselves wanting in respect, were we not to tender our friends our most greatful acknowledgements for their support and interest, in patronizing our infant undertaking. . . It must certainly appear very obvious to the public, that an establishment of this nature, is attended with a great deal of expense, especially in a country so remote from the source we have to procure almost every article of any consequence essential to the printing business; and consequently without energy and promptitude on their part, in coming forward with their support, numberless difficulties, as may be naturally supposed, will devolve on the undertakers. . . We rest however with a considerable share of confidence, that the judicious discernment of an enlightened public to the many advantages the country will derive from the present establishment, will, by a generous encouragement prevent the occurrence of any difficulties, anticipated by the enemies of its existance.

To win a place in *The Messenger* local news had to be of vital importance to the community. In so small a settlement the happenings of the neighborhood were known to everyone, and space in the paper was given over to outside events. Many causes contributed to delay in the receipt of this news: "We have been informed, by several persons immediately from Slippery-Rock creek, that Mr. Tucker, one of the carriers of the U. S. mail between Pittsburg & Erie, was unfortunately drowned in attempting to cross that water."

In spite of difficulties, *The Messenger* continues:

Thursday-morning January 2,

The patrons of THE MESSENGER, by reverting to the head of the first page, will observe that this number (52) completes one year since its commencement—Grateful for the encouragement with which he has been favored; he takes the liberty of reminding them, that tho' subscribing tends to encrease the credit of the paper, yet there is another little *article* on which it must depend for support—he need hardly remind his readers that this little article is the *necessary* evil we are all in pursuit of—MONEY is the life of trade, punctual payment is the printers sure defence against the paper maker[1]—without it the expense incurred by the publication cannot be paid off— Our readers will therefore recollect the terms on which we en-

---

[1] Print paper, like other supplies and merchandise, was brought by packhorse over the mountains from eastern cities.

ENTERPRISES BEGIN 125

gaged—ONE dollar every six months in advance—A considerable number of our patrons have neglect to favor us with the first dollar, such we trust will speedily oblige by a punctual payment of their respective dues.

Country produce will be received in payment at the cash price.

EDITOR.

Thursday-morning, March 30. (1809)

Business requiring the attendance of the editor at court, has prevented him from issuing more than half a sheet.

This issue appeared without a heading and contained besides news items four advertisements.

After December 29, 1813, no paper was issued until

Thursday-morning, February 16.

The editor regrets most sincerely, the interruption that has occured in the publication of his paper. The duties which devolved on him by the late sudden and unexpected call of the militia, rendered it absolutely unavoidable.

Few communities of the size of Meadville could boast of five citizens of sufficient classical, literary, and scientific prominence to enable them to be members of The American Antiquarian Society of Worcester, Massachusetts, one of the oldest and foremost historical societies in the United States. The records show that Timothy Alden was elected a member in 1813; Reverend Robert Johnston, one of Meadville's earliest clergymen, Major Roger Alden, and Honorable Jesse Moore, in 1815; and

Honorable Patrick Farrelly, representative in the State Assembly and the National Legislature, in 1820.

With the growth of the village and the increase of industry there was difficulty in keeping enough specie for the convenience of trade and the citizens determined to establish a bank.

The North Western Bank of Pennsylvania at Meadville.

In the winter of 1813-14 the Legislature granted a charter to the North Western Bank of Pennsylvania[1] with an authorized capital of $200,000 and 4,000 shares of stock. Of this stock, Erie, Crawford, Mercer, and Warren Counties were each to be awarded 1,000 shares. The bank was to be located in Meadville.

The books were opened for subscription at Meadville on May 4, 1814, by Thomas Atkinson, Henry Hurst, John Brooks, and Samuel Torbett, Commissioners. The first board of directors—William Clark, John Brooks, Roger Alden, Samuel B. Magaw, Henry Hurst, Jacob Shryock, Patrick Farrelly, Eliphalet Betts, John Reynolds, James Herriott, Wilson Smith, and Rufus Reed of

[1] The Records of the North Western Bank are in the possession of John E. Reynolds, whose grandfather, John Reynolds as receiver, liquidated the bank. These records consist of the Charter and ten volumes: Minute Book of the Board of Directors, two volumes; Stock Subscriptions, two volumes; Transfer Book; Dividend Book; and Discount Book, four volumes.

Erie, and William Connelly of Franklin—held their first meeting on October 31, 1814. Samuel B. Magaw was elected president and also treasurer pro-tem. Joseph Morrison of Philadelphia was elected cashier with a salary of $900 per year, which afterward was raised to $1,400, provided he should pay his clerk hire and provide stationery, firewood, and candles.

The commissioners succeeded in obtaining the entire stock subscription, but a very considerable portion was never paid in full. There were in all 369 subscribers, and the actual amount of stock paid for totaled $63,138. The bank issued $1,000 in fractional notes of 50, 25, 12½, and 6¼ cents, also denominations of $20, $10, $5, $2, and $1. There were about $200,000 of notes actually engraved, but there is no record of the actual amount placed in circulation, which in 1821 was $57,-000. Prior to 1820 the amount of specie gold and silver for redemption of notes varied from $15,000 to $22,-000. The discounts embraced nearly the entire business of the four counties, although the deposits never exceeded a very small sum, not more than $3,000.

November 5, 1821, Dividend No. 11, the last of the regular six per cent dividends, was paid on all outstanding stock. The unusual scarcity of specie in the middle of the 1820's, together with the demand for the redemption of notes in gold and silver, placed the bank in straightened condition and, while in 1828 its discounts were between $80,000 and $90,000, the specie reserve dropped to fourteen cents. Under these conditions it became necessary to go into liquidation, and John Reynolds was appointed receiver by the court. It required many years to liquidate the affairs of the bank. The last meeting of the officers was held on March 6, 1838, when the bank notes on hand were counted and burned. Stockholders were reimbursed in full for the stock paid in, and all notes of the institution were redeemed. So ended the North Western Bank of Pennsylvania, one of the first and one of the very few banks in all the great west.

Shortly before this occurred, the Bank of Pittsburgh had been established with a capital of $400,000. Pittsburgh then boasted 5,000 or 6,000 inhabitants. Meadville had a population of 400 or 500 in 1814, and Crawford County 5,000. Cincinnati was a village of a few hundred people. These were the conditions of the west when the enterprise of the early citizens of Meadville established the North Western Bank of Pennsylvania. Not only was it profitable to the stockholders, but it also gave banking facilities to this part of the state and aided greatly in public enterprises, such as the building of the Susquehanna and Waterford Turnpike, the Mercer Turnpike, and helped the agricultural community in establishing a profitable wool industry in northwestern Pennsylvania.

CHAPTER XII

LOCAL TALENT

"The friends of vocal music in Meadville and its vicinity are requested to meet at the house of David Compton, on Friday evening next, in order to make arrangements for the commencement of a Singing School."[1]

When darkness brought the close of a day of strenuous living to the pioneers it is not surprising that they sought some form of relaxation and amusement. Music formed an important part in their religion as well as in their celebrations and other entertainment. The school room could be had in the evening, and there the singing school flourished. Under the direction of Colonel Joseph Stockton were enrolled Mrs. Reynolds, Mrs. Huidekoper, Mrs. Mead and her daughters, the Misses Heron, Mrs. Foster, and others. Later instructors came from other parts of the country to earn a precarious living and encourage the love of music in the community. Some of these were apparently not as good as they might have been.

STOP THE RUNAWAY[2]

RAN AWAY from Meadville on the night of the 17th inst. *Selah Wilcock*, about

---
[1] *Crawford Weekly Messenger*, November 27, 1805.
[2] Ibid.

five feet eight inches high, of a dark complexion, about 21 years of age, blue eyes, professes to be a singing-master— He took with him two body coats, one blue nearly new, the other brown, about half worn, one pair of cossack boots and one pair of shoes, one pair of blue nankeen pantaloons with some other clothes unknown. Whoever apprehends the said runaway and brings him back to Meadville so that his creditors may punish him for his ingratitude and the money he owes shall receive a reward of five dollars, by

    FREDERICK HAYMAKER,
    LUKE HILL.
Meadville, August 19th, 1806.

Not all of the citizens were in favor of music when pursued beyond the status of amusement and used as a vocation. Daniel Shryock, frank in expressing his opinion, did not hesitate to tell a young man of the same name who came to teach a singing school that it was small business for a man and that if he could not find a more worthy employment of his time he had better leave town.

Amusement in that early day was frequently combined with a serious trend for improvement. By efforts of the members of the community 150 books were gathered to start the Meadville Library in 1812. This nucleus was made up of standard works, history, biography, and travel, but no fiction was included. This collection of volumes was placed in John Reynolds' office and furnished food for thought and meditation until the library of Allegheny College was established.

This example was followed when the Crawford County Sabbath School Union was organized in 1821 with eleven Sunday Schools, and rapidly increased in membership. During the first year a library of more than 100 volumes was established for the exclusive use of pupils —with restrictions:

Those pupils[1] who may distinguish themselves by their acquisitions in the sabbath schools of the Union, and who shall have recited memoritor 5000 verses from the Bible shall have the right to take one volume, those who shall have recited 10,000 verses memoritor, shall have the right to take two volumes, and those who shall have recited memoritor 15,000 verses shall have the right to take three out at one time and this right duly certified by the patron to continue for life.

By the close of 1829 life certificates had been issued to 68 for 5,000 verses, 4 for 10,000 verses, and Anne Lovitt and Anne Pickett attained the award for 15,000 verses. If the Union still functions and the rules have not been modified, it is exceedingly doubtful if there has been much wear and tear to damage its volumes of recent years!

That persons outside might share in knowledge and enjoy the spiritual benefit as well as those in the community, there was formed the

[1] Quoted in William Reynolds, Public Enterprises of the Early Citizens (Reynolds Collection)

MEADVILLE BIBLE SOCIETY.

CONSIDERING the incalculable benefits, which have resulted to the world from a dissemination of the truths of the gospel; the obligation upon all, who enjoy the advantages of this glorious dispensation, to use the means within their reach for extending its blessings to their destitute fellow creatures; ... and that there are many in this region, to whom, we have good reason to believe, a donation of the Holy Bible would be a most suitable, acceptable, and profitable charity;

WE, THE SUBSCRIBERS,

voluntarily associate ourselves together . . .

Following the Constitution the article continues:

The foregoing constitution was drawn up, on the 20 of July, and having been signed by a considerable number, a meeting of the members was held, agreeably to publick notice, at the court house in Meadville, on the 15 of August (1815), when twelve directors were elected for the present year, who immediately organized themselves according to the terms of the third article.

DIRECTORS.

Roger Alden, esq., President,
Hon. Jesse Moore, Vice-President,
Rev. Timothy Alden, Cor. Sec.,
Rev. Robert Johnston, Rec. Sec.,
John Reynolds, esq., Treasurer,
Dr. Daniel Bemus, Auditor,
Hugh Cotton,
George Davis,
James Hamilton, esq.,
William Hammond, esq.,
Col. Robert Stockton,
Peter Shaw.

Jesse Moore, President Judge for the 6th Judicial District for Crawford and Erie Counties. 1803-1825.

DISTRIBUTING COMMITTEE.
Roger Alden, esq.,
Rev. Timothy Alden,
Rev. Robert Johnston.

A like desire to help their fellow creatures animated those who organized the

FEMALE CENT SOCIETY OF MEADVILLE.[1]

Considering the infinite importance of religious instruction to the present and future generations; the unhappy condition of thousands, in our own as well as far distant climes, who are perishing for lack of the knowledge of God and of Jesus Christ, whom he has sent; and being conscious that the oracles of God, which contain the inestimable treasure of grace and truth, can be neither read nor preached among the parishing multitude, without the aid of christian benevolence, we have felt it our duty, and humbly hope it will not be considered ostentatious nor assuming, to add our names to the numerous list of those, who are coming from every part of christendom to the help of the Lord against the mighty, and to cast our mite into his treasury, if so be we may be instrumental, in any degree, in enlightening a dark, reforming a wicked, and blessing a miserable world. Animated by the example of those daughters of Zion, who have led the way, and encouraged by the success, with which Heaven has crowned the efforts of benevolent female societies, we have resolved to unite ourselves under the name of the Female Cent Society of Meadville and have agreed to adopt the following

CONSTITUTION.

Article 2. Any female may become a member of this society by subscribing the constitution and paying into the treasury

---

[1] Alden, *Alleghany Magazine* (August, 1816), 36-37.

one cent per week. Any person subscribing and paying ten dollars shall be a member for life; and, if any member shall pay more, than a cent, a week, it shall be entered to her credit as a donation; and, if any other person shall contribute to the funds of this society, more or less, he or she shall be numbered among its benefactors and due entry thereof shall be made in the records of the society. Any member may withdraw her name by giving notice to the secretary and paying up the arrears to the time of such application. . .

This society, highly honorable to the ladies of Meadville, was formed, on the 11 of last December, and its officers were chosen agreeably to the terms of the constitution. On the first of January, the society held its first publick meeting, when a discourse, by request of the ladies, adapted to the occasion, was delivered by the rev. Robert Johnston. At present the number of members consists of fifty five. The amount of money, already collected in the way of tax and donation, exceeds seventy dollars, and, by a resolve of the society, on the fifth of July, their first anniversary, it is to be forwarded to Calcutta to aid in the noble work of translating the holy scriptures into the languages of Asia. If the ladies of every village in the United States would follow the laudable example of the ladies of Meadville and of a multitude of other places in this western world, how vast would be the sum of money and how glorious would be the result.

DIRECTORS.

Mrs. Jannet Mead, President,
Mrs. Sarah Mead, Secretary,
Mrs. Eleanor Johnston, Treasurer,
Mrs. Catharine Torbett, Auditor,
Mrs. Elizabeth Alden,
Mrs. Elizabeth Compton,
Mrs. Margaret Cotton,

LOCAL TALENT 135

Mrs. Mary Cotton,
Mrs. Sarah Cummings,
Mrs. Elizabeth Davis,
Mrs. Sarah Perkins,
Mrs. Agnes Smith.

Both of these societies were active religious influences in the community for many years following their organization. The same spirit of helping was manifest in other societies, although not stressed in their organization.

> A meeting of the members of the MEADVILLE THESPIAN SOCIETY is requested at the hou of R. Patch on Saturday evenig next (March 1,) half past six. Punctual attendance is requested.

This notice appeared in the *Messenger*, February 28, 1828. Mistakes like the above were seldom found in its pages.

> On Thursday[1] evening will be performed, by the "Meadville Thespian Society," at the tavern of Mr. George Hurst,[2] the comedy called "Who Wants a Guinea?" after which will be performed the farce called "A Pedlar." The doors will be open at half past six, and the curtain will rise at a quarter to seven. Admittance 25 cents. Tickets to

---

[1] *Crawford Weekly Messenger*, March 31, 1824.

[2] Spread Eagle on the northeast corner of the Public Square and Chestnut Street.

be had at the different inns of Meadville. The front seats to be occupied exclusively by the ladies.

This notice in the *Messenger* was of one of the early performances of the Thespians. The membership was confined to the young men of the town and included David Dick, Wilson Dick, Archibald Stewart, George King, John Clark, Robert Adrain, W. P. Shattuck, James Buchanan, Sebastian Chappotin, and others. Robert Adrain, a merry and witty young Irishman, was the comedian, and the lovely ladies were played by W. P. Shattuck.

Performances of the Thespian Society were given wherever a large room could be secured, usually at one of the taverns. On the second floor of Livi Barton's Hotel there was an unfinished room, bare walls lighted only by tallow candles in tin sconces, a stage of rough boards with a row of footlights which needed constant trimming with snuffers, and rows of plain wooden benches for the audience. Here in April, 1827, a performance was given which ran three nights to help raise funds for the purchase of the first fire engines for the village; they were named the "Vigilent" and the "Dilligent."[1] At another time money raised by giving plays

---

[1] "Our Borough this year (1830) purchased its first fire engines—two small crank machines which were filled by buckets, from pumps or wells—very inefficient." (Cost $500) William Reynolds, *Home Life-- Life Time Memories*, 16 (Reynolds Collection)

was sent to the "Greek sufferers" at the time of their struggle for freedom from Turkey.

In the beginning of this year (1834) the Meadville Lyceum[1] was organized for a series of public lectures by the citizens weekly at the Court room. John Reynolds was President, David Dick, Vice President, Alfred Huidekoper, John Stuart Riddle, David Derickson and Prof. A. W. Ruter (Prest. of Allegheny College) Managers. This Lyceum was continued for several winters always with a well filled room, notwithstanding the gloom and discomfort of the old Court room, seated with bare pine benches and lighted only by tallow candles in sconces on the walls & candlesticks on the tables.

In the early twenties there were many young people in the town. They were a gay and lively set full of spirit and seeking amusement. In the winters a dancing master came from Pittsburgh to teach the newest steps and conduct a dancing school. Weekly cotillion parties were held at Mr. Torbett's hotel, "The Sign of the Stag," and were attended by all who could arrange to be there.

Came a new minister to guide and care for the congregation of one of the largest churches who viewed this happy condition with dismay. Weekly denunciations from the pulpit of all amusement together with the circulation of tracts bearing a similar import had the sad effect of closing the only ballroom at "The Sign of the Stag."

Energetic young men were not to be easily discouraged and soon found a way to combat the propaganda

[1] Ibid., 20.

against their "sinful" amusement. On Center Street a building was put up in which the first floor was to be rented for offices and an "assembly" room handsomely furnished on the second, where the weekly balls could be continued.

But the influence of the Sabbath sermons had weight with a growing number of the young ladies. The threatened punishment for the sin of dancing diminished their attendance. The "assembly" room as an assembly room was finally abandoned and later used by the Meadville Grays as a drill hall.

CHAPTER XIII

TIMOTHY ALDEN'S DREAM

The journey across the mountains was so difficult and dangerous that there was little in the way of possessions which the pioneers could bring with them, only meager necessities. As they prospered, pride of possession in goods and chattels grew and children were not allowed to forget that their forbears had been the "first" in each particular event and owned the "first" of each article. It was only natural that succeeding generations exulted in this inheritance, so that any chronicle of that period by way of accent is bound to bristle with "firsts"—if there were any.

While this busy frontier town was swelling with pride at having the only banking institution in the northwestern part of the state, there arrived at the public dock of Meadville one evening, the 24th of April, 1815, to be exact, a most important personage and his family—one destined to play a distinguished part in the civic, religious, and educational development of the community. The Reverend Timothy Alden was a lineal descendant of John and Priscilla and of course a native of Massachusetts; also, like his father and grandfather before him, a graduate of Harvard College in the class of 1794. While a student he was the secretary of one of the oldest college societies in the United States, the Institute of 1770, a society which in those days not only required popularity but scholarship as well before membership could be attained. The Reverend Timothy Alden was ordained a Congregational clergyman and up to the time of his departure for the western country had, in addition to filling several charges in rural New England, acted as missionary among various Indian tribes in the east.

A distant cousin, Major Roger Alden, had settled in Meadville 22 years before, so it was possibly at his suggestion that Timothy made the journey west with the idea in mind of establishing an institution of learning. A log house on the northwestern corner of Walnut Street and Chancery Lane became his home shortly after his arrival, and here he lived for many years. He quickly endeared himself to the people by his kindly and dignified manner, which was also democratic enough for a frontier town. He was a man of broad ideas, had traveled extensively through New England, and made a seven-weeks trip to the west in the fall of 1812, going as far as Cincinnati. Being a member of the New York and Massachusetts Historical Societies, as well as the American Antiquarian Society which he had assisted Isaiah Thomas in organizing, his reputation as a scholar won him a wide acquaintance with distinguished men of the east.

Before coming west Timothy Alden had printed sev-

Timothy Alden, Founder and First President of Allegheny College

Bentley Hall, Allegheny College. Built in 1820.

eral treatises on various subjects and published one book, "A Collection of American Epitaphs and Inscriptions with Occasional Notes," in two volumes.

A most progressive citizen, he quickly took his place as a leader in civic as well as spiritual affairs, ready as far as his means would permit to aid every public enterprise of merit. He considered it right and proper that both he and Allegheny College should support the North Western Bank of Pennsylvania by subscribing for stock in that institution. Although he had no permanent charge he frequently held services in the village and also in the country communities. He married a large proportion of the youth, christened their children, and buried their dead. At political celebrations and on national holidays he officiated as toastmaster, and when not serving in that capacity invoked divine blessing. Owing to his popularity, on more than one occasion he was urged to be a candidate for political office in the state.

Two years after Alden made his trip to the west, an entry was made under the date of January 25, 1814, in the diary of William Bentley of Salem:

> Alden here[1]. . . . He also brought the project of a settlement at a place to be called Aldenburg, upon the Allegheny, 90 miles from Pittsburgh and about 30 from Presque Isle. He had all the locations and plans with him.

---

[1] Diary of William Bentley, January 25, 1814, quoted in Ernest A. Smith, *Allegheny—A Century of Education* (Meadville, 1916), 10.

A comfortable fortune which came to the Alden family after the death of Mrs. Alden's mother made possible their removal to Meadville. From records of those early days real estate speculation seemed to be the principal means of making a livelihood in this western country. Not immune from temptation, it was several years after his arrival before his project began to materialize. He secured a tract of land and laid out a new village on paper which he called Aldenia, on the western shore of Konneyaut Lake,[1] "for the accommodation of purchasers, and which, from the eligibility of its location, looking forward to the canal operations which are to give it a water communication with Philadelphia, Pittsburgh, and the great northern Lakes, is worthy of the attention of merchants and mechanics." With the *"odd numbers* being on the right, and the *even numbers* left hand of the street," a thrill of recognition would have awaited the New Englander in looking over the names of Winthrop or Salem Streets and Yarmouth Alley.

In the centre of the block between South Lake street and North Lake street on the west side of Winthrop street *two lots* are reserved, in a very commanding situation for a *Church*. All the *lots*, six in number, between the two *Lake streets*, extending from Winthrop street to the lake are reserved for a public Common—a part of which is to be a *Mall*, or a public walk, 25 feet in width along the margin of Winthrop street, to be ornimented with a row of Trees on each side. . .

That orniment, comfort, and convenience may be consulted

---

[1] Dr. Alden's advertisement in the *Crawford Messenger*, May 1, 1828.

TIMOTHY ALDEN'S DREAM 143

and promoted, it is stipulated in the sale of these *Village Lots,* that the purchasers shall not set their buildings nor fences, nor place any obstructions on these ends of their *lots* which front on Winthrop street or Bentley street, nearer than *eight feet* from the boundry line of the street—and that they shall severally be at the expense of setting out opposite to the corners of their respective lots on the boundry line of the streets, *Locust* or some other trees—and of securing them by stakes suitably guarded with pieces of boards nailed to the same, and by all reasonable care preserving them from injury. . . These *side walks* ornimented with *trees* will add much to the symmetry and beauty of the village and at the same time reflect honour on the taste of its inhabitants. . .

The plan of this village may be seen at the store of Mr. Robert Stewart—For terms of purchase application may be made to

TIMOTHY ALDEN.

Meadville, 26 April, 1828.

N. B. Winthrop and Bentley streets are so named in memory of the late Hon. James Winthrop, LL.D. and of the late Rev. William Bentley, D.D. the two greatest benefactors of Alleghany College—and Thomas Alley in respect to Isaiah Thomas, LL.D. the founder, magnanimous benefactor, and President of the American Antiquarian Society, who became the executor of his own will by a very liberal donation to Alleghany College—names ever to be had in grateful remembrance by the present and future generations of Crawford county.

Apparently planning for "the city beautiful" did not originate with the present generation.

Finding Meadville such a flourishing village it is not surprising that Timothy Alden upon his arrival considered it a possible place in which to carry out the dream of his life. Only a few weeks elapsed when he wrote and the *Crawford Weekly Messenger*[1] published the notice of a meeting to be held in the Court House on the evening of June 20 to consider "the expediency of systematizing a plan for the foundation of a collegiate institution" in northwestern Pennsylvania.

On the evening of the meeting the capacity of the Court Room was taxed to accommodate the assemblage. General David Mead was there, the erect carriage of his six feet six inches heightening the dignity of his appearance in dress coat and knee breeches. With martial bearing Major Roger Alden, veteran of the Revolution, Honorable Jesse Moore, President Judge, Harm Jan Huidekoper, Honorable William McArthur, Crawford County's first representative in the General Assembly, William Clarke, Henry Hurst, Ralph Marlin, Thomas Atkinson, William Foster, Daniel Perkins, Honorable Patrick Farrelly, Samuel Torbett, John Dick, John Brooks, Associate Judge, Samuel Magaw, Samuel Lord, James Hamilton, James Dickson, Joseph Morrison, and Dr. Bemus were prominent among the many citizens present. The meeting was organized and elected Major Alden chairman and John Reynolds secretary, after which the following preamble to the business of the evening was read and unanimously approved:

[1] 1815.

... Be it known[1] to all whom it may concern, that we, whose names are affixed to this instrument, have voluntarily associated ourselves together for the purpose of establishing a collegiate institution.

The importance of advantages for a classical education and the want of an institution, where such an education may be obtained in the extensive region watered by the Alleghany River and its numerous contributary streams, and destined in all human probability, to be overspread at no great distance of time with as many inhabitants as any interior section of the United States, of equal magnitude, are sufficient reason for awakening our attention to this subject.

The example of our venerable ancestors who early made provision for the liberal and pious education of their sons; the nature of our government, the welfare of which depends, in no small degree, under Almighty God, on the prevelance of knowledge, virtue, and religion; the eventful period in which we live, plainly indicating that the time is nigh at hand when there will be an unprecedented call for the labors of the heralds of the Gospel, afford additional arguments of the expediency of our present undertaking.

As friends to the best interests of our fellow creatures, and influenced as we trust, by a desire for promoting the glory of God, we will cheerfully exert ourselves to lay the foundation of a seminary, in which a regular course of the liberal arts and sciences shall be duly taught.

From the patronage we hope to receive, and from a reliance on the smiles of Heaven, we indulge the expectation that our endeavors for the literary and scientific, moral and religious benefit of the rising and future generations will not be in vain; and that many young men of genius and piety in this part of our Republic, will soon enjoy the desired advantages for ac-

---

[1] *Crawford Weekly Messenger,* June 24, 1815.

quiring such an education, as will enable them to become an honour to their country and a blessing to the world. . .

The foregoing statement, designed to excite the fostering attention of the friends to literature, science, and religion, is respectfully offered to the publick.—By order.

R. ALDEN, *Chairman.*
JOHN REYNOLDS, *Sec'ry.*

It was resolved in the meeting to name the future seminary Alleghany because the greater part of the region for whose benefit it was designed is watered by the numerous streams which make the Alleghany River. It was resolved that Meadville be selected as the site of the college, and further it was resolved that the Reverend Timothy Alden be named as President, Professor of Oriental Languages and Ecclesiastical History. Also, it was resolved that the Reverend Robert Johnston of Meadville be the Vice-President and Professor of Logic, Metaphysics and Ethics. A committee was appointed to address the legislature of Pennsylvania praying for the granting of a charter to the college. Subscription books were to be immediately opened by the Treasurer, John Reynolds, for donations of any kind of property useful to the institution. The Reverend Timothy Alden was authorized to visit the eastern states and solicit gifts toward the founding of the college.

Thus was Allegheny College organized. The town meeting was ended, the candles in the sconces were extinguished, the citizens wended their several ways homeward through the dark, silent, summer night, little realizing the blessings that were to follow their deliberations of the evening.

Soon after this meeting Timothy Alden left for the east where he spent some time soliciting funds with which to start the institution. In this he proved his ability, for he returned with many donations of books for the starting of a library, besides $4,103.30 largely given in small amounts, ranging from 22 cents to land valued at $2,000, by friends in Massachusetts, Rhode Island, New York, New Jersey, and Pennsylvania. To this amount the citizens of Meadville added the sum of $5,685. Also he was successful in obtaining a most valuable bequest, a theological library from Reverend William Bentley of Salem. It is rumored that before his interview with Dr. Alden the Reverend Bentley, a graduate of Harvard College, had intended giving his library to his Alma Mater. With the gifts received and an appropriation from the General Assembly the Trustees determined to erect the main building and call it Bentley Hall. Laying the corner-stone for this was an event to which the *Crawford Messenger* did full justice:

> On Wednesday, 5 July, 1820,[1] the ceremony of laying the *corner stone* of Bentley Hall, the first public building of Alleghany College, took place in the presence of the most numerous assemblage of gentlemen and ladies, ever known, except perhaps on one occasion, in the county of Crawford.

---

[1] *Crawford Weekly Messenger*, July 14, 1820.

The smiles of Divine Providence marked the business of the day. About 12 o'clock a fine shower of rain laid the dust, which otherwise would exceedingly have incommoded the procession. No showers, however, fell, until the various exercises of the day were over, and the procession had returned to the village, when the rain came down most plentifully and most opportunely for the vegetable creation.

People from this and the adjacent counties were collected together on the diamond[1] long before two o'clock, the time appointed for forming the procession. The several divisions were received by the committee of arrangement, consisting of Messrs. T. Alden, P. Farrelly, R. Marlin, J. Brooks and D. Bemus, and were committed to the marshals of the day who promptly formed the procession, which began to move a little before three o'clock. The route taken was from the front of the court house on the centre of the diamond through Mechanics' Row and Water Street, by the dwelling house of Samuel Lord, esq. and through his field to the elevated and beautiful five acre lot, generously presented by this gentleman for the site of Alleghany College.

ORDER OF PROCESSION

1. Meadville Blues under the command of capt. C. Long.
2. Male pupils of the academy and of the schools kept by messrs. Kerr and Law, under the direction of Mr. Leffingwell, preceptor of the academy.
3. Citizens.
4. Band of music under the direction of Mr. Jennings.
5. Choir of singers under the direction of Mr. R. Temple.
6. Students of Alleghany College with a sprig of laurel in their hats.
7. Officers of the county of Crawford.

---

[1] The public square.

8. Magistrates and other officers of the commonwealth of Pennsylvania.
9. Officers of the United States' government.
10. Strangers of distinction.
11. Young misses of the academy under the direction of Miss Benedict.
12. Ladies, of whom there were many, who were pleased to honor the occasion by their attendance.
13. Clergymen and elders of the churches.
14. Benefactors of Alleghany College.
15. Trustees of the College.
16. Hon. Wm. MacArthur, treasurer, and maj. gen. R. Alden, president of the board of trustees.
17. Committee of arrangement, appointed by the board.
18. Knights Templar, officers and companions of Western Star Chapter with proper badges.
19. Officers and brethren of Western Star Chapter with their appropriate habiliments.
20. Rev. Timothy Alden, president of the faculty of arts, appointed by the board of trustees to perform the ceremony of laying the corner stone of Bentley Hall, supported, on the right, by the hon. Jesse Moore, presiding justice of the northwestern judicial district of Pennsylvania, and, on the left, by Hugh Brawley, esq. sheriff of the county of Crawford.
21. Capt. David Molthrop, M. E. H. P. of Western Star Chapter and Stephen Barlow, esq. W. M. of Western Star Lodge.

When the procession began to move, the 148th psalm was sung in the tune of Newburgh. The band then performed until capt. Long's company, approaching from the west, came within four rods of the northeastern corner of the site for Bentley Hall, where due preparations had been made for laying the corner stone, when the whole procession stopped, opening to the right and left. The marshals passed down to the rear, which with the successive divisions fell in, and following them, moved to the place of operation.—Flowers of various kinds held in the hands of the ladies and young misses were strewed along the path, as the rear approached.

Arrived at the corner stone, the president of the college addressed the throne of grace. Samuel Lord, esq. presented to the president of the board of trustees a deed, executed in legal form, gratuitously conveying five acres of land, bounded, for twenty rods on the western side of the Susquehanna and Waterford Turnpike, to the president and trustees of Alleghany College, for the location of the public buildings of the institution, which was publicly read, by George Selden, esq. one of the marshals of the day. The Ode on Science was sung. The president of the College was appointed W. M. of Western Star Lodge, protempore, and was invested accordingly. He then proceeded, with the kind aid of the officers, brethren, and companions of the two fraternities, to the ceremony of laying the corner stone, which was done to the satisfaction of the craft and the numerous attendants. He sprinkled it with corn and wine and oil, according to the ancient usage, and pronounced it "well laid and sure." He closed this ceremony by kneeling down with the Senior and Junior Wardens at the corner stone and supplicating the blessings of heaven on the work undertaken, and on the benefactors, officers, instructors, and alumni of the institution, of the present and all succeeding generations and on the vast assembly convened on the joyous and interesting occasion. He then resigned his temporary appointment, returned his investments to Mr. Barlow, W. M. of W. S. Lodge, assended the corner stone, and made an address. In doing this he read an extract from a letter he received from the late rev. William Bentley, D.D. a munificent patron of the college, in which he passed an exalted encomium on the people and the territory of the state of Pennsylvania; and an extract from a letter, he had recently received from Wm. Bentley Fowle, esq. of Boston, expressing his high sense of the honor conferred on the name of his distinguished relative, by the government of Alleghany College, in naming its first public edifice *Bentley Hall.* An account was given of the Bentley legacy, estimated at something more than three thousand dollars, and of the donation of Isaiah Thomas, LL.D. president of the American Antiquarian Society, amounting to seven hundred and fifty dollars. Some remarks were made on the beauty of the surrounding scenery; the flourishing village at the foot of this intended hill of science; the mountains round about like Jerusalem; French Creek, the In-nun-gaeh of the Senecas, upon the bosom of which Washington once was born, meandering through the extensive and fertile meadows, which stretch to the south; and Kussewaugoa rolling in silence from the west.

It was stated that a more eligible site for the institution could not have been found in this part of the country. A modest intimation was given to the numerous and respectable auditors, that, to judge from their approving aspect, on the joyous occasion, nothing but the opportunity was wanting, to contribute munificently, as God had prospered them, to aid in rearing the spacious fabric so auspiciously begun, and to be devoted to the best interests of the literary, scientific, moral, and religious welfare of the community.

Previously to laying the corner stone, the president of the college held in his hand certain articles to be deposited in an excavation on the underside of the stone, of which he gave some account. These consisted in an elegant plate of silver about six inches in length and four in breadth, wrought and engraved by captain Jacob Hull, the inscription on which is subjoined, and presented by him for the purpose; and a bottle containing foreign and domestic coins; a concise history of the origin of Alleghany College; sundry small rolls of parchment exhibiting lists of the names of the benefactors and officers of the college and the members and officers of Western Star Lodge and Chapter; several newspapers giving notices of the proceedings of the board of trustees; a piece of the rock, upon which the pilgrims of Leyden first stepped, in 1620, when they reached the shores of this western world; a piece of marble from a column of queen Dido's temple in ancient Carthage, and a specimen of mortar from the tomb of Virgil, presented by J. H. Steel, M.D. U. S. Navy; a piece of sundried brick from the Tower of Babel and of the reeds, which were laid, three thousand years ago, between the bricks and are as sound as if the growth of the last year, presented by capt. David Molthrop, whose son William Molthrop accompanied capt. Austin, in 1816, in his expedition to the Euphrates and brought these couriosities of antiquity to America, &c.

This being the anniversary commencement of Alleghany College, the appropriate exercises of the day, by resolve of the board of trustees, took place on the corner stone, over which was erected an arched bower, handsomely ornamented with wreathes of flowers displaying the taste of several young ladies of Meadville, who kindly prepared them for the purpose.

* * * *

The 78th psalm was sung in the tune of Mear and a benediction pronounced. The procession returned in a reversed order, except captain Long's company, which, followed by the band, led the whole. Decency and order marked the movements of the numerous train and reflected honor on the activity and attention of the marshals of the day, who, by appointment, were col. R. Marlin, col. R. Bean, G. Selden, esq. and capt. Jacob Hull.

The central part of Bentley Hall is to be sixty feet in length, twenty-six in width, three stories in height with a cupola rising from the centre of the roof. The wings are to be thirty feet in length, twenty in width, and two stories in height with a cellar under each seven feet deep. The wall already built by Mr. Jas. Lowry, is two feet in thickness from the foundation to the top of the corner stone. The face of it above ground consists of handsomely hewn grit stone. The corner stone is four feet in length facing east with the following inscription, elegantly wrought by Mr. John Birth:

TIMOTHEUS ALDEN
Praes. Pri. Coll. All. Lap. Angy. Hvj.
AVLAE BENTLIENSIS
Posvit, V JVL. MDCCCXX.

The college received about 3,000 volumes from the Bentley bequest; Isaiah Thomas, LL.D., President of the American Antiquarian Society, presented about 700; and the William Winthrop library followed. The Boston Patriot said, "The college beyond the mountains stands a fair chance of possessing the best collection of books of any seminary in the Union."

On the 28th of July, 1817, the first annual commencement took place, at which time with proper ceremony Dr. Timothy Alden was inducted into office.

A Mr. Temple was the architect for Bentley Hall.

The trustees were so pleased with the donation of land by Samuel Lord that Mrs. Lord was presented with a "handsome Canton crepe dress" which cost fifteen dollars.

CHAPTER XIV

THE ALLEGHANY MAGAZINE

It was in this little pioneer settlement which within a generation began to assume the aspect of a cultural oasis in the wilderness of northwestern Pennsylvania that one of the most ambitious dreams of Timothy Alden came to materialization—a monthly magazine. Designed for the people in the valley of the Alleghany it was given the name of *Alleghany* by its founder, and though published for only one year it was astoundingly well edited and composed. The material was original, an unusual fact for even the seaboard magazines of that day, and the contents were extremely enlightening on the conditions of the region. The *Crawford Weekly Messenger* introduced Dr. Alden to Meadville by publishing the following notice:[1]

TO THE FRIENDS OF JUSTICE.

ON the 15th of Feb. last, I left New York with my family in a coachee, and followed a waggon load of my effects, which was carefully driven by Jonathan Kirtley from the vicinity of Monticello, in Virginia, to Pittsburgh. At Myerstown a trunk burst open, containing a variety of articles of value. Among these was a small neat trunk, without a lock, about five inches in length, containing many plain gold rings, mostly very ancient. In the collection was one with a very brilliant light

---

[1] *Crawford Weekly Messenger*, May 13, 1815.

purple stone, and two with white stones—one with *"Let virtue be your guide,"* one with *"Love and live happy,"* and another with *"Remember the giver"*—Two mourning rings, one of which was embellished with hair, the other with a painted device, both having the name *"Martha Roads"*—a string of gold beads—a gold coat clasp—a pair of very small sleeve buttons —several pairs of earrings, one of which was paste—two Cornelion pins—several strings of beads—and a pair of silver barred spectacles. The most of these articles were peculiarly valuable from the circumstances that they had belonged to those, who in life were very dear to me and my family, and were preserved with fond veneration. From the difficulty of traveling in our circuitous route, we did not reach this place till the 24th of April, and it was not till after that time it could be ascertained where the foregoing articles were purloined. As it is possible some, if not the whole of these, may have been offered for sale at Pittsburgh, or on the road to Philadelphia, or in that city, or elsewhere, I have thought proper to publish this notice, hoping that in due time they may be recovered. Ample satisfaction shall be made to any one, having it in his power, who will afford me the information necessary for regaining these articles, or any of them, which though of some value in themselves, would be inestimable to their late owners, from the circumstances before mentioned.

TIMOTHY ALDEN.

Meadville, May 3rd, 1815.

Astonishing as it is that a man of the talents and culture of Timothy Alden should leave the centres of learning and commerce of the east and take his family to a remote little village on an undeveloped frontier, it shows that he had a flare for romance and unusual vision. Willingly enduring the hardships of travel and the inconvenience of life in a settlement, he entered immediately into activities of the community with a spirit which carried the leading citizens with him. In another column of the same issue of the *Messenger* reporting the meeting at which Allegheny College was started, there appeared the

PROSPECTUS[1]
Of a new periodical publication, to be entitled
THE
ALLEGHANY MAGAZINE,
OR
Repository of Useful Knowledge.
BY REV. TIMOTHY ALDEN.

To the Citizens of Crawford, and of the Counties adjacent.

HAVING, for a considerable length of time, purposed to settle in some region west of the Alleghany mountains, I have brought my family to Meadville, intending to fix my abode wherever Providence may direct. My object is to find a situation, where I may devote my life to the cause of religion, literature, and science.

From the friendly suggestions of many in this part of our country, I have been led to contemplate an establishment in this place, as favorable to the design which I fondly cherish. In case of my perminent residence here, it has occured, that, with the means in my power, I may rationally hope to be instrumental of good to my fellow citizens, by conducting a Religious and Literary Magazine. I therefore respectfully offer to the publick this Prospectus, not doubting but all, who are disposed to encourage the proposed undertaking, will shortly

---

[1] *Crawford Weekly Messenger*, June 24, 1815.

forward their names to me at Meadville, or to Mr. Atkinson, who is to execute the typographical part of the work. . .

As soon as the patronage shall be sufficient to warrant the publication, and a new fount of types procured, the work will be commenced, of which notice will be given in the "Crawford Messenger."

The first number of the *Alleghany Magazine* appeared in July, 1816, with this

PREFACE [1]

AS this work is expected to circulate, principally, in the region watered by the numerous streams, which in the aggregate, form the Alleghany river, it takes the name of the *Alleghany Magazine.*

The object of the editor will be to furnish his patrons with a variety of information relative to the state of religion in all parts of the world; notices of the present unprecedented exertions of the friends of the Redeemer for the spread of the gospel; dissertations on moral and religious subjects; elucidations of certain passages of scripture; accounts of attempts for increasing the literature and science of the United States, especially in the north western judicial district of Pennsylvania; results of American antiquarian researches; biographical, historical, and topographical sketches; articles for the benefit of farmers, herdsmen, and mechanicks; such domestick and foreign intelligence as may be deemed of general interest; and other miscellaneous matter.

The actual number of patrons, who have kindly subscribed for the encouragement of this undertaking, is far inadequate to the pecuniary expense, which the editor must encounter to conduct it; but, knowing the want of some publication in the

---

[1] Timothy Alden, *The Alleghany Magazine* (July, 1816), v.

extensive region, for which it is designed; and hoping, after its commencement, to receive all due fostering attention from the friends of morality, religion, literature, and science; he offers, to the publick, *his first number,* on the forty second anniversary of the independence of his beloved country.

CONDITIONS.

1. ONE number of 24 pages 8 vo. is to be published at the beginning of each month. The 8 vo. rather, than the 18 mo. form, is adopted, on the suggestion of friends, to the publication, though the latter form was contemplated in the original prospectus; still, the same quantity of paper and letter press will be given as was promised.
2. The price is two dollars, a year, or, for twelve numbers. *One dollar* is to be paid on the delivery of the *first number,* and the *other,* on the delivery of the *seventh.*
3. Those, who become responsible to the editor for ten copies, shall be entitled to one copy of this Magazine, gratis.
4. With the twelfth number as index to all the articles and a list of the names of subscribers to the work will be given.

The energy and effort put into the Alleghany Magazine did not meet with the public support for which the Reverend Alden had hoped although he put forth a publication of unusual merit. The twelfth number for June-November, 1817, contained an index of articles published for the year and a list of the subscribers, followed by this paragraph:

The editor[1] having fulfilled his engagement to his patrons is

---

[1] Alden, *Alleghany,* 304.

conducting this work till a volume has been completed, he hopes they will fulfil theirs by the payment of whatever is due. A want of patronage induces him to suspend the publication of the All. Mag. and whether it will ever be resumed depends upon circumstances, which time will unfold.

Like many men who have devoted their lives to the uplift of the human race, he found that few persons had reached a place in their development where they could accept what he was so ready to give. A notice published in the *Messenger,* December 19, 1817, listed the contents of the twelfth number:

LITERARY NOTICE.

THE XII num. of the Alleghany Magazine is published and contains an account of the second anniversary of the Meadville Bib. Soc. an extract from an address delivered by S. Hays, jun. esq. before the Newark Bib. Soc. a notice of the hieroglyphicks on the Dighton rock in Massachusetts; Asiatick antiquities; account of a missionary tour among the Senecas and Munsees; instalation of the Western Star Lodge; incarceration of a toad for sixty years; historical notes on the county of Crawford, the township of Mead, and the town of Meadville; laudable zeal of the ladies in Meadville; Aboriginal, num. XII; inauguration of the first president and professor of Alleghany College and a description of the seal for that institution; notice of the late execution; an index to the volume and a list of subscribers to the work.

For want of that encouragement which is indispensable in conducting such a work, the Editor, having fulfilled his engagement to the publick, by completing a volume, now relinquishes his editorial task and requests all subscribers, who kindly gave their names as patrons to the publication, to do him the justice to pay the trifling sums, which are still due.

This issue described the town in which the magazine was published.

NOTES ON MEADVILLE.[1]

That portion of the section of land, which the late general Mead chose for his settlement, constituting the town of Meadville, is on the eastern side of French Creek, the In-nun-ga-ch of the Senecas, and adjoining it. At this place, French Creek assumes a handsome serpentine bend, on the west of which is an island of sixty acres, made by a division of the waters taking nearly a semicircular sweep, and into which the Kossewauga empties, about ninety rods above the confluence of the two parts.

The town gradually rising towards the east is delightfully situated. The first improvement was begun by the pioneer to this region, whose name it perpetuates, in 1787. The original plan was conceived in 1790, but was matured and much enlarged by the magnanimous exertions and influence of major Alden and the late doctor Kennedy, in 1795. It is divided into seventy-five squares, by streets, alleys, and a lane. One of these, more correctly speaking, a parallelogram, six hundred by three hundred feet, including the streets, by which it is circumscribed and intersected, and designed for publick use, is called the Diamond, and is located in a central part of the town plot. Each of the squares is divided into townlots fifty feet in width and two hundred feet in length, except those on Water Street, which are one hundred and fifty.

One tier of lots is abutted by the margin of French Creek, westerly; and, easterly, by Water Street, which runs north, fifteen degrees east. Taking the streets, alleys, and lane, in

---

[1] Alden, *Allegheny Magazine* (June-November, 1817), 293.

Henry Baldwin, District Attorney, 1800-1804; Associate Justice of the United States Supreme Court, 1825-1844.

loeal order, from west to east, the following list exhibits their names, widths, and distances apart.

	Water Street, in width	50 feet
150 feet from this is	Mulberry Alley	20
200	Second Street	50
200	Crab Alley	20
300	Plum Alley	20
300	Main Street	100
300	Chancery Lane	20
250	Liberty Street	50
200	First Alley	20

At right angles with the foregoing, and beginning on the northerly side, the first publick road is called

	North Street	50
200	Stear's Alley	20
200	Walnut Street	40
200	Strawberry Alley	20
200	Cherry Alley	20
200	Chestnut Street	50
200	Dock Alley	20
200	Arch Street	50
200	South Alley	20

Main Street crosses the Diamond longitudinally. At the north end of this street Mill Run enters the town and, meandering southwesterly, crosses Water Street between Dock Alley and Arch Street. A canal, passing a little without the limits of the town, on the north side of it, receives a sufficiency of water from Mill Run to carry a grist mill,[1] which is the first built in Pennsylvania north of the Alleghany river.

---

[1] Built by General Mead on the bank of French Creek just south of The Terrace.

Meadville is bounded by French Creek, on the west; by land belonging to the heirs of the late general Mead and of the late Thomas Kennedy, M.D. on the north; by land belonging to major Alden and the Meadville Academy, on the east; and by land belonging to colonel Hackney, mr. Macarthur, the heirs of doc. Kennedy, and mr. Huidekoper, on the south.

It contains eighty families, which probably include four hundred and fifty inhabitants. These are made up of people from different parts of the United States, and of Europe, and are of various pursuits, languages, and sentiments religious and political.

In mechanical employment we find located, in this pleasant and flourishing village, tanners, curriers, shoemakers, carpenters, joiners, cabinet-makers, winsor chair-makers, turners, coopers, boat-builders, wheelwrights, millrights, blacksmiths, whitsmiths, gunsmiths, silversmiths, watchmakers, nail cutters, tinmen, masons, stone cutters, brickmakers, wool carders, weavers, tailors, hatters, painters, etc.

In this village there are six stores, containing a variety of merchandise, some of which are wholesale as well as retail.

Of hotels and other houses for publick entertainment there are eight.

Of gentlemen of liberal education there is an uncommon proportion considering the population of the place and comparing it with most others equally new.

The presiding justice of the northwestern judicial district of Pennsylvania resides in Meadville, one of the associate justices of Crawford county also resides in this village and the other in its vicinity. The deputy attorney general for this district is an inhabitant of the town. Here too are the offices of five gentlemen of the bar, of several, who are extensively engaged in the sale of land and the settlement of the surrounding country, of magistrates, and of various county and town officers.

Henry Shippen, President Judge, 1825-1839.
Alexander Addison, First President Judge, 1800-1803.

A block house built in time of the Indian wars still remains. The courthouse, the lower apartments of which constitute the gaol, is a large hewn log building. An elegant brick courthouse, as is contemplated, is to be erected on the centre of the Diamond. The academy is a one story brick building. The state arsenal, one hundred feet in length, two stories in height, now rearing under the direction of the hon. William Clark, and of brick, a little without the town plot, on land presented by the late general Mead, north of Main Street, will be a conspicuous ornament to this part of the country, as well as an evidence of the wise, judicious, and magnanimous policy of the legislature of the commonwealth.

The North Western Bank of Pennsylvania is located in Meadville. Other publick institutions are a College, recently organized and in operation, a Bible Society, a Female Cent Society, a Social Library, and a lodge of free and accepted masons, called the Western Star Lodge.

A printing office established here, in the year 1804, by T. Atkinson, esq is still owned and conducted by him, at which the Crawford Messenger is published every friday morning.

The only churches formed in this village are one presbyterian and one German Lutheran, but no meetinghouse has been erected for either. As pastor of the former the rev. Joseph Stockton was settled here in 1801. In 1810 he removed to Pittsburgh. His successor was the rev. Robert Johnston, who left his charge for another on the forks of the Youghiogany in the spring of 1817. The writer of this article has statedly officiated, one half of his time, as a preacher to the presbyterian church and congregation, since the first of July 1817, yet has ever declined as acceptance of the pastoral charge. The rev. Charles William Colson was the only German Lutheran minister ever stationed in Meadville. He was a gentleman of amiable and endearing manners and respectable talents. Had his days been prolonged, there is reason to believe that he would have proved an important blessing to the German population in this place and its vicinity; but the great Head of the church saw fit to remove him from his sphere of useful labours, 29 December, 1816, a few months after his establishment, we trust, to a happier clime. [See memoirs of mr. Colson, pp. 173-176.]

Of the traces of French settlements near the waters of Innungach; of the remains of the fortifications of unknown antiquity in their region; of the numerous indications of the general deluge in all directions from Meadville; of the hardships sustained by the first settlers of this town and its neighborhood; of the painful apprehensions, in which they lived, for several years, from the hostile disposition of the encircling savage tribes; and of many other particulars in reference to this part of the country, the editor of this Magazine intended to have written fully for its pages, but the want of patronage induces him to forbear and with the present number to conclude his editorial task, at least, for the present.

For information concerning events, names, locations, and boundaries, the *Alleghany Magazine* continues to be an undisputed authority for the period in which it was published. It was cited as evidence in the case of the Conneaut Lake Ice Company against Amos Quigley, et. al., before the Supreme Court of Pennsylvania.

The high hopes of the Reverend Timothy Alden were only partially realized by him. Publication of the *Alleghany Magazine* was never resumed. Another dream faded when in 1832 he was no longer able to finance Allegheny College, and when that institution passed into other hands he left Meadville, for which he had done so much. After a year in Cincinnati the balance of his life was spent in teaching and preaching in Pittsburgh, where he died July 5, 1839, and was buried. In appreciation of the founder of Allegheny College, Dr. William H. Crawford while president of that institution brought Dr. Alden back to rest in the Allegheny College lot in the Meadville cemetery.

CHAPTER XV

WATER STREET

Even before and for years after David Mead laid out Meadstown, the Venango Trail was the principal thoroughfare, later the center of business and the place of residence of prominent citizens. This Indian trail followed the east bank of French Creek; when Mead arrived he built his log house with its fifteen-foot stockade surrounding it on a bluff above the Creek so that it had a clear view south along the trail. His mills were close by, part way down the embankment. With the coming of other settlers who built houses near for protection, the trail widened into a road, and when the town was surveyed it became Water Street.

Meadville was incorporated as a borough in 1823, and Squire Lord was still living in a durable log house shaded by a great maple tree which leaned over the pond beside it. The land of Mt. Hope, as his patent was called, extended from French Creek well up the slope of the hill. The old Indian trail over which Washington traveled northward to Le Boeuf lay between the Lord house and the Creek, and when the town grew out to it it was called The Terrace, being designated by a sign nailed

168   IN FRENCH CREEK VALLEY

to an oak tree, "To Erie 36 miles." Lord's spring, south of the pond, was the scene of many a celebration at which there was a collation aided and abetted by a barrel of rye whiskey together with numerous toasts.

Samuel Lord was a soldier in the garrison at Venango and on coming to Meadville he opened a store which attracted a large country trade. Many Indians also traded with him as he spoke their language. Of medium height, he was somewhat stooped and always carried a drab tree cane. Austere in looks and abrupt in speech, he was genial and kind and had many friends. He was a valuable citizen as well as a Justice of the Peace.

Going toward town the only house between those of Squire Lord and David Mead was that of James White, with only the Trail between it and the Creek. Bricks for his house[1] were made from clay obtained on his own property, and the lime for mortar was made by calcining mussel shells from the Creek.

David Mead's second house was on a rise of ground at the head of Water Street, where the street preempted the Indian Trail. Built for him in 1797 by William Dick, it was one of the earliest clapboard houses, showing in line and proportion the builder's skill.

[1] The north wall was cracked by the earthquake in 1811. When A. C. Huidekoper built a new house this one was moved back to form the north wing.

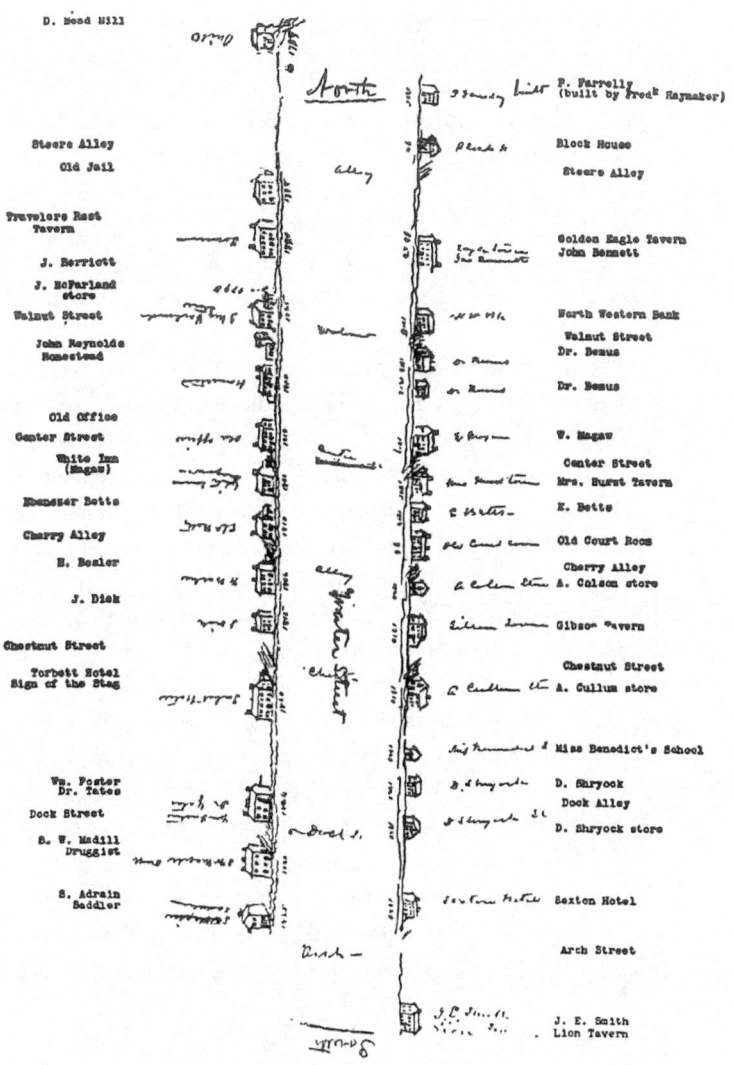

Water Street Sketches by William Reynolds.

After Jared Shattuck purchased this house and moved in, he built a store west of it, which faced down Water Street, and there he did a thriving business. This was only one of his numerous enterprises; he purchased large tracts of land, built distilleries, a foundry in which he introduced a steam engine, and operated a haypress, sending his products to the lower Mississippi by flatboat.

Going down Water Street a deep ravine was crossed by a bridge. Mead's mills on the south bank of the Creek were pulled down at the time of the construction of the canal and the ravine filled in where the bridge was removed. At this time the "Red Mill" replaced the old one and a mill race brought additional water from Mill Run to the mill pond east of the Street.

Further down Water Street on the same side as the pond and across North Street, John McFarland built a frame house some years after he had married a daughter of Thomas Atkinson. Born in Erie County, he at the age of fourteen was a clerk in the store of Major James Herriott, and when his employer failed he carried on the business, using for his motto, "A smile and full weight to customers." He also manufactured and sent  down the river quantities of potash and pearl ash. For a long time treasurer of Allegheny College, president of the Merchants National Bank, he later was one of the first Board of Directors of the Atlantic and Great Western Railway.

WATER STREET

An excellent classical scholar and an eloquent orator, Patrick Farrelly began practice at the Crawford County bar in 1803. He lived in a house built by Frederick Haymaker south of John McFarland's and north of the Block House, marrying successively daughters of General Mead and Timothy Alden. A major in the War of 1812, he served one term in the State Legislature and subsequently was elected to Congress.[1]

Built of logs in 1794, the Block House for defense against the Indians was on the northeast corner of Steers Alley. After the Indians were defeated by General Wayne it was used as a school until  the Academy was opened. Turning utilitarian it sheltered a blacksmith shop, a carpenter shop, and various families. One morning the citizens were surprised to discover the former formidable Block House toppled over and lying on its side. Just who the spirited youths were who assisted its recline is not certain; perhaps no other building in the village could so well have served as an outlet for their excessive zeal for celebrating.

A one-room log cabin on the south side of Steers Alley a short distance west from Water Street was rented for the first jail.

[1] William Reynolds, *Fifty Years of the Bench and Bar of Crawford County* (Meadville, 1904), 18. "When in Congress, Mr. Farrelly offered an amendment to the general appropriation bill appropriating four or five thousand dollars for the improvement of the harbor at Erie. After an explanation by Mr. Farrelly . . . the amendment was carried. This appropriation was the *first appropriation* of money by Congress for the improvement of Harbors and Rivers. . . ."

During a trial in 1801[1] one of the citizens with an ... overflow of spirits was singing a song in front of the court room, to the great annoyance of the Court. The Sheriff, ordered by the Judge to silence him, returned with an answer more forcable than courteous. For this contempt he was committed to jail. The door of the cabin was securely locked on the prisoner, who, without trouble, made his escape by the primitive stick and clay chimney, and followed his jailor down the street with his song.

 Diagonally across the street from the Block House a log tavern was built in 1790 and kept by Henry Reichard, a Hessian soldier of the Revolution.

South there was built four years later another tavern, the Traveler's Rest, which had sheltered Audubon; it was presided over by J. E. Smith.

Directly opposite was the Sign of the Golden Eagle, John Bennett's yellow frame tavern. There were three Bennett brothers, all of fine physique and ranging in height from six feet three inches to six feet five.

On the same side of the Street at the corner of Walnut Street was the North Western Bank of Pennsylvania, so important in the business activities of the district, with courteous and efficient Joseph Morrison the cashier. He was a public-spirited man and associated with many of the projects for social and business betterment.

[1] Ibid., 7.

At this time James Herriott lived in part of the Bank building—a small and decrepit old gentleman who was often seen on the street speaking to few and seldom recognized, although he had been a successful merchant and identified with most of the early enterprises. At the opening of the War of 1812 he locked his store across the Street and entered the service, returning at the end of the War with the rank of major and honorable mention. At one time he was extensively interested in river traffic on the Ohio and the Mississippi. Later financial reverses ended his business career.

The little frame store south of the Traveler's Rest was occupied successively by Joseph Hackney, Conner Clark, James Herriott, and John McFarland, merchants.

Dr. Daniel Bemus came from Chautauqua County, New York, and studied medicine with Dr. Thomas R. Kennedy. For a time he and Dr. Kennedy were the only physicians in the county. He occupied the building on the southeast corner of Walnut Street as an office and apothecary shop, building his residence south of it in 1816. He married a daughter of James Miles of Erie County. A man who made many friends and possessed of great energy, he built a saw and a grist mill two miles above the town at Bemustown Dam on French Creek, which he replaced with larger mills after the construction of the canal by the State.

In the frame building on the opposite corner of Walnut Street was the law office of Henry Baldwin, Jr., one of the early members of the Crawford County bar, a son of the Honorable Henry Baldwin of the United States Supreme Court.

On the property extending south to Center Street was the home of John Reynolds. A portion of the house had been built by Samuel Lord, one room being used by him as a store. The house and land were purchased by Dr. T. R. Kennedy, and after his widow married John Reynolds it became the Reynolds home. It was a one-and-three-quarters-story cottage built near the Street, like most of the homes at that time, with sweetbrier roses trained over the front, and in the back a large shed over the summer oven and soap kettle, and just north, a storeroom. Dr. Kennedy had planted a row of lombardy poplars on the Street front. The property extended from the Street to French Creek, having flower and vegetable gardens and fruit trees. John Reynolds' office was in the building on the corner of Center Street. It had also been the office of the first prothonotary of Crawford and Venango Counties, and there the first mail was received for distribution.

In 1819 Colonel William Magaw built a brick house directly opposite this office, using the corner room on Center Street for his store. In proportion and design this building was outstanding, and the interior exhibited many beautiful examples of the carpenter's skill. William Magaw first came here as a clerk in the store of his uncle, Samuel B. Magaw, and when in business for himself sent quantities of lumber, farm produce and whiskey down the Mississippi by raft and flatboat. After  building a paper mill on Woodcock Creek he invented and manufactured straw paper, later converting the "Red Mill" into a paper mill.

The Crossed Keyes Tavern across Center Street was kept by the widow of Henry Hurst, who had built it in  1802. Serving through the War of 1812 he returned with the rank of brigadier general. In his home town he held the offices of commissioner, sheriff, and postmaster. During this time when everyone took politics seriously and party spirit was bitter, the Democrats used Hurst's Tavern as their headquarters.

The Federalists met at the tavern of Bartholomew White on the opposite side of Water Street. It was here that a colonel and a captain of the Burr expedition had a recruiting office. After the death of White this weatherboarded log house became the home of Dorothea (better known as "Dolly"), the widow of Samuel B. Magaw, and her son William A. V. Magaw.

On the same side of the Street the frame building occupying the corner of Cherry Alley was built in 1800 by Samuel B. Magaw for a residence and store. Later it became the home of Dorothea Magaw's brother, Ebenezer Betts, who had his nail factory back on the bank of French Creek.

The Betts family was a united one, for another brother, Eliphalet, in 1804 built a log house across the Street south of the Hurst Tavern. A tailor by trade, Eliphalet was a public-spirited man and took an active interest in all affairs for promoting the welfare of the Settlement.

Robert L. Potter and his two maiden sisters lived in the house which he built next south, after coming here from New Haven, Connecticut. A few years after he was admitted to the bar in 1820, he was appointed justice of the peace. Squire Potter succeeded in having the first continuous board walk built in the town, on Center Street from Water to the public square.

William Dick started building a house for himself on the northeast corner of Cherry Alley which was unfinished at the time Meadville became the County Seat. As no place had been found for the first court session, arrangements were made for William Dick to finish his building so that the ground floor might be used as a court room by July, 1800. Court continued there until a new Court House was built in 1805, when the Dick family occupied the old house as was originally intended.

On the other side of Cherry Alley was the frame store of Augustus Colson. It was in this store that a grain bin was converted into a studio for John James Audubon where he made crayon portraits of the citizens while the curious and the interested watched his rapid fingers.

The entire front of the two-story log house across Cherry Alley from the Ebenezer Betts house was covered with sweetbrier and occupied by Henry C. Bosler, his family and his mother Mrs. Wahab. It was shaded by fragrant locust trees and convenient to his store across the Street. The Bosler household was known for its hospitality and had a wide reputation for the excellence of its suppers.

John Dick's house came next, having been built in 1815 by James Gibson, with a garden extending on to Chestnut Street. General Dick had a prominent part in all the affairs of the village. Merchant, manufacturer, with his brother James R. he established the town's first private bank, J. & J. R. Dick & Company. Four times he was elected burgess of the town, and later he was sent to Congress. The house at present retains its original position but not its shape, for the roof sags badly. The Dick family lived here until John purchased the Roger Alden cottage and built a new house under the old sycamore trees.

Midway between the Colson store and Chestnut Street on the east side of Water was the Gibson Tavern, two stories and of frame construction, with vegetable gardens north and south of it and locust trees for shade.

It was known as the best hotel between Pittsburgh and Buffalo, being patronized by prominent persons who came to the village, including visiting lawyers attending the court. James Gibson, a resident since 1798, was a popular landlord and held the esteem of his fellow-townsmen. He married Polly McGunnegle of Pittsburgh.

Arthur Cullum had a store in the frame building built by Jacob Shryock in 1816 on the southeast corner of Chestnut Street. Before coming west he had manufactured carriages on Chambers Street opposite City Hall in New York. A man of energy and ambition he took contracts for building the aqueduct over French Creek and part of the construction of the canal, which owing to his death were finished by his son Oscar.

Built and operated by Samuel Torbett in 1815, the Sign of the Stag was the finest inn of its day and had a very select patronage. After Lafayette had dined at Mr. Gibson's Tavern and greeted the citizens on the Street, he was presented to the ladies of the village at Mr. Torbett's hotel. In the evening of that eventful day a grand ball was held in the Assembly Room— but without the guest of honor who had departed earlier. In this room the Western Star Lodge of Masons held their meetings. The Stag barnyard was opposite just south of the Cullum store and enclosed by a high board fence. There at one time was exhibited a menagerie, a real novelty in the town. It consisted of an elephant, a lion, and a "Dandy Jack." It was after the failure of the Hill and Torbett store and before the days of the Stag that Samuel Torbett manufactured nails. In the rear of his hotel where Chestnut Street met the Creek he built a wharf and warehouse for merchandise carried by flat and keel boats. He too was a director of the North Western Bank.

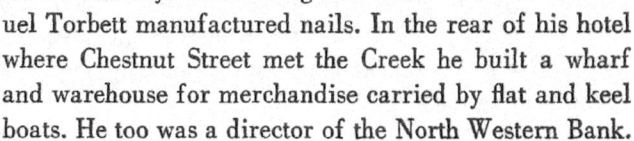

Miss Benedict's school was in a one-story building on a little knoll south of the barnyard of Samuel Torbett.

On one side of the school room[1] was a row of desks, ornimented with carvings by the boys with jack-knives during leisure moments. Benches without backs, for the younger pupils, high four-legged desk for the teacher, a lath nailed to the floor for a toe mark for the spelling and reading classes, a "dunce block" in the center of the floor completed the furnishings of the room. A huge dunce cap with peacock feather and leather spectacles, ornamented the wall. Within the teacher's desk were deposited the insignia of honor to be worn to their homes by the meritorious scholars.

It was a successful school and in it most of the children of the village acquired their primary education. The girls were also taught sewing and ornamental needle work. Like all schools of that day, it was conducted on the line of reward

---

[1] William Reynolds, Water Street and the Residents of Olden Times, (January, 1907), 15 (Reynolds Collection)

and punishment—or punishment and reward—for the memory was much stimulated by the use of the ferule.

Across Dock Alley from the school was the house of Colonel Daniel Shryock with his store south of it. He helped in cutting the timbers for Commodore Perry's ships at Erie, and with William Magaw manufactured salt in Beaver township from wells drilled 180 feet deep and producing ten to twelve barrels a day. He also had made wooden pumps before going into the mercantile business.

Dr. C. M. Yates started to practice medicine in 1825 and purchased the handsome two-story brick house which William Foster had built the year before on the northwest corner of Dock Street. The next year he married Mrs. Maria Magaw of Lancaster, a sister of James Buchanan who became president of the United States. Dr. and Mrs. Yates entertained many friends and President Buchanan was a frequent guest at their house.

On the other corner of Dock Street, Samuel W. Magill lived and had his drug store. He had for a time been editor of the Democratic paper.

Robert Adrain, a native of Ireland, built his home and saddle shop south and nearer Mill Run. His many friends appreciated his Irish humor and genial disposition.

The yellow frame tavern of Roswell Sexton was on

the northeast corner of Arch Street. Extending north from the tavern to Mill Run there was an orchard where many a Fourth of July celebration was held. The Sexton Tavern was noted for the excellence of its food.

South of Arch Street Andrew Smith had his store and dwelling. And

South of the store lived an eccentric man[1] of middle age, crippled with rheumatism, Brasilla Goodrich—the useful man of the town. He was a veritable "jack of all trades," from blacksmith, carpenter, cabinetmaker to repairer of clocks and watches. His workroom was a curiosity shop containing varieties of tools, and models, the result of his inventive genius, ropes and pullies for moving buildings. He was a right hand man in all mechanical difficulties. He built the first billiard table in the town and opened a room in his dwelling for those fond of the pastime.

Next was the Guilded Lion, the tavern built by its landlord, John E. Smith, an old resident. He had formerly been a teamster driving his four-horse Conestoga wagon from Meadville to Pittsburgh in from ten to fifteen days, and the trip to Philadelpiha taking from four to six weeks. He was a genial, popular landlord, and on election, military training, and other days of celebration his house was patronized by country people. Many

---

[1] William Reynolds, Water Street and the Residents of Olden Times, 16 (Reynolds Collection)

feuds and neighborhood quarrels were settled in the tavern barnyard.

John Radle lived over his smith shop south of the Guilded Lion. And the house of Bailey Courtney, one of the earliest tailors to come to the village, was nearer Pine Street.

Occupying the other side of Water Street, with a board fence extending from Mill Run to Arch Street, was the tannery established by Patrick Davis in 1805. This was being operated by George McFadden in the thirties.

The Barton House was a three-story frame structure built by Livi Barton about 1820 on the northwest corner of Pine Street. It was at this tavern that the stage from Erie and Pittsburgh stopped to discharge and take on travelers.

David Mead in laying out his town started at his mills with Henry Marley carrying the chain and worked south cutting out the hazel bushes in their path. Late in the afternoon they reached the bank of Mill Run and Mead looking at his watch remarked, "Well Henry,[1] we'll stop here. I guess the town will never go farther south than this creek." Harm Jan Huidekoper had a larger vision when he purchased his acres some years later and built his house a quarter of a mile south of the village, and still later Water Street was extended down past it. Pomona Hall was a two-story frame house

[1] Samuel P. Bates, *History of Crawford County* (Chicago, 1885), 372.

with wings north and south and a wide veranda extending along the entire front. Between it and the Street there was a broad semicircular lawn planted with a variety of trees; one old oak still grows as it did when surrounded by the original forest. Just north of the Hall the building used as the office of the Holland Land Company also remains. To the rear the stable, sheepfold, smoke house, kennel, chicken and carriage houses, with gardens and a large orchard were to be found.

Since its founding Meadville has grown into one of the larger and more important towns in Pennsylvania's northwest. From the beginning Water Street had been its busiest and principal thoroughfare, and the 1820's found this Street continuing to occupy its prominence. Those who had stores or lived upon it built well for the generations which were to follow.

CHAPTER XVI

VILLAGE LIFE

In looking over the record of events and achievements in the growth of pioneer settlements in western Pennsylvania, the most impressive factor is the character and intelligence of those men and women who made it possible. The instinct for adventure which dominated one element of the white race made possible the colonization of many parts of the world, but the type of colonist chosen for North America was marked by a quality of character higher than the ordinary. The rapidity with which the United States has risen to leadership of the nations of the world is proof of this fact.

Not all who helped in this courageous work were animated by the vision of a better condition than was known at the time of their venturing—many followed the urge solely for combat and gain—but a sufficient majority of those who came first and many who came later possessed a nobility of character which dominated the movement as a whole. Beginning with Washington a greater number of the men who came to the French Creek Valley were of the finest quality that their civilization had produced. This is attested by their love of freedom, of justice and of the arts, and most of all by the God-given desire for the best that man could produce and be.

Pomona Hall, Water Street, Residence of H. J. Huidekoper, built 1806.

First Brick House, built on The Terrace, 1807, by James White. Later the A. C. Huidekoper residence. Now the home of Phi Delta Theta Fraternity.

Naturally these traits were more noticeable in the communities than in the open country; since Mead's Settlement was older and larger than any of the others it became a leader in building up this new territory. Daily life reflected the sterling qualities of its inhabitants. They made their simple homes as comfortable as was possible, gathering in them the best furniture and food which they could make or procure. Furniture being bulky was consequently difficult and expensive to transport across rough mountain roads. It was much easier to bring a cabinet maker to a place where the forests furnished an abundant supply of wood of the best quality. These artisans had learned their trade in the shops of the best workmen of the east.

One cabinet maker advertised his artisanship in the *Crawford Weekly Messenger*:

C. CUNNINGHAM

CABINET MAKER

RESPECTFULLY informs his friends and the public in general, that on the 7th of May next, he intends opening a shop in the town of Meadville, where he proposes carrying on the above trade in all its various branches, and flatters himself, that from having served an apprenticeship of five years, with a first rate workman, and afterwards improved himself in the most reputed *shops* in the city of Philadelphia, will be sufficient to recommend him to public patronage.

As it has been currently reported, that his charges, for work, are extortionary, and in order to remove such report, he respectfully submits to the public the following

Statement of Prices:

	Dol.	Cts.
Desks, plain	24	
Do. elegant	30	
Beaureaus, from 12 to	14	
Circular, do. from 18 to	20	
Serpentine do. do. do. to	20	
Secretary, plain from 26 dollars and 50 cents to	37	50
Bason-Stands for taverns	2	
Corner do.	3	50
Breakfast tables	6	
Dinging do.	8	
Circular card do. sash-cornered and commode per pair	16	
Northumberland tables per set	24	
Book-Cases after Chinese mode, from 12 to	16	

Drafts for Sideboards of every description may be seen by applying to him.

The prices of a number of other articles might be mentioned; he deems it however unnecessary, but pledges himself to the public, they shall be in proportion to those above stated.

> Dry boards from this date, cherrey or walnut, will be received at 1 dol. 67 cts. per hundred feet, and half inch poplar at 75 cts. per hundred.
>
> Meadville, March 6, 1805.

Pieces of this early American furniture still in use exhibit the skill and artistic taste of their makers. Meadville soon acquired a reputation for cherry and birch-crotch furniture which found a market as far away as New Orleans. The whole countryside was stripped of birch trees and much of the lumber was shipped down the river to Pittsburgh, Cincinnati, and Louisville to be made into veneer.

By 1820 the parlors of these homes had carpets from the loom of a local weaver which were often bright with stripes in colors, while those in the other rooms were a product of the home and dyed brown with butternut. The colonial mantle over the ample fireplace held candlesticks with extinguishers and snuffers. In the summer time its vases were kept filled with flowers, while over it there was the usual "looking glass." In the winter the brass andirons held a cheerful fire of logs. The chairs and settee were more often painted than polished, except in the houses of the more prosperous where there were tables, sideboards, and bookcases of mahogany.

The chief furnishing of the "spare room" was a four-poster bed spread with a patchwork quilt of many colors and ingenious design which had required many stitches by the wife and daughters in the making. Crisp dimity or chintz curtains completed this picture.

On the broad hearthstone of the fireplace in the huge chimney of the kitchen were great andirons and a swinging crane with pothooks on which the kettles hung.

When the table had been set with Irish linen, steel knives and forks, china and cut glass, all the food except the dessert was placed upon it. Meats, poultry, game, and vegetables were all prepared under the supervision of the mistress. This was only one of her many duties as few persons could be obtained for domestic service. Even indented servants were hard to keep after they had been obtained, as is seen by advertisements in the local press.

25 DOLLARS REWARD.[1]
RAN AWAY from the subscriber, on the 24th instant, a black indented servant, named *Robert Davis;* born at or near Pittsburgh; eighteen years of age next June, according to his agreement with Alexander M'Intire, and witnessed by his father; five feet seven inches high, and left handed. Had on and took with him, a dark brown cloth roundabout; a white Marseilles vest, and one of white woollen; one pair of check cotton, and one pair of new tow cloth pantaloons; two shirts, a felt hat, and a handsome fowling piece; well made, strong, active, and fit for any service in a

---

[1] *Crawford Messenger.*

family or on a farm. All persons are hereby forbid harboring, protecting, or concealing him; and those who have aided and advised him, may expect to be called to answer for their conduct. The above reward will be given to any person who will secure him in Meadville jail, or in any other jail in the state, and give notice so that he may be delivered in safety to the subscriber.

R. ALDEN.
Meadville, May 29, 1815.

N. B. The above described boy is in company with another of the same name, and nearly the same age, a servant of Mr. Samuel Davis, near Meadville; both the boys are left handed.

The expense and difficulty of obtaining help and necessities from outside sources compelled the mistress of a household to be largely dependent upon herself. Spinning wheels were to be found in homes on which the family supply of yarn was spun from wool prepared by a carding mill. "Our Mother[1] was very fond of spinning and spent many hours at the wheel near the glass door opening on the porch and while spinning the yarn told stories to the children gathered about her. She was a most gifted story teller and her fund of tales of the fairies and genii was almost inexhaustible. Her power of improvisation was also remarkable." Mothers and daughters knitted stockings for the household. At an

[1] William Reynolds, Life Time Memories (Reynolds Collection)

early age, all girls were taught plain and fancy needlework, both at home and at school.

From the Indian the early settlers had learned to tap the sugar maple in the early spring as the snow was melting and boil down the sap into syrup and maple sugar. As the summer berries and fruit ripened they were preserved to be kept for winter use. Apples having been pared and cut in pieces were strung on a cord to be hung from the kitchen ceiling to dry. In the autumn pork was made into sausage, head cheese, and liverworst against winter, hams pickled for the smokehouse, and bacon salted and packed to be ready for the coming summer. Beef was bought by the quarter and corned in barrels. Wicking dipped in tallow made candles for ordinary use but for special occasions they were poured in moulds. With the coming of spring tubs were brought out and filled with the winter's accumulation of wood ashes, the lye run off and enough hard soap boiled in large kettles to supply the household for the year. Every cellar had its cask of soft soap. These with the routine duties of the household devolved upon the housekeeper —and today when all supplies can be purchased from a shop we think living is complex!

Acorns from the oak trees furnished "mast" for fattening hogs and turkeys. Huckleberries, blackberries, and raspberries were abundant, and the thickets of wild plum contributed their fruit for jam. After frost the plentiful wild grapes were sweet enough to gather and eat, and also made jelly. Honey from the blossoms of the basswood or linden was especially prized.

Weddings were an event in the small community and always celebrated in the evening at the home of the bride, to which friends were invited. After the ceremony the house was open to all who desired to extend their congratulations to the bride and groom. As everyone was acquainted practically all the inhabitants availed themselves of this privilege.

In most cases these marriages were happy ones but occasionally they did not end in harmony and public print was resorted to, to-wit:

>   CAUTION
> WHEREAS my wife *Deborah*, has left my bed and board without any reasonable cause—This is therefore to caution all persons from trusting her on my account.
>   DAVID THURSTON.
> Oct. 17, 1817.

>   November 14, 1817.
> DAVID THURSTON, sorry I am, that you pay no respect to decency; for you have proven yourself a liar *my* dear by advertising me.
>   DEBORAH THURSTON.

In several issues of the *Messenger* these notices appeared sometimes on the same page and at others following one another as they do here.

Funerals were attended by all the inhabitants of the

community, but eulogies were seldom made as the occasion was considered more as a reminder to the living of the uncertainty of life and the necessity of preparation for what was to follow. Where the services were held the house was made as sad in appearance as possible. Mirrors, pictures, and ornaments were either removed or covered with white muslin. Flowers were considered inappropriate. The services were simple but quite melancholy. The hymns selected were often of the most gloomy character and sung by all present—the lines being read by the minister. The coffin was placed on a bier and borne on the shoulders of friends to the "Grave Yard" on Randolph Street.[1] There was no service at the grave. The first hearse was brought to the village by Thomas McDowell, but it was little used as it was considered disrespectful to the deceased to be drawn to the last resting place by horses instead of being carried by neighbors and friends.

As an act of hospitality in private homes, visitors were usually offered a glass of wine or spirits, and for this purpose a decanter and glasses were kept on the sideboard. It was also a custom in every store to have a decanter of whiskey, a pitcher of water and glasses on the counter that customers might refresh themselves. Although this privilege was sometimes abused, yet on the table of the moderator at meetings of the Presby-

---

[1] Those buried in the old "Grave Yard" were removed and the property was sold when Park Avenue was opened through it.

VILLAGE LIFE

The John Reynolds House, Water Street. Drawn by William Reynolds.

terian Synod there was always a decanter of whiskey and a pitcher of water. However, as time moved on and drinking of free whiskey in the stores became excessive, the custom was finally abandoned after H. J. Huidekoper and John Reynolds had visited and made a personal appeal to each merchant in the town.

At this time the use of snuff was prevalent also, and it was but an act of courtesy to offer an acquaintance an open snuffbox. The merchants bought Scotch snuff by the barrel and snuffboxes in quantities. Used by both men and women these boxes were often beautiful and expensive. Smoking too was general and indulged in by some of the women as well as the men. With the laboring and farming communities the most popular form in use was a white clay pipe.

In the town the houses were built on the street line so that the land for gardens and orchards was behind them. Board fences enclosed these lots to protect vegetation from the numerous cattle and swine which roamed at large through the streets. While a majority of the families had a cow to supply milk and butter, every family owned a pig, all of which were turned loose to forage on the public highway in the summer. This privilege obtained from the beginning of the settlement until the early 1840's, when the question of liberty was brought to a vote. After an animated and exciting election an ordinance was passed limiting the grazing of cattle on public thoroughfares from 6:00 a. m. to 8:00 p. m., and finally, in this land of the free, pigs and cows lost all their liberty when they were banished from the free pasturage on the streets.

CHAPTER XVII

FAMOUS VISITORS

People living in small villages in remote situations usually cherish the memory of visitations of personages who have attained prominence or fame. It sometimes occurs that men who attract no attention in passing through later achieve praise and it is from then on that they become notable and worth remembering. Washington created no undue stir in the Indian town of Cussewago as he journeyed toward Le Boeuf, but later generations appreciate the importance of what he did then and afterward. George Croghan[1] in July, 1760, accompanied Bouquet and Mercer when they went north from Fort Pitt to occupy the forts in the Valley lately abandoned by the French. Again in October he set out from Fort Pitt with a band of friendly Indians for Presque Isle to join Major Robert Rogers on an expedition to occupy Detroit. Colonel Croghan as Indian Agent and as trader knew the French Creek Valley and had title from the Indians for land within it included in his great acreage.

On his way to Meadville Jan Huidekoper[2] with another Dutch gentleman and Prince Tallyrand traveled

---
[1] Albert T. Volwiler, *George Croghan and the Westward Movement 1741-1782* (Cleveland, 1926), 153-154.
[2] Older brother of Harm Jan Huidekoper.

from Philadelphia to Pittsburgh in 1794. What would be more natural than to try to interest Prince Tallyrand in land recently purchased by the Holland Land Company, especially as Jan Huidekoper was continuing his journey on to visit relatives in the Genesee valley in New York and the only route lay through the Valley.

The visit of another Frenchman who figured in world history is referred to in an address[1] celebrating the centennial of the Mt. Nebo Presbyterian Church near Whitestown in Butler County.

Between 1815 and '20 Joseph Bonaparte,[2] once King of Naples and afterwards King of Spain, brother of the great Napoleon, with a retinue of attendants and servants, making a company of thirty or more, in wagons and carriages passed along this highway. They stopped over night, and part of a day, at Whitestown. Napoleon had placed his brother upon the throne of Spain against the wishes of the Spanish people, and the allied English and French armies expelled him from Spain in June, 1813. In 1815 after the overthrow of Napoleon at Waterloo, Joseph emigrated to the United States, and lived at Bordentown, New Jersey, under the name of the Count-de-Survilliers. My grandfather told me that they bought what provisions they needed, such as ham, butter, chickens, eggs, milk, etc., from him, and that he had to make out an itemized bill of same, and receipt it, when the purser paid over the

---

[1] Andrew White McCollough, *An Address: Historic and Reminiscent* (Greenville, 1905), 22-23.

[2] Search of the files of the *Crawford Messenger*, 1816-18, produced no reference to Bonaparte; and search of the *Pittsburgh Gazette* was also fruitless. The *Niles Register*, March 23, 1816, records Joseph Bonaparte in Ogdensburg, New York, where he had purchased a tract of land. Denunciation of Napoleon was so bitter at that time it is possible that the papers made no mention of his brother Joseph.

Pieter Huidekoper. Heretofore unpublished portrait by Audubon, 1824

money. They had their beds in covered wagons and slept there. He was of medium size, large head, stern visage and historians say that he was a statesman of marked ability, scarcely surpassed in talent by the distinguished Napoleon himself. Wishing to crystallize into history the tradition of his driving over this road, I wrote, several years ago, to Charles J. Bonaparte, of Baltimore, now Secretary of the United States Navy, who is a grand nephew of Napoleon and Joseph Bonaparte, asking him if he knew what business could have brought his grand uncle over this highway. He replied, that "Joseph Bonaparte owned large tracts of land that he had purchased in Western New York, and that his route, at that time, from Philadelphia to his landed estates, lay over the pike to Pittsburgh, thence to Erie, and thence to Western New York." He said also that his grand uncle kept a diary, or journal, of each day during his lifetime, comprising several volumes, which were in the French language, and never had been translated into English, and that it would be quite a task to go over these books in search of the memoranda made of this trip.

Having journeyed through western New York state while engaged in making studies for his famous "Birds of America," John James Audubon traveling south came to the French Creek Valley and stopped for the night at a farm house south of Waterford. In the morning he continued on to Meadville with funds at low ebb and hope for their replenishment high. His own account of this experience is worth repeating.

In our voyage[1] we had safely run the distance to Presque Isle Harbor, but could not pass the bar on account of a violent

---

[1] *The Life of John James Audubon, the naturalist.* Edited by his widow (New York, 1869), 110-113.

gale. The anchor was dropped, and we remained on board during the night. How long we might have remained at anchor I cannot tell, had not Captain Judd, of the United States Navy, commandant at Presque Isle, sent a gig with six men to our relief. It was on the 29th of August, 1824, and never shall I forget that morning. My drawings were put into the boat with the greatest care. We shifted into it and seated ourselves according to directions. Our brave fellows pulled hard, and every movement brought us nearer to the American shore; I leaped upon it with elated heart. My drawings were safely landed, and for anything else I cared very little at the moment. After a humble meal of bread and milk, a companion and myself settled to proceed upon our journey. Our luggage was rather heavy, so we hired a cart to take it to Meadville, for which we offered $5. This sum was accepted and we set off.

The country through which we passed might have proved favorable to our pursuits had it not rained nearly the whole day. At night we alighted, and put up at a house belonging to our conductor's father.[1] It was Sunday night. The good folks had not yet returned from a distant church, the grandmother of our driver being the only individual about the premises. We found her a cheerful dame, who bestirred herself actively, and got up a blazing fire to dry our wet clothes, and put bread and milk on the table. We asked for a place in which to rest, and were shown into a room in which were several beds. My companion and myself were soon in bed and asleep; but our slumbers were broken by a light, which we found to be carried by three young damsels, who, having observed where we lay, blew it out and got into a bed opposite ours. As we had not spoken, the girls supposed we were sound asleep, and we heard them say how delighted they would be to have their portraits taken, as well as their grandmother, whose likeness I had prom-

---

[1] Maxon Randell lived beyond Waterford on the road to Meadville.

ised to draw. Day dawned, and as we were dressing we discovered the girls had dressed in silence and left us before we had awakened. No sooner had I offered to draw the portraits of the girls than they disappeared, and soon returned in their Sunday clothes. The black chalk was at work in a few minutes to their great delight; and while the flavor of the breakfast reached my sensitive nose I worked with redoubled ardor. The sketches were soon finished and the breakfast over. I played a few airs on my flageolet while our guide was putting the horses to the cart, and by ten o'clock we were once more on the road to Meadville.

The country was covered with heavy timber principally evergreens; the cucumber trees loaded with brilliant fruits and the spruce throwing a shade over the land in good keeping with the picture. The lateness of the crops alone struck us as unpleasant. At length we came in sight of French Creek and soon after we reached Meadville. Here we paid the $5 promised to our conductor, who instantly faced about, and applying the whip to his nags, bade us adieu.

We had now only $1.50. No time was to be lost. We put our luggage and ourselves under the roof of a tavern keeper known by the name of J. E. Smith, at the sign of the "Traveler's Rest" and soon after took a walk to survey the little village that was to be laid under contribution for our support. Putting my portfolio under my arm, and a few good credentials in my pocket, I walked up the main street, looking to the right and left, examining the different heads which occurred, until I fixed my eyes on a gentleman in a store who looked as if he might want a sketch. I begged him to allow me to sit down. This granted, I remained perfectly silent and he soon asked me what was in that portfolio. The words sounded well, and without waiting another instant I opened it to his view.

He was a Hollander,[1] who complimented me on the execution of the drawings of birds and flowers in my portfolio. Showing him a sketch of the best friend I have in the world at present I asked him if he would like one in the same style of himself. He not only answered in the affirmative but assured me he would exert himself in procuring as many more customers as he could. I thanked him and returned to the "Traveler's Rest" with a hope that tomorrow might prove propitious. Supper was ready and we began our meal. I was looked on as a missionary priest, on account of my hair, which in those days flowed loosely on my shoulders. I was asked to say grace, which I did with a fervent spirit. Next morning I visited the merchant, and succeeded in making a sketch of him that pleased him highly. While working at him the room became crowded with the village aristocracy. Some laughed, while others expressed their wonder, but my work went on. My sitter invited me to spend the evening with him, which I did, and joined him in some music on the flute and violin. I returned to my companion with great pleasure; and you may judge how much that pleasure was increased when I found that he also had made two sketches. Having written a page or two in our journals we retired to rest. With our pockets replenished we soon afterwards left for Pittsburgh where we arrived in safety.

None of the portraits drawn by Audubon remains in the town where they were made; they were probably taken with the descendants of the original sitters when they removed elsewhere.

Early Thursday morning—it was the second of June in 1825—there were unusual signs of activity. Eager expectancy filled the air of the village of Meadville.

[1] Augustus Colson.

Flags were flying from windows and doors, and all signposts along Water Street flaunted the national colors. People young and old were dressed in their Sunday best with the addition of blue badges inscribed in gold letters. One building was the center of attraction—William Foster's new brick dwelling at the corner of Dock Street. Its two stories towered above all its neighbors and from the roof an unobstructed view of Mercer Turnpike could be had as it came over the top of Kennedy Hill. Excitement ran high for at last the day had arrived and the inhabitants were to welcome the Nation's guest and hero as he passed through this village. The watchers on the roof were to run up a flag as a signal at the first sight of the stage bearing this distinguished man. It had been arranged that this signal should be answered by a national salute from the cannon at the arsenal. And so General Lafayette, his son George Washington Lafayette, and his suite were welcomed to Meadville.

The *Crawford Messenger* of June 9 did justice to the occasion:

The venerable *Lafayette*, and suite, arrived at Mr. Gibson's Hotel, in the village, on Thursday last, between the hours of 1 and 2 o'clock, on his route from Pittsburgh to Erie. He had reached Mercer the night preceding after 1 o'clock, rose at 6, and took his departure for this place at 7. He appeared evidently fatigued. His arrival was announced by the thunder of cannon. A numerous assemblage had collected at an early hour—but the moment the first gun was fired, old and young— maid and matron, one and all hastened with rapid strides to get a sight of "The General." The throng of persons collected in and in front of the house were soon given to understand that he meant to pay his personal respects to them. They were accordingly formed in lines, when "the man of the people" made his appearance, passing each line from right to left, exchanging a kind and familiar shake of the hand with each and every individual, whether old or young, that came within his reach. This ceremony being over, he was conducted to Mr. Torbett's Hotel, where he paid his respects to, and was received with the most marked attention by a numerous assemblage of ladies, who had collected to honor the illustrious hero, notwithstanding the unfavorable state of the weather. Many of our revolutionary worthies attended, who were invariably received, by the General, with expressions of peculiar kindness, followed by several extra cordial shakes of the hand. A public dinner had been proffered to the good man, by the citizens of the village; but lest it might retard his progress, and thereby interfere with the solemn duty which had been assigned him, of assisting in laying the corner stone of the monument about to be erected, at Boston, to the memory of Gen. Warren, on the 17th inst. he was under the necessity of declining it. Ample and excellent provision, however, had been provided for the occasion by Mr. Gibson. He took his departure between 3 and 4 o'clock amid cheers and blessings of hundreds, whose hearts were warm with gratitude, and who had felt an intense anxiety to behold the distinguished companion in arms of *Washington*, and the gallant and disinterested champion of their freedom and independence.

It may have surprised Lafayette to recognize among the men of this outlying country waiting to greet him Dr. William Magaw who had dressed his wounds at the battle of Brandywine forty-eight years before.

At the reception at Mr. Torbett's Hotel, Mrs. Sebastian Chappotin was the only lady to greet Lafayette in his native tongue. William Reynolds, then a small boy, in after years remarked: "I was taken to the latter place[1] by Sarah A. Kennedy and thus saw and received a kiss from the distinguished guest of the Nation." And in describing the wedding of Sarah Ann Kennedy to Augustus Colson in September of that year: "Most of the ladies wore belt ribbons with long ends on which were embroidered a printed memorial emblem of the visit of Lafayette."

Before leaving town Lafayette found time to visit Allegheny College, where his and the signatures of his party are still shown upon the register.

The *Messenger* further recounts events of the day in the same issue:

GRAND FETE AT THE FAYETTE ASSEMBLY ROOM.

The arrival of Fayette in our village afforded much gratification to all classes of people, and all participated in the good man's thanks and greetings; every veteran hero, who grasped his hand, recalled to his recollection the stormy period of the revolution, and reminded him of achievements in which both were promiscuously engaged; it was no less gratifying to the General to hear, than the decrepid sage to relate to him events long passed but not forgotten. The remark of an old revolutionary soldier in particular pleased me very much—"Gen-

---

[1] William Reynolds, Life Time Memories (Reynolds Collection)

eral," says he, "there have been three happy periods in my life, one was the declaration of independence, the other the peace, and the third the present interview with you." The General with his accustomed condescention and familiarity thanked him in the strongest terms of respect: thus agreeably passed the short period of the General's stay; and on his departure he was greeted with three cheers and *"long live Lafayette."*

In the evening the young people assembled at a grand fete (beyond description) at the Fayette vault, in honor of the General, and his presence only was required to add lustre to the scene and enhance the enjoyment of the evening; the grand display of badges, the taste and elegance with which the ladies were ornimented, in addition to their own natural beauty, the lively glow of enthusiasm and vivacity which enlivened their countenances, the noble and manly appearance of the young men decorated with all the elegance of dress—in fact everything combined to render the scene most interesting and sublime; this joy and hilarity did not extend to those alone who were engaged in the promenade, but the Fayette-inspired African, whose music spoke pleasure of the soul, evinced the emotions of his breast, by various contortions of the countenance.

It is useless to attempt a description of such a combination of interesting circumstances as took place at the assembly: The established reputation of the young men for sobriety and decorum, renders it superfluous in me to make any comments upon the manner in which things were conducted. However innocent and harmless amusements like these may be, yet there are many illiberal minded persons, who reprobate them on the severest terms, open the batteries of invective against them, and give them the appellation of vice and dissapation, as destroying the morals of young men, and derogating from their characters; they are not aware, however, that times have altered

FAMOUS VISITORS 205

vastly since the days of their youth, that society has become more polished, and that its views concerning delicacy and decorum are much more refined; but when the mind of man becomes depraved by superstition and biased by prejudice, reason takes its flight, and no course of conduct, however consistent, can prove a barrier against observation, or can vindicate man's character from the foul aspersions of malicious envy, every trivial circumstance has a tendency to aggrave the feelings of animosity, and time alone will consign them all to oblivion.

A Spectator.

Other visitors, native sons who had attained fame, came in later years. The morning of August 24, 1849,

Lafayette
G. W. Lafayette
Levasseur
J. Alph. de Syon
Chas. I. Israel
Harmar Denny

From the Register at Allegheny College.

found Honorable J. W. Farrelly, Honorable Gaylord Church, Colonel John Bliss, and General John Dick going down the Mercer Pike. They were a committee formed to welcome to Meadville the President of the United States, Zachary Taylor, and William F. Johnson, Governor of Pennsylvania. These unusual visitors

. . . met at Custard's tavern[1] near Mercer Co. line were welcomed to Crawford Co. by J. W. Farrelly in a brief and appropriate manner. . .

The approach of the distinguished visitors to town, was announced by the discharge of artillery, and, as the procession advanced up Water Street, the view was really imposing. The long planked street, bordered with beaming faces—the national flags strung across at various points, and the spirited portraits of the visitors, suspended in the air from the Hotel of Mr. DUMARS—all formed a *tout ensemble,* that made us feel proud of our Borough.

After being paraded through the town the presidential party was taken to the Sherwood Hotel on Water Street where John Dick made a short welcoming address. In the evening the Hotel was crowded with people of the town and its environs who came for the reception to the honored guests. And that was not all, for at seven in the morning they were escorted on their way to Erie.

At Woodcock Borough they were handed over to the Erie Committee, where the President expressed himself highly gratified with the attention he had received in what he termed our "beautiful Borough of Meadville," in which the Governor also joined.

---

[1] *The Crawford Democrat,* Meadville, August 28, 1849.

This account on the front page was followed by the announcement of the impending visit of another famous person:

Gen. Tom Thumb.—this celebrated man in miniature will visit Meadville, on next Monday; the 3d of September; he is 17 years old, 28 inches high and weighs 15 pounds.

James Buchanan and his niece Harriet Lane had often visited the former's sister, Mrs. C. M. Yates, before his election to the presidency and were known by the inhabitants of the town. Miss Lane was popular in Meadville, as she afterward was when mistress of the White House.

CHAPTER XVIII
TROOPS AND TRUMPETS

No complete account of pioneer days and early settlements can be entirely separate from the military activities of the times, and in this instance at least part must be included in the history of the Nation. Before there were any settlements the armies of France and England had marched down and up the French Creek Valley in attempts to establish their claims to possession. The expedition led by General Contrecouer was the largest in point of numbers which descended the flood waters of the Creek in the attempt to reach the site and establish Fort Duquesne on the forks of the Ohio River. War parties of the Six Nations and other tribes were still a menace after Mead's Settlement had been made. Many who came there as pioneers were Revolutionary soldiers and some had seen service with the English as Hessian mercenaries.

The following letter[1] was addressed to General Presley Neville by General Mead:

CUSSEWAUGA,
July 11th, 1793.

Sir:

We are Just informed that the Federal troops at this Station have orders to March in a few Days down the Ohio; of Course

---

[1] *Pennsylvania Archives* (Harrisburg. 1890), Second Series, IV, 631-2, Edited by John B. Linn and William H. Egle.

the Post will be evacuated and the settlement of the Country much Discouraged.

Therefore we request that you will be pleased to Order a Surjeant's Command of State troops to support the Post, But should it not be in your Power to grant us any relief, we wish you to let us know by the first Opportunity what Prospects we can have, and also that you forward the Inclosed letter without Delay.

I am, in behalf of the inhabitants,
Your most obedient and,
very Humble Servant,
DAVID MEAD.

TO Col. NEVILL.

The names of the men who willingly volunteered in Militia service for the defense of their lives and homes are shown in the reports of Sergeant Van Horn:

A RETURN[1] OF THE NAMES AND CONDITIONS OF THE MEN AT PRESENT WHO VOLUNTARILY SIGNED MY INLISEMENT THE 29TH DAY OF OCT'R LAST AT AND FOR THE DEFENSE OF THE INHABITANTS OF COSWAGO AGAINST THE ENEMY THEREOF (TO WIT THE INDIANS) AND HAVE CONTINUED IN READINESS TO THIS DATE NOV. 29TH 1793.

&ME CORN'S VAN HORN. SERGEANT.

Thomas Ray,
James Dickson,
Rob't Randolph,
Rorah Frazer,
John Welsh,

---

[1] *Pennsylvania Archives* (Harrisburg, 1907), Sixth Series, V, 64-65, edited by T. L. Montgomery.

Rob't Finney,
John Wentworth,
John Beal,
John Clemons,
Dan'l McCormac,
Luke Hill,
David Mead,
Corns. Vn. Horn, Sargeant,

I do certify that the above Sargeant & 12 men, as Volunteers, from the Allegheny County Militia, were directed by me to protect the infant Settlement at Cassawago, after the failure of the negotiation for peace by the United States with the Hostile Indians, or otherwise the Settlement would have been deserted.

     JOHN WILKINS, JUNR., Brig. Gen'l.
          Allegheny County.
Pittsburg, 2d Dec'r., 1793.

The following year the number of men for defense was greatly increased, as is shown by the pay roll:

PAY ROLL[1] FOR A COMPANY OF MILITIA INROLLED AT COSSAWAGO ELLIGHANY COUNTY. FOR THE DEFENCE & PROTECTION OF THE SAME, AGAINST THE INSULTS OF INDIANS

Corn. V'n Horn, Ensign,
James F. Randol, Sergt.,
Jno. Brooks, Corporal,
Robt. Finney, Private,
Matt. Wilson, Private,
Robt. Wilson, Private,

James Dickson,
Roarah Fraiser,
Henry Ricard,
Wm. Mead,
David Mead,
Luke Hill,

---

[1] *Pennsylvania Archives*, Sixth Series, V, 78-80.

Natl. Wilson,
John Wilson, Senr.,
John Wilson, Jur.,
Robt. Fitzrandol,
Taylor Fitzrandol,
Robt. Fitzrandol,
Edward Fitzrandol,
Nicholas Lord,
Joseph Griffin,
Wm. Jones,
Jno. Mead,
Wm. Mead,
John Beal,
Wm. Dick,
Wm. Black,
Thos. Black,
Thomas Ray,
Abner Evans,
Matthias Colsher,
Aron Wright,

John Baum,
Thomas Cambel,
John Fredinbach,
Matt. Laughlin,
Christ. Bair,
Jno. Shoop,
Danl. Ringal,
Henry Ringal,
Frederick Baum,
Sol. Ginnings,
David Rolya,
Wm. Clemons,
Wm. Johnston,
Elisha Harris,
Jos. Parsons,
Thos. Black, Senr.,
Jno. Anson,
Joseph Dickson,
Jno. Robinson,

Pr. me COR'S VANHORN, Ensn.
Jan'ry 1st, A. D., 1795.

I do Certify that I ordered Ensign Vanhorne and the men Enrolled in his pay roll is to Service at Cussawagoe, having Considered that settlement as a very important post to Maintain and that from the hostile disposition of the Six Nations, the Garrison of Le Bauf was in a precasius Situation had Enssewagoe Been deserted as it could not be supported by drafts from the Militia from its very remove Situation.
Pittsburgh, Jany. 5th, 1795.

JNO. GIBSON, Major,
Gen'l of the Militia Wes'tn County.

The War of 1812 brought military activities to Meadville, which on account of its strategic position was selected as the training place of all troops for the protection of the frontier along the Great Lakes area. Three thousand men encamped there during the summer and fall of that year. They were drilled and equipped for the defense of the post at Niagara; also some were sent to join General Harrison's command in western Ohio.

This mobilization camp laid out in the form of a crescent was in a clearing on land owned by Samuel Lord southwest of the present site of Allegheny College. Captain Cochran's company and two companies of militia from this vicinity volunteered, but these troops do not include the volunteers who marched from Meadville to Erie in the summer of 1813 for the purpose of protecting the shipyards from a threatened raid.

During the war period special messengers passed through the village with dispatches for the front. Keelboats loaded with freight for Erie went up French Creek to Le Boeuf. Wagon trains hauling ammunition and supplies traveled up, while prisoners marched down the road through the settlement. These were days of activity and excitement which kept the citizens tense with expectation.

On July 12 a town meeting was held at which Colonel Hackney, Major Farrelly, and General Mead were deputed to visit the Indians on the Allegheny Reservation to make explanation of facts and learn their reaction.

A council was held at Genestongue with much speaking, at which Cornplanter replying for the Senecas said in part:

Brothers[1]—We are very glad to see you today. Our forefathers made an agreement which we hoped would be lasting. If any bushes grow up in the road we will cut them down. You have now come forward to renew our friendship. We made this agreement with the United States—that we should have our lands together and should always be friends as long as the sun shines and the water runs.

A letter[2] was received by express last night from Erie, directed to Gen. Mead, informing him that six sail of the enemy's armed vessels had appeared off that place crowded with troops, with the evident intention of destroying our shipping &c. and soliciting the general to send on a reinforcement of militia. Anxious to repair wherever our duty calls us, we have anticipated our usual day of publication.

---

[1] Quoted in William Reynolds, *Crawford County*, The *Tribune-Republican* (Meadville, May 12, 1888).
[2] *Crawford Weekly Messenger*, Tuesday, July 20, 1813.

CITIZENS TO ARMS

Your state is invaded. The enemy has arrived at Erie threatening to destroy our navy and the town. His course hitherto marked with rapine and fire wherever he touched our shore, must be arrested. The cries of infants and women, of the aged and infirm, the devoted victims of the enemy and his savage allies, call on you for defence and protection. Your honor, your property, your all requires you to march immediately to the scene of action. Arms and ammunition will be furnished to those who have none, at the place of rendezvous near Erie and every exertion will be made for your subsistence and accomodation.

Your service to be useful must be rendered immediately. The delay of an hour may be fatal to your country in securing the enemy in his plunder and favoring his escape.

DAVID MEAD,
July 20, 1813.　　　　Maj. General 16th D. P. M.

This appeal met with immediate response from the patriotic citizens of the Valley, and that afternoon a large number of men left Meadville and after marching all night arrived at Erie on the morning of the twenty-first.

The Messenger.
Wednesday-morning September 22.
SPLENDID VICTORY!!

It will be a source of pride and heart-felt gratification to every American breast, and more especially so to the inhabitants of this section of the county, to read the following account of Commodore Perry's brilliant victory, unequaled by anything of the sort that history records. It was to protect this fleet, and assist it over the bar, that the militia of this country left their harvest fields, and repaired to Erie. The sacrifice made has been amply rewarded, and the confidence reposed in the gallant commodore and his little fleet has been fulfilled to the utmost extent.

This letter gives a detailed account of the engagement, ending the last paragraph with—"You may tell Mr. Lord that his son Samuel is well; he was among the seven who were unhurt on board the Lawrence; Mr. Lattimore saw him, and was told by one of the officers that he behaved nobly."

Owing to its location, Meadville, being a safe distance from Lake Erie and on the routes of highway and water transportation between Erie and Pittsburgh, was chosen as the site of an arsenal for which the state appropriated $10,000. Building was commenced in the summer of 1816 and completed the next year. In it were kept all the military stores, small arms, uniforms and other equipment, such as reserve ammunition and field pieces for use of the militia of the state in case of invasion by foreign or domestic enemy.

Two days of each year were set apart for training the militia from early times until the Civil War occurred. These "training days" were events in the community. All men of military age in the county were assembled on the Public Square in Meadville and drilled in the manual of arms and military maneuvers. During this period there were many independent volunteer military companies ready for service at the call of the state. The regiment composed of these companies usually had their training day just before the regular Muster Day of the ununiformed County Militia. David Mead was the Major General with William Clark and Patrick Farrelly acting as his aids. Late in the 1830's General John Dick was in command.

The Honorable A. B. Richmond[1] pays a tribute to the volunteer militia who helped to make the early history of northwestern Pennsylvania:

It is meet in this our centennial year that the glory and power of the ancient military of Crawford county should not

---
[1] Centennial Edition, Meadville *Tribune-Republican*, May 12, 1888, 56-57.

General John Dick, Three Times Burgess of Meadville.

The Arsenal, Built in 1816, on the northeast corner of North Main and Randolph Streets.
Drawn by W. D. Craig.

be forgotten. Fifty years ago, when I was a boy, the great day of the year, the day that in my youthful opinion was that for which all others were made, was general "training day." It was usually appointed the last of June, at which time it was supposed the farmers would have their corn hoed and could well afford to spend one day for their country's glory. At that time the military of the commonwealth was divided into volunteers and militia. There were a number of uniformed volunteer companies in our county, but the general mass of bone and sinew—male—was mustered under the militia law, and were compelled to practice the art of war two days in each year. This was for the purpose of educating the yeomanry in the science of military tactics; so that, if called out to defend our country from sudden invasion of foreign foe, they might be termed veterans in the science of war. Of course it was not expected to give the average farmer a West Point education in two days' time, yet it was expected that they could be taught to execute the complicated military maneuvers of "right and left wheel," "shoulder arms," "stand at ease," and "break ranks," in a manner that would strike terror to any invading foe that might land from foreign ships into the "back woods" of Pennsylvania.

I have said that there were a number of uniformed companies in the Volunteer Regiment, and these were marshalled in battle array the day before the "general militia training day." The uniforms usually varied according to the taste of the soldiers. Many of the companies, however, preserved their characteristic style and color to such an extent that a naturalist would have been able to determine their genus, even if he failed to detect their species. He at least would know that they were uniformed volunteers, no matter what doubts he might have as to the company to which they belonged. Several of the companies were well and even handsomely uniformed. The

Meadville Grays was the "crack company" of the regiment. Their uniform was white pants, gray coats, with buff crossbelts, to which were suspended a cartridge box, a priming wire, and a small brush to clean the pans of the formidable flint lock muskets that were a terror to those who held them, while *accidental* death was the *probable* fate of those at whom they were aimed. But the crowning glory of the equipment was the hats. Words fail to convey to the present denizens of earth even a faint conception of their shape or gravity. Verily, "they were fearfully and wonderfully made," bell crowned in the widest sense of the term, of the size of an ordinary camp kettle, a rigid frame covered with shining black leather, on their front a metallic shield as large as those carried by the crusaders of old and, blazoned with the form of our national bird. This shield supported a lofty plume of scarlet wool. From the projecting eaves of the crown were suspended festoons of white cotton cord, curiously braided, and from them white tassels depended in tasteful profusion. A metal clasp passed from the sides of the crown under the chin. This was of sufficient size and strength to ensure the artillerymen on a battle-field that if he could only hit a hat the soldier would be decapitated.

The military band of this company consisted of a fife, tenor and bass drum; and its inspiring strains, even at this distant day, echo through the recesses of my memory with painful distinctness, while Yankee Doodle has become an important factor in the formation of my now educated musical taste. Many of our old citizens will remember little Jesse Baldwin, whose distinguishing uniform was a scarlet coat, and who beat the tenor drum so skillfully, while grim-visaged war was delineated on his every feature. Well do I remember with what feelings of mingled awe and admiration I gazed upon him as he marched along in all the glory of his position, and how my boyish ambition coveted the attainment, in the distant future, of his fame, skill and uniform. To reach such a point in military greatness seemed to me to be the consummation of human glory, and I determined to attain it or perish in the attempt. But alas! while ambition urged me on, ability lagged behind and I never reached the goal.

The "Cussewago Rifles" wore a neat uniform consisting of a green hunting frock and leather leggins fringed with yellow, a light wool hat or cap with a short yellow plume, and a black leather belt in which was hung a tomahawk and scalping knife. Suspended by a strap from the shoulders was a powder horn, so thin and transparent that its contents could be distinctly seen; a bullet pouch and charger completed their equipment. Each member of the company carried a long American rifle; the pride of its owner, with which their skill was such that they could hit a squirrel's head on top of the highest forest tree. The members of this company were farmers, well skilled in the woodcraft of those early days, and would have been formidable adversaries to the trained troops of France and England. It was such men as these that gave Lexington and Bunker Hill their renown, and rested our forests from savagery and wild beasts. Every bullet forced by sturdy hand into those long slender iron tubes was a death warrant, and every man who carried them was skilled in its execution.

The Saegertown company presented a neat and soldierlike appearance. Their uniforms consisted of white pants, black swallow-tailed coats with white cross belts sustaining cartridge box and bayonet sheath; black fur "plug" hat, on the side of which was fastened a white cockade, in the center of which was a ten-cent piece. Well do I remember how my boyish avarice coveted the wealth thus publicly displayed. They carried muskets which were supplied to the troops from the government aresenal, situated where the North Ward School House now stands.

IN FRENCH CREEK VALLEY

Next in the roll of fame . . . was the "Meadville Light Dragoons." Here my pen fails me in an attempt to accurately describe the gorgeous equipments of this celebrated body of warriors or their martial appearance on days of parade. Their coats and pants of steel gray, the former glittering with globular buttons of brass; their leather helmets surmounted with a crest of horse hair that hung down their backs to the crupper of the saddle, afforded a complete protection against invidious sword cuts from an enemy in the rear; their ponderous swords of polished iron, like that of Sir Hudibras:

> "With basket hilts, that would hold broth
> And serve for fight and dinner both,
> In which could be melted lead for bullets
> To shoot at foes and sometimes pullets."

Holster pistols with flint locks and bores the size of small artillery; dangerous weapons to the troopers themselves, what must they have been to an advancing foe! The horses were of all colors, size and sex, from mustang to the plow horse, or the high stepping blooded charger, to those that "were without pride of ancestry or hope of posterity." I well remember one June morning that a member of the company appeared on parade with a maternal dam and her playful offspring. The juvenile steed somewhat interfered with the military evolutions of the company and was promptly ordered under guard by the captain. The mother and son were accordingly led to the stable of the Crawford House,[1] at that time the fashionable hotel of the place. The colt, (against loud maternal protests) was confined in a vacant stall, and the mother and rider took their place at the head of the column near the *band,* a "single bugler." The order "forward march; music" was given. The column started across the public square; the *band* blew an

---

[1] Earlier the Spread Eagle Tavern of George Hurst.

inspiring blast, in which the disconsolate mother thought she recognized the plaintive appeals of her imprisoned offspring and answered with an affectionate response that completely drowned the bugler's cheering notes. A halt was called, and the owner of the mother and colt was ordered out of the ranks, whereupon he refused to go, in a style of language highly ornamental. For the balance of the day the deceptive notes of the bugle continued to mislead the maternal mind, and were affectionately answered by the bereaved mother. From that time the company was known as the "Meadville Stock-raising Dragoons."

Of all the volunteer companies none was more patriotic than the Meadville Dragoons. Afterwards, in 1845, when the war cry "54-40, or fight," resounded over the land, I was orderly sergeant of the company, very young in years but aged in military ambition. Well I remember how the cry fired the hearts of the Dragoons. Our swords almost leaped from their scabbards with patriotic zeal. Our pistols rattled in their holsters with an ominous war-like sound, while every horse hair on the crests of our helmets "bristled on end like the quills of a fretful porcupine." We all regretted when the white hand of peace smoothed war's frowning face and corrugated brow, and continued to regret until the news came that war had been declared against Mexico, when the Meadville Dragoons suddenly disbanded. *"Sic transit gloria mundi."*

There were several fragmentary portions of other uniformed companies at that time that seemed to be fossiliferous remains of past ages. Their uniforms were diversified and unique; but were generally composed of the ordinary holiday suits of the farmers, ornimented with white belts and colored scarfs. I remember a fragment of a company called the "Washington Guards." The only distinctive feature that remains in my recollection was a large shield of painted tin in front of their hats.

These were kept in place by cords passing through holes in the top and bottom of the shields and around the hat crown, where they were tied in a bow with pendant tassels. The front of the shields were ornamented with the letters W. G. in yellow. There was also a company called the Greenwood Rifles, with a uniform similar to the Cussewago Rifles. A company called the Liberty Guards from Blooming Valley mustered in members. Their members were expert with their rifles, their uniform hunting frocks and leggins well suited to the times and forest warfare.

The Meadville Artillery, commanded by Captain Samuel

The Diamond, Meadville, 1840.

Doud, was a formidable array of twenty-five or more veterans, uniformed in gray coats and white pants. Their gun was a brass six-pound cannon, with a "vent" almost as capacious as the muzzle, rendering the feat of "spiking" it one of great difficulty unless a cannon ball was used. This company was very popular with young "pioneer America" of that day.

But Oh! the gathering of the militia or "flood wood" as they were sometimes called. The "diamond" was the parade ground, and at that time it was a sea of dust whose surface was as restless under the summer's wind as the ocean's water in a storm. Promptly at 10 o'clock a. m. the citizen soldiers were called to arms. These arms usually consisted of old shot guns, dilapidated muskets, rifles, and bean poles. The line was formed three deep and extended from end to end of the public square. After a short practice in the "manual of arms" the soldiers were put through a system of evolutions that must have been copied from a western cyclone. This continued an hour or two, when the line was again formed and the inspection of arms took place. While the brigade inspector passed along in front of the men, numerous bottles of liquid refreshments were surreptitiously passed from hand to hand in the rear, and when the final order "break ranks, dismissed" was given, a more happy and "inspired" array of men never rallied under the flag of any nation.

They were true soldiers in the best sense of the word; inured to hardship, brave, independent and patriotic. They were ever to be relied upon when danger threatened either their neighbors or the country. Kindly to each other and hospitable to strangers, they were honest and truthful, always to be trusted as friends and to be feared as foes. They were in fact the germs of a great people sown in the virgin forests of a new world, and from which has been propagated a great nation whose institutions will eventually mould and model the future governments of the earth.

A nobler race of men than the early pioneer soldiery of America never lived. Alone with the Creator in this sublime forest temple, they were naturally reverential and religious. The evening prayer daily ascended from many a rude cabin in the wilderness, while the family Bible was read by every fireside. They prayed on the eve of battle, yet took good care to "keep their powder dry." Theirs was "faith with works," and the result is a nation of freemen, a Christian people who acknowledge no supremacy on earth; no sovereign but Him whose throne is on high.

It was a day long to be remembered, and what citizen of our country who has almost reached the alloted period of human life, does not recollect the relish with which we, boys, feasted on "general training days," on a quarter section of good old Jacob Fleury's ginger bread, washed down with that "nectar fit for the gods," a bottle of small beer; and how anxiously we longed from month to month, from week to week, and finally from day to day for a return of those, the happiest days of our boyish life; and how we sorrowed when a cruel, malicious legislature, by one fell swoop, repealed the militia law and made us miserable forever.

CHAPTER XIX

POLITICAL BATTLES

Men who lived at the time the thirteen colonies united to form the United States and in the years that followed felt deeply on subjects affecting their country's welfare. Differences of opinions were freely discussed and often bitterly. Politics furnished a fertile field for opposing ideas and these men and their descendants believed in defending their rights. The Federalist and Democratic parties of that time were quite diverse from those which now exist.

In 1806[1] Meadville was visited by Comfort Tyler (a confidential Agent of Aaron Burr); his object was to enlist men for the enterprize. Bart^w White[2] (a federalist) built & kept tavern in the house now owned & occupied by M^r McNamara, at his house Tyler established his headquarters—it was also the prominent Federal club house. Many of the enterprising men of Meadville & vicinity, thoughtlessly embarked in the scheme without further knowledge than that it promised enterprize & profit. Late in the fall they decended the river; all subsequent is history—some returned, if not better, wiser men, some remained south & some died.

---

[1] John Reynolds, MS (Reynolds Collection)

[2] A relentless prosecution was instigated against Bartholomew White in the United States court, causing him great expense and several journeys to Philadelphia—and rendered him bankrupt. He was killed in the War of 1812. His tavern was on the southwest corner of Water and Center Streets.

This occasioned much political bitterness in the community, and the Democrats did not overlook an opportunity to score their enemies the Federalists.

The 4[1] of March following a grand rally of the Democracy was convened in Meadville to denounce Burr and mortify the family & friends of those men who had enlisted in the enterprize, all having been known as Federalists. A well got up effigy of Burr was made and draped in military garb; the procession headed by the two associate Judges, with drum & fife passed up Water and Walnut Streets to the public square, in the centre of which had been erected a gallows, and where the hangman[2] was in readiness to compleat the farce. The assembly then entered the Court house and Pat[k] Farrelly, Esq. delivered an address prepared for the occasion—a public dinner enlivened with toasts & sentiments closed the pagent.

The next morning the Democrats were surprised to find hanging from Garber's sign post on Water Street the figure of an Irishman with flaxen cue, knee breeches, and other habiliments. That there might be no mistake about this figure representing the Honorable Mr. Farrelly, it was adorned with many placards with impertinent remarks. It was a day of disorder and personal encounter, with neighbors and fellow-townsmen in hot dispute.

The editor of the *Messenger* expressed his feelings in no uncertain terms in the next issue, witnesseth,

---
[1] J. Reynolds, MS (Reynolds Collection)
[2] Jack Ketch.

POLITICAL BATTLES

On Wednesday[1] the fourth of March (1807) a vast concourse of republican citizens from different parts of Crawford County, assembled at the court house, in this town, to testify their approbation of the wise and salutary measures pursued by our general government, and to express their destation of traitors, by burning the effigy of Aaron Burr, a man who has attempted to destroy its repose and tranquility.

Gen. Mead was appointed president and

Major Clark, vice president.

After the address delivered by P. Farrily, esq. the effigy of Burr paraded through the different streets, was taken to the public square and commited to the flames.—Toasts were given, accompanied by the discharge of platoons of riflemen, under the command of capt. Wilson—a liberal repast was then partaken of, after every citizen retired in perfect peace and good order.

Notwithstanding every scheme which malice could invent to prevent the assemblage—altho' muskets were loaded and the idea held out, that our object in meeting was to destroy offices, plunder and conflagrate houses—altho' every dirty artifice was resorted to, in order to inflame and alarm the citizens— the day was closed in a manner highly honorable to the democracy of Crawford county.

Succeeding issues for several weeks contained caustic comment in reference to those who were the instigators of what was turned into party antagonism. The editor asserted that,

It would be a matter of satisfaction[1] could we close the sub-

---

[1] *Crawford Weekly Messenger,* March 12, 1807.

ject of the recent celebration, without noticing the infamous and dirty conduct of a pack of scoundrells whose conduct prove them to be a reproach to the American character— Not satisfied with the abuse of every person who chose to participate in it, they must single out a worthy and respectable citizen, whose patriotism and inflexible firmless to the principals which govern the present administration, have created him all the enemies he can boast of, to reek their envenomed malice upon. He was represented in effigy, which was found hanging to a sign post, with the most opprobrious devices the English language could possibly invent, on the morning of Thursday last. After letting it hang until about ten o'clock, they took it down, and to crown the scene of infamy and satiate their brutal appetites, it was carried with drum and fife past his house, in a triumphant and insulting manner for the purpose of wounding the feelings of a young and amiable wife. This not being sufficient he must be attacked and beat in a ruffian like manner. However gross and villianous this outrage on the feelings of humanity, we cannot but deprecate the mode of retaliation inasmuch as we believe the laws, if applied to, will afford the individual ample redress who sustains an injury in his person or property,—this being the course contemplated to be pursued by the parties who consider themselves injured, we think it therefore improper to say anything further on the subject.

The last remark apparently referred only to the issue in which it appeared, as will be seen from quotations taken from subsequent ones.

It is a notorious fact,[1] that Jabez Colt, agent for the Pennsylvania Population company, continually associated with,

---

[1] *Crawford Weekly Messenger*, March 19, 1807.

and entertained the vagabond, Davis, emmissary of Burr, who was in this town last summer, beating up recruits for the expedition.

It is a notorious fact, that Jabez Colt gave Hugh Allen a letter of recommendation to the said Davis, then at Pittsburg, who introduced him to Comfort Tyler, one of Burr's principal agents.

It is a matter of fact, that Jabez Colt, with a number of others from this town, warm advocates of an energetic government, went to Beaver, the place of rendezvous for the conspirators, and actually had an interview with Comfort Tyler.

It is a subject of notoriety, that Jabez Colt, after his return, did unequivocally declare his intention to embark in the expedition.

But it is equally notorious, that on the appearance of the presidents proclamation, his whole frame was siezed with a universal trepidation, his cowardly heart failed, which we suppose, had just been feasting itself with the pleasing ideas of *energy*—the titles of *lord's*, *duke's*, *earl's*, &c. the little emperor would establish and lavishly confer upon his "host of choice spirits"—All these agreeable sensations, so pleasing to those "above the dull pursuits of civil life," vanished in a moment—nothing now remains to be heard, but imprecations against the high handed tyranny of a government, which but a few months since, he had the unblushing impudence to declare, aught to be damn'd for its pusilanimity and want of energy to guard against the machinitions of traitors.

Some of the *choice spirits*[1] who left this town last fall, to aid the little emperor in the establishment of his *empire*, have returned, and again commenced the *dull pursuits of civil life*, to wit—Wm. Davis, Owen Afton, and hugh Allen. They were

---

[1] *Crawford Weekly Messenger*, May 7, 1807.

amongst those who were taken prisoners by order of the executive of the Mississippi territory immediately after Burr's elopement.

It is positively asserted[1] that two men in this town actually received a large sum of money to fit out boats on French creek, and furnish men and provisions for Burr's expedition—*Query—could not Jabez Colt furnish a clue to this?*

The flame of party spirit did not grow less in the years that followed. In 1812 it was still burning brightly when war was declared in June. The celebration of July 4th of that year reflected it. Noon found the Federalists seated under a bowery constructed of leafy branches on the east bank of French Creek, not far from the public docks and Water Street. The tables were bountifully supplied with excellent food from the Inn of Samuel Torbett, and decanters of brandy to fill and refill the tin cups for drinking the toasts which followed. The president of the day started with—"The Constitution of the United States—The ark of our safety—may it ever be held sacred and inviolate." The rattle of the tin cups was drowned by the roar of cannon. When quiet was restored another toast—"The memory of George Washington"—was offered, and tin cups were drained and the booming cannon smothered the clatter as they banged on the boards of the table. Each of the thirteen toasts were hailed with noise and hearty approval, which grew louder and jollier with all the succeeding volunteer ones.

[1] *Crawford Weekly Messenger*, March 19, 1807.

POLITICAL BATTLES 231

The Democratic Republicans celebrated in like manner but chose another part of the town, so they would be undisturbed. One of the toasts which they drank was —"Party spirit—may it be extinguished in the love and support of our country."

In writing of the mobilization camp at Meadville, John Reynolds mentions the effect of party spirit.

On the 18th of June, 1812,[1] the alarm of war sounded from Washington in a declaration against Great Britain, and although expected, a thrill of apprehension passed as an electric shock through the nation.

Meadville was selected as a convenient point at which to collect a force for service in the contemplated invasion of Canada. Accordingly orders were issued to accept companies of Pennsylvania volunteers to rendezvous here in early autumn, form a brigade, elect officers and await orders.

Ground for the camp was offered and accepted from Samuel Lord, Esq. On it the companies as they arrived formed their encampment, beginning at the Creek Road near where Race Street now connects with The Terrace, and extending in a crescent form to a point eastward of Allegheny College. These companies were from the western counties of the state, and each had a political homogeneity. Several of them had been long organized and were well disciplined.

Squire Samuel Lord.

Adamson Tannehill, of Allegheny County, was by the brigade elected their General. He was at home, and several

---

[1] J. Reynolds, *Olden Times*, Meadville *Daily Republican* (1867)

weeks elapsed before he arrived to take command. In the interim Colonel Thomas Forster, of Erie, in command of the Erie Infantry, being a good draughtsman, and with the view of facilitating ulterior arrangements when the General should arrive, on a fine morning commenced at the west end of the encampment to make a plan of the situation and strength of each company with the names of its officers. He had proceeded to the second company, when several officers of democratic companies confronted him with the demand "for what purpose he was taking notes." He explained his design, but could not allay their suspicions. They ordered him to desist, and charged him with the treasonable purpose of conveying information across the lines to the British; so rank became the suspicion, that until the arrival of the General he did not feel safe from violence by day or night. The arrival of the General relieved Colonel Forster, by his immediate appointment to the post of Brigade Major, for the duties of which the General knew him to be eminently qualified. He had been the nominee of the Federalists at a recent election and the honor of the brigade would not have suffered had he succeeded.

The inaction of several weeks in camp waiting organization tended to produce anarchy and insubordination: Gardens and orchards suffered, also poultry yards and beehives. These depredations were much complained of by the farmers.

A few days before their departure for the frontier a poor fellow who was detailed for duty on the General's guard, stole onions in the night; the Sergeant reported him in the morning to his Captain, who had him tried by court-martial and he was sentenced to be dismissed from the service and drummed out of camp with a wreath of onions around his neck—all of which was done. Inasmuch as the owner of the onions was a Federalist and the culprit was a Democrat, it was made a political issue. Although the owner of the onions had taken no action in the matter, yet in the estimation of the democratic part of the brigade he was a proper object of retribution for the shame and penalty suffered by their comrade, and to whom their pledge was given that they would avenge his wrong. Accordingly on the morning of the day previous to the breaking of camp, and the march of the brigade for the Niagara frontier, it was evident that mischief was brewing. An unusual issue of whiskey was reported by the sutler; and that he had heard threats of vengence to be visited on several of the prominent citizens of the town, who were Federalists (in their vocabulary, Tories) ere they left the encampment. This evidence the sutler communicated to Major Herriott, officer of the day, who communicated it to the officers of the several Federal companies. Upon consultations it was resolved to make provisions against any mutinous attempt, and the Erie, Meadville, Pittsburgh and Chambersburg companies—nearly all Federalists, and being the best disciplined—were provided with ball cartridges to be used in case of necessity. As was feared, about 8 P. M., a drum beat in the encampment, and the officer of the day was prevented from going or sending a message to the General by sentinels the insurgents had placed on the south side of the camp.

The General was soon advised that the camp was in motion and his presence was required. He ordered his guard to load, every man his musket, and follow him. It was not well in the night and the excitement had become general in the encampment and in the town.

At the head of Water Street in that day, was a narrow bridge over a deep ravine into which the water fell over the breast of a dam situated on the East line of the street to supply the mill with water (this site being near where the old Red Mill formerly stood). The General reached the South end of the bridge as the insurgents entered it at the North end. Then commenced a parley, the General entreating them not to commit an act that would disgrace them and bring upon him censure. That having elected him their General he had the right to insist on their obedience. They eventually agreed for his sake they would desist if it was understood that they were not forced to retire. By this time their spokesman had well nigh reached the South end of the bridge, pushed forward by the crowd. At this juncture the guard arrived under the command of William Anderson of Pittsburgh. He brought them to a halt, ordered them to deploy in single rank and to make ready and immediately the click of the gun locks was heard—Anderson called in a loud voice—"General, shall we fire?" This ended the parley; the rabble broke and in wild confusion fled for their tents and thus ended what had well-nigh been a scene of arson and murder on the part of the insurgents, and in the perpetration of which, many of them would by short shift have made expiation, for many loaded muskets were prepared for defense of the property and lives of the doomed Federalists.

As Mr. Lord had suffered much by them in the destruction of his fences which they used for fuel, he had complained to their officers; he was marked, therefore, as one that should be punished. What rails they could conveniently carry they made piles of to which they set fire as the insurgents left the camp to burn the doomed houses in the town.

The morning of departure after striking their tents and firing their bedding straw, from amid the smoke a rifle ball whizzed near the head of Mr. Lord as he with several citizens was standing looking at the movements. It was supposed to have been aimed at him, it may not have been, but he took the hint and retired. In the democratic companies were many honorable men who took no part in these movements and discountenanced them entirely, but they were so greatly in the minority that they were powerless, and their political feelings would not permit them to act with the Federalists against men of their

CHAPTER XX

RELIGIOUS BUILDING

Of those who came to the wilderness to establish new homes most had been prompted by a propelling desire for freedom in thought and the privilege to worship their God in a manner not bound by rules of sect. The arduous labors of the day ended and the simple evening meal over, before retiring for the night a prayer was offered and a passage read from Holy Scriptures. If there was a book in the household, more often than not it was a Bible, and by its aid many children learned to read. A deep religious feeling and a practical attitude of devotion underlay their undertakings and gave them courage to overcome the hardships of their new life.

It was a rare occasion when a traveling missionary sought shelter for the night in a settler's cabin and those of the neighbors who could came to listen and learn. Such gatherings were fostered by the missionaries from the Presbyterian Synod of Ohio. When the Reverend Elisha McCurdy and the Reverend Joseph Stockton visited Mead's Settlement in 1799, the latter was invited to preach, dividing his time between Meadville and Sugar Creek,[1] so the following summer he moved to the former place, serving there until June in 1810. Services

---
[1] Cochranton.

were held in the house of William Dick on Water Street, just as the first Episcopal services in Pittsburgh had been in the "parlor" of his wife's father, George W. McGunnegle. Meetings in this house were the beginning of the Meadville Church of which Robert Stockton, John and Hugh Cotton were the first elders. This was the meeting place until the erection of the second court house[1] furnished better accommodation for the growing congregation, and services continued in the court house until the completion in 1820 of a building for religious purposes only.

A new pastor was installed October 11, 1811, having in his charge the congregations at Meadville, Little Sugar Creek, and Conneaut.[2] The Reverend Robert Johnston was a lineal descendant of Bridget, the eldest daughter of Oliver Cromwell. He and Thomas Atkinson organized a Sabbath School in December, 1814.

The determination to have a community church in Meadville which could be used by people of all religious creeds persisted through the early years and was encouraged by the many pioneers who had removed from New England, New York, and New Jersey where the idea had long been familiar. That some of the inhabitants sought to have those of their belief meet by themselves is shown by a notice[3] dated September 20,

---
[1] 1804, on northwest corner of Public Square and Cherry Alley.
[2] Conneaut Lake.
[3] *Crawford Weekly Messenger*, September 22, 1813.

1813, requesting all members of the "congregation under the ministry of the rev'd Mr. Johnston" to meet "to take into consideration the necessity of building a church

The Brick Church, Liberty Street. Meadville's first building for religious purposes.

in the town of Meadville." In those days when the scarcity of money was so great a handicap, the community plan was carried through, and on February 5, 1818, a contract was awarded to George Davis for $6,500 to erect a brick building 60 by 70 feet to be completed within two years for the Meadville Church.

The Brick Church, as it was usually called, was finished in the summer of 1820 and prior to occupancy the pews were sold.

CHURCH PEWS.

THE PEWS in the Meadville Church will be offered for sale on Monday the 14th day of August next, being the Monday of the court—The sale is to be at the church, and to commence precisely at 4 o'clock P.M. The conditions of the sale will be made known at the time to the purchasers.

JOHN REYNOLDS,
STEPHEN BARLOW,
JOHN BROOKS,
JAS. HAMILTON,
H. J. HUIDEKOPER,
Committee of sale.

July 24, 1820.

The building had a seating capacity of approximately five hundred. The committee in charge of the sale sold the pews at auction, and the money so obtained was applied to payment of the cost of construction. Money to build many early churches in Pennsylvania was raised by authorized lottery, and it has been rumored that this method helped to pay for the building in this instance.

The Meadville Church, outstanding among public buildings of this part of the state, was on the west side of Liberty Street between Center Street and Cherry Alley. It was there, under the auspices of the faculty of arts of Allegheny College, that the Second Centenary of the landing of the Pilgrims of Lyden was celebrated on

December 22, 1820, with a program including music, orations, and an ode written for the occasion. Robert W. Alden, David Derickson, and Timothy J. Fox Alden, a son of President Timothy Alden, members of the first graduating class of Allegheny College, were the orators. New England with Philadelphia and New York also celebrated this second centennial.

The custom of selling church pews outright with title in fee continued after other denominations had established churches of their own. This practice obtained in the Episcopal Church also. There is recorded an interesting document,[1] a deed poll Hugh Brawley, Sheriff, to Daniel Shryock and John McFarland for pew number 62 in the Meadville Church, which was sold on the ninth day of June, 1826, at public vendue or outcry, for the sum of twenty-four dollars.

A request was sent to the Erie Presbytery in 1802 from Oil Creek for "supplies" to preach to them. Again the next year the request was repeated by Johnathan Titus, the first man to settle in the eastern part of Crawford County. It was in his barn that Joseph Stockton and Samuel Tait held religious services. The Reverend Amos Chase, a graduate of Dartmouth College, came to western Pennsylvania in 1814 after filling several charges in the east. The following year he established two churches, at Oil Creek[2] and Centerville, and remained their spiritual director until 1830.

[1] Sheriff's Deed Book, A, 57.
[2] Titusville.

It was in 1798 that a Methodist class was organized on the head waters of Shenango Creek with Robert R. Roberts as leader. He was a man of ability, being licensed in 1801 as an exhorter, in 1802 licensed to preach, and in 1816 consecrated a bishop in the church. It was not until 1825 that the Methodist Episcopal Church was started in Meadville with a membership of eighteen, by the Reverend Robert C. Hatton. Samuel Gehr's log tavern[1] with a Black Bear painted on its sign stood on the north side of Center Street a short distance west of the Public Square, and there the meeting for organization was held. There was no regular place of meeting until John Luper erected a building for a blacksmith shop on the southeast corner of Main and Arch Streets. There was a large room over this shop which he finished and furnished for a church at his own expense. A part of this building is still in use—but not for religious purposes.

Five years after coming to America from Germany with the "Von" dropped from his name, Karl Wilhelm Colson was sent as a missionary to Ohio and when returning visited French Creek Valley where settlers were glad to hear the gospel in their native tongue. In the spring of 1816 his family was brought to Meadville where he proceeded to form a Lutheran congregation,

---

[1] It was near this tavern during the construction period of the canal that a riot was started by Irish laborers. Wives rallying to male support pulled off their stockings and with a stone in the toe began smashing heads.

with others at Erie, Conneaut Lake, and one ten miles north of Meadville. Prior to that year meetings were held at Venango, where the first church was built of logs in 1820, the Reverend Mr. Mueckenhaupt being pastor. Later Mosiertown and Saegertown had churches also, and congregations were formed at Cambridge, Drakes Mills, and Blacks Corners.

It was through the efforts of H. J. Huidekoper that an Independent Congregational Church Unitarian was organized, and in the fall of 1825 the Reverend John M. Merrick began services on alternate Sundays in the Brick Church; services were also held at times in the Court House. Young men who came as tutors to the Huidekoper children were often preachers for the church. The church building was dedicated in August, 1836. Four acres were donated by a son of Harm Jan, the Reverend Frederic Huidekoper, at the junction of Chestnut and Arch Streets, to the Meadville Theological School which was founded in 1844. As Professor of Literature and Ecclesiastical History his services were gratuitously given to the school for many years and earned him a wide reputation as a Greek scholar.

John B. Wallace persuaded his friend John Henry Hopkins, D.D., the rector of Trinity Church in Pittsburgh, to come to Meadville in January, 1825, and at that time he organized Christ Protestant Episcopal Church. During the twelve days of his stay thirty-two adults and forty-three children were baptized. The following year the Reverend Charles Smith became rector, and in 1828 the new church building was completed on the Public Square at the corner of Walnut Street.

Three years after settling in the Cussewago valley northwest of Mosiertown, Lewis Thickston and others of similar religious beliefs had started the Carmel Baptist Church in 1805, but it was five more years before the logs were hewn and put in place for a church building. It was not until 1831 that the First Baptist Church was organized in Meadville and a meeting held at the house of Samuel Kirkpatrick on Arch Street. Within two years a small frame building was erected and opened for service at the corner of Arch and Liberty Streets. Not ashamed of their meager beginnings, the early worshippers used sawhorses with planks laid across them as seats until better ones could be provided.

A strange manifestation at religious meetings in Kentucky[1] in the spring of 1800 caused great excitement as it spread to neighboring states and extended to the whole of western Pennsylvania in the years of 1801 and 1802. Worshipers often in numbers fell down and remained as though in sleep for sometimes an hour, while others were violently agitated. This exhibit of loss of emotional control was the antithesis of the religious stamina which customarily marked those sturdy people in the French Creek region.

[1] John Reynolds, *Olden Times*, Meadville *Daily Republican*, June and July, 1867.

The staunch courage and steadfast faith of those men and women who fought and endured to establish themselves in this wild country was seated in their Christian belief. It was this which gave them the strength to overcome all difficulties and discouragements. Differences of opinion as to the mode of worship were set aside when numbers were few as the desire to worship was strong and sought communion of interest. As the population increased each group withdrew and found a place of meeting with those of like thought, so churches increased in number as the community prospered.

CHAPTER XXI

GENERAL DAVID MEAD IN RETROSPECT

David Mead, the invincible founder of the first permanent settlement in the Valley, died in 1816 after guiding the destiny of the little town for more than a quarter of a century. The newly established *Alleghany Magazine* took occasion to recount his career and contributions in an obituary which is worthy of reproduction.

MEMOIR OF THE LATE GEN. MEAD.[1]

The honourable David Mead, the pioneer to the waters of French creek and the first settler of the pleasant village, which bears his name, was born at Hudson in the state of New York.

His father, Darius Mead, a native of Connecticut, as was his mother also, whose original name was Ruth Curtis, purchased a farm in Hudson, to which he removed before the birth of any of his children, and there resided till his eldest son, the principal subject of this memoir, had arrived at the years of manhood. He then sold his estate and left New York for Pennsylvania. In connexion with this son he became proprietor, under a Pennsylvania title, to some valuable lands in Wyoming; but, in consequence of adverse claims under Connecticut titles, they with the rest of the family took up their residence on the western shore of the north branch of the Susquehanna, about six miles above the town of Northumberland. This was a few years before the commencement of Indian depredations in that region.

---

[1] Alden, *Alleghany Magazine* (September, 1816), 77.

About the year, 1774, David Mead married Agnes Wilson, sister of the present hon. Thomas Wilson, a daughter of Janet Wilson, widow of John Wilson, who had been dead about a year and who had been one of the earliest settlers of Northumberland county.

At an early period of the revolutionary struggle, the incursions of the Indians were become so frequent and terrifick, on the then frontiers of Pennsylvania, as to put the inhabitants to flight. For a time, during the war, numerous were the scenes of savage bloodshed and carnage and great were the distresses of the people in that part of the country. Asahel Mead, the second son of Darius Mead, fell, a victim to his valour and Indian barbarity, and was mangled in a most shocking manner.

The subject of this article removed his family to Sunbury, where he commenced business, as an inn-keeper, and also erected a distillery. By great industry, he, not only, supported his own family, affording occasional assistance to his connexions; but, he had accumulated a handsome property by the close of the war, shortly after which he returned to his estate at Wyoming, thinking the disputes, as to his title, at an end. In this, however, he found himself under a great mistake. After expending large sums, in making improvements, and three years in conflicting with various perplexities in reference to his possessions, he was forced to flee for safety, with great difficulty getting away his family and a very inconsiderable portion of his household furniture.

He returned to Sunbury, in 1787,[1] where he immediately renewed his exertions in the same pursuits, which he had formerly found successful. Destitute, however, of capital, and a change of times rendering business, in a great measure, unproductive, his utmost efforts could effect little more, than a bare support.

---

[1] Probably 1786.

In these periods he carried on an extensive correspondence with the government of Pennsylvania and with the best informed individuals relative to the two contending claims to the Wyoming lands, and, in other ways, devoted himself with the utmost perseverance to this subject.

In 1788,[1] accompanied by his brother, John Mead, he visited the country north and west of the Ohio, Alleghany, and Connewango creek, then a wilderness. In 1789,[1] he removed with his family to the banks of French creek. Some time afterwards, he obtained, from the state, a remuneration, in lands, to the amount of an official valuation of those, at Wyoming, of which he had been dispossessed.

After several years of incessant trouble, toil, and hardships, his prospects began to brighten, but they were soon overcast with a dark and gloomy cloud. Another Indian war began, which bore a menacing aspect upon all the infant settlements in this western country. Many had fled beyond the reach of the savage foe; but those, who remained, were exposed to constant perils and were obliged to submit to various privations. In these times of alarm and danger, the subject of this memoir was conspicuously distinguished by the firm and undaunted part he was called in providence to act. Having an important interest in this country and being almost without means of removal, to a place of greater security, and of subsistence, in case he could have effected it, he continued on his plantation resolutely determined to brave every danger and to yield to every inevitable privation, while the war should exist. It may here be remarked, that few have had a greater share of disheartening difficulties, in private life, and that few have ever borne them with greater equanimity. The war was, at length, happily terminated, by general Wayne, in 1794.

---

[1] Mead came west a year before he settled at Cussawago which was in 1788.

General David Mead's Second House, Randolph and Water Streets.

For several months, in 1794, when the Indians were daily expected to attempt the utter extermination of the people on French creek, mr. Mead with his family resided at Franklin, which is twenty-five miles from Meadville, in order that he might have it in his power to repair to the garrison in that place, as the dernier resort. During this period, his father was taken by two Indians from a field, where he was at work, and carried to the vicinity of Conniaut Lake. Some days after, he was found together with one of the Indians, both dead and bearing such marks of violence, as showed that they had had a contest; and it was deemed probable, that the other Indian had been wounded, in the encounter, from the circumstance of his companion being left unburied.

In 1796, the subject of this memoir, having some time before lost his wife, married Janet Finney, a daughter of Robert Finney, who survived him. By his former wife he had nine children,[1] four only of whom are living; by his second, six, five of whom are living.

Mr. Mead was appointed a justice of the peace at Wyoming and was re-appointed, among the first, in this part of the country. He held the latter commission till 1800, when he became one of the associate judges for the county of Crawford. He was appointed major general of the militia by governour M'Kean and was re-appointed by governour Snyder. He continued to discharge the duties of this station until the commissions in the militia were vacated by law.

In person, mind, and deportment, general Mead was remarkable. His height was above the ordinary standard, being six feet, three inches, and a half; he was large in due proportion. He was a man of uncommon bodily strength. His

---

[1] Mrs. Elizabeth Farrelly, consort of Patrick Farrelly, Esq., the only one among the deceased children of gen. Mead, who had lived to enter a family state, departed this life, 24 August, 1811, in the 25 year of her age.

features were masculine, regular, and strongly marked with the lines indicative of reflexion. In his deportment, he was generally sedate and grave; but, he was always affable, easy of access, and a total stranger to every thing like ostentation.

He was a kind and faithful husband, an affectionate father, an inflexible friend, and a patriotick citizen. His vigorous mind was ever active and was constantly occupied upon business either publick or private.

For his youthful instructions, he was almost entirely indebted to his mother, who was a lady of distinguished excellence and attachments. Had he been favoured with a liberal education, his talents would have entitled him to the first offices in the gift of his country. Highly appreciating the advantages of such an education, he was one of the associaters for founding Alleghany College and was one of its generous benefactors.

His house was a mansion venerable for its hospitality; and, in the latter years of his life, the morning and evening sacrifice of prayer and praise daily arose from his family alter.

The general was a man of strong passions, and, sometimes, he was irritable; yet his great characteristicks were those of persevering patience under the trials of life, and unrelaxing application to whatever he considered his duty. It would be untrue to state, that he was without failings; yet, it may be justly said, that there were many things, amiable and of good report, in his character, which will endear his memory to a numerous circle of relatives, friends, and acquaintances, and his name will be had in grateful remembrance in future generations.

He died in full vigor of body and mind, on friday morning, the 23 of August, 1816, in the 65 year of his age, after a short illness, which excited no special apprehensions of danger till a few hours before his death. On the following day, his funeral was attended, with becoming solemnity and respect, by a numerous concourse of people.

W. O.

In addition, John Reynolds gave the following information:

David Mead[1] was the proprietor of the two tracts on which Meadville was by him located. He came here as an adventurer in 1789[2]—and obtained these tracts & Cussawago island, from the state in settlement of Wyoming claims he held. His first residence was on the site of Ja^s E. McFarland's house.[3] It was stockaded to protect from Indian hostilities.

In person he was large in height I think 6 f^t 7 or 8 inches & stout in bodily frame. He was the first commiss^d Justice of the peace; and as illustrative of his prompt method of dispatching business, the following was related to me by an early settler—

"A man became indebted to him, Mead issued his summons & in default of a constable he served it on his debtor. On the day of appearance entered Judgm^t, then issued execution, made levy, cried the sale & himself bid in the property, and satisfied the docket." Thus he appeared in the position of creditor, magistrate, constable & purchaser—this may have been an exagerated story.

Wm Miles (Father of present Judge Miles of Elk Creek) related to me his first knowledge of Mr Mead, it was also his first passing through Meadville. Himself & a fellow travellor at the head of Water Street, enquired of two men the way northward to Le Beuff. These men were Mr Mead and another

---

[1] John Reynolds, MS (Reynolds Collection)
[2] 1788.
[3] West side of Water Street on the bank of French Creek, south of Mead's saw and grist mills.

well known man of the early times (Jn⁰ Wentworth,) they were in hot dispute about the question of damages claimed by Mead of Wentworth for neglect in the cultivation of a field of corn, on the flats, Mead landlord Wentworth tenant. It was proposed by one and accepted by the other, that it should be submitted to the two strangers whose decision shᵈ be final. Miles & his companion took off their knapsacks. Mead opened his case, was frequently contradicted by Wentworth, when he woᵈ approach Wentworth in a menacing manner, the latter a small but very irascible & determined man, woᵈ seize his rifle & thus keep at bay his powerful antagonist. Several such episodes occured before the matter was left with the arbˢ, they stepped aside made their decision announced it to the parties, took up their knapsacks & proceeded on their Journey. Mʳ Miles settled & built mills, where now is Union village, Erie Coʸ.

It will always be regretted by the citizens of Meadville that there is no portrait or sketch of General David Mead, its founder, to occupy the place of highest honor in a collection of early settlers.

CHAPTER XXII

DAVID DICK, INVENTOR

Among the first of the white children born in Mead's Settlement a boy started his career in one of the few log houses in the village on the corner of Water and Center Streets, March 1, 1797. David Dick was the third son of William Dick and Anna McGunnegle, who with their sons George and John had removed from Pittsburgh to Meadville two years before this event. David, educated in the frontier settlement school of this village, had at mid-life earned a reputation as a man of learning. In business his interests were many and varied. He took an active part in the affairs of the community and lent his support to many enterprises for its betterment and welfare. He had passed his fortieth year before turning his attention to mechanics and invention which brought him medals and highest awards in his own country as well as in Europe.

Any man would be proud to have said of him what John Reynolds wrote[1] at the time of his death in 1870.

Meadville has produced no more honorable and upright man than David Dick. He was noted for his integrity, industry, enterprise, purity of character, and thorough unselfishness, and he will be mourned, not only in our community, but by scien-

---

[1] David Dick, Meadville *Daily Republican*, March 23, 1870.

tific men both in this country and in Europe, with many of whom he enjoyed an intimate acquaintance and held friendly intercourse. . . . This has been his home during his long and busy life. From youth to middle age he was an intelligent merchant, in which vocation he was enterprising and popular, unselfish and liberal. Every public improvement had his aid and influence.

Robust and healthy, he was always active in the pursuit of some favorite study, either in Mental Philosophy or Mechanics; nor did he amid the bustle and business of life, neglect the higher duties of spiritual life. He read and studied the Scriptures, and was a firm believer in the revealed truth.

Colonel Magaw was a partner in David Dick's initial business venture. Later, with his brothers John and James R. he was in a mercantile business, a "general store" on Chestnut Street. At this time these brothers also operated an ashery manufacturing potash which was shipped to Pittsburgh.

He was a man of initiative. It was while still a member of this partnership, on the thirty-first day of December, 1827, that a contract was entered into by him with the President and Trustees of Allegheny College: "to finish and complete the superstructure of Bentley Hall[1] now in an unfinished state, with internal partitions, walls, floors, supporting columns, fire-places, stairs, &c."

Engaged to lecture at the Smithsonian Institute at

---

[1] David Dick Papers: Articles of Agreement with Allegheny College, Copy of Articles of Agreement, Specifications, Three-measurements and estimates; Nine letters to his wife and brothers; Letters patent, October 19, 1848 (Reynolds Collection).

David Dick.

DAVID DICK, INVENTOR

Washington, D. C., one December when the ground was covered with snow, David Dick awaited with others the arrival of the four-horse stage to take them to Pittsburgh. The stage was late and he grew restless, so as he enjoyed walking he told the others that he would start ahead and the stage could pick him up when it caught up with him. Pittsburgh was ninety miles distant—David arrived there before the stage.

David's interests were varied after leaving the partnership with his brothers. Becoming interested in mechanics his attention was later turned to invention and he obtained patents for a number of ingenious machines. He was for several years a member of the firm of Dick, Fisk & Company, Founders and Machinists, and at the time of his death he was still working to perfect what he called a "hot air engine," in which power was generated by the combustion of petroleum. This was a forerunner of the motor which made possible automobiles, airplanes, and submarines.

October, 1848, a patent was granted to David Dick for an "Anti Friction Press," which later won him an enviable reputation and was probably his greatest success. The following year he wrote to his brothers of a demonstration at the New York Navy Yard.

New York, Dec. 20, 49.

... I yesterday experienced a great triumph in the operation of the Sampson I had constructed for the Navy yard. Previous to trying it an experiment was made with an immense lever to

D. DICK'S ANTI-FRICTION PRESS.

The public are now offered an arrangement of mechanical power, by which any given amount of force can be exchanged for any other amount of force or power that may be required, and no material discount lost in the trade for friction, and yet cheap and effective in all cases where the simple lever becomes inconvenient, either from its weight, or want of room. It is peculiarly adapted to pressing Cotton, Hay, Tobacco, Paper, all classes of Oils, Baling Goods, Packing Flour, Pressing Cheese, Printing, Embossing, Stamping, Coining, Shearing, Punching, Riveting, making Lead Pipe, &c. It can be graduated so as to produce motion at one point of its action, and intensity at another, is more effective than the hydrostatic press, for the same initial force, can be constructed for half the cost, and is not liable to get out of order.

With these advantages, we expect to see it displacing all the other combinations for producing force, and offer it confidently as the great improvement of the age in mechanical power.

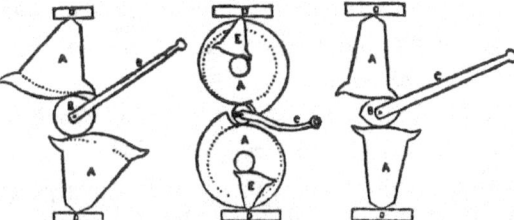

In addition to the United States, measures have been taken to secure the right in England and her Provinces, and in most of the States of Europe, and the public are particularly cautioned not to infringe. Each Machine sold, no matter through what agency, will be accompanied by the direct right of the inventor, to use the same for its specific purpose.

Address
DICK & HOLMES,
MEADVILLE, CRAWFORD CO., PA.

extract one of the piles of the cofferdam. The lever was 20 feet long & 20 inches by 16. The fulcrum was 1 foot from the end. At the other end was appended a Six fold tacle & operated by a powerful capswain with all the power of men that could be put to it but without starting the pile a hairs breadth. Engineers & all now despaired of my machine. They determined however to try it. They accordingly got all the fixtures ready & yesterday commenced to try it. The first operation started the pile about ¾ of an inch when their powerful graplings broke. New & stronger graplings were made fast to it, second trial shivered them again. New graplings as strong as iron could make them were put on & secured by three heavy iron bolts passing through iron straps 10 feet long 1½ inches thick 5 inches wide & of every precaution made use of to secure them to the pile. There were a great many Officers of the Army & Navy & distinguished Engineers & citizens present. The excitement became intense breathless stillness the machine was put in operation by 5 men at the two cranks groaning among the heavy irons, every person expecting a crash of the machine pile began to come, The earth trembled for some distance around the agony was over, machine all safe from the dreadful effort. It was now discovered that the piles had been dowelled together by heavy iron spikes which the Sampson had to sever in the effort before the pile could start. The piles have been about 7 years driven they are 70 feet long 50 feet in the ground & 15 inches square. In drawing up the one three or four of the piles on each side were started & drawn up 1 or 2 inches before the spikes gave way which secured them together. Couriosity on the part of a great many had been on tiptoe for some days previous to this trial to know the result.

   The first pile being out the rest can be drawn by 2 hands at the machine with ease.

The axles of the eccentrick wheels of the machine are of cast steel three inches diameter & the centre roller of cast steel also four inches in diameter. The whole weight only about two tons. The effort made by the machine is about equivalent to lifting a column of cast iron 4 feet square & 100 feet high or your dwelling house back building & all lifting it up bodily...

The machine is in such perfect credit now that I am able to occupy a strong position & parties must come to my terms. I will reserve a place for you should I make any arrangement. An Old Gent. worth a million who has taken quite a fancy for me offers to loan me 10, 15 or 20,000 on interest should I desire it to extend my business. . . .

D. Dick.

Messrs. J. & J. R. Dick,
    Meadville,
       Penn[a]

In discussing American steamers in a speech before the United States Senate on April 27, 1852, the Honorable William A. Seward commented upon Dick's Anti Friction Press as follows:

The machine[1] used to hoist the coffer dam at the Navy-yard, only weighed 3500, yet it exerted the force of 650 tons lifting power by the aid of four men. We have seen a stump machine that weighs only about a ton, that will draw any stump in America; worked by three men.

Writing to his wife from New York in July, 1850, after telling of an "excursion to the Sea Shore at Rockaway," he mentioned the reason for this trip.

---

[1] Rogers, Charles T., *American Superiority at the World's Fair*, Philadelphia, 1852. (Report of Commissioner)

DAVID DICK, INVENTOR

... My machine is constantly growing in the knowledge of the people & in importance... My main object now is to secure my French patent & I have fortunately met with an American gentleman who resides at Paris whose business it is to attend to all such matters & who has agreed to defray all expenses in procuring the French patent, making sale &c. for one half. He is well acquainted with many of the Savans of Paris & can easily get their certificate of the great superiority of the machine over all others.

The following March he was again in New York and in a letter to Mrs. Dick mentions that it has been suggested that he exhibit his Anti Friction Press at the great fair to be held in London in the fall. "I have seen Mr. Leonard the Agent of the Matteawan Co. who expressed himself very much pleased with my invention & proposed at once a Manufacturing arrangement."

This suggestion became an actuality and in September, 1851, he wrote from Liverpool of his safe arrival after a stormy passage, mentioning "a Mr. Bigelow from Boston, the inventor of a wonderful carpet loom," a fellow passenger who had taken the sea voyage for his health. On going to his hotel he met an acquaintance from New York, who asked if he "had heard anything about the medals. I told him nothing official." He wrote frequently, keeping Mrs. Dick informed of the progress made in the sale of the English rights to his patent and giving his impressions of London.

United States Commission
Industrial Exhibition
London, Sep. 19, 1851.

... You will no doubt have seen by the papers how completely the Americans have beaten all creation at the Exhibition. The Times newspapers has within a few days most wonderfully altered its tone in reference to America . . . .

From the invitations he received and the cordiality which he met everywhere David Dick had reason to be pleased with his reception in London. His comments were both interesting and humorous.

London Sep 26 1851

... I have become quite intimate with an American gentleman Doct. Black who has been in London about 17 years. He is a talented man & has had much to do both with getting up the Great Fair & the conducting of it. He has taken a deep interest in my press. . . .

I had a letter of introduction from N. York to Sir Henry De la Beache but I found he was absent & in Ireland on a Geological Survey which I regret as I expected through him to get introduced to Sir Micheal Fareday & other Scientific gentlemen. This however I will probably accomplish through Doct. Black.

London, Friday 30, Oct. 1851.

When last I wrote I expected to have sailed on Wednesday last on the Baltic. But I did not succeed in time in getting my negotiations to a close. It takes about as long a time to complete an operation of Selling a patent here as to negotiate a treaty of Ghent.

... dinner at the house of the American Minister Mr Law-

Obverse: VICTORIA D:G: BRIT: REG: F:D: ALBERTUS PRINCEPS CONJUX. MDCCCLI.
W. Wyon R:A: Royal Mint

Reverse: EST ETIAM IN MAGNO QUAEDAM RESPUBLICA MUNDO MDCCCLI
H Bonnardel Inv.   Domard Sculp.

Rim: D. DICK. CLASS VI. COUNCIL MEDAL OF THE EXHIBITION.

Medal Awarded to David Dick, Industrial Exhibition, Crystal Palace, London, England, 1851.

rence . . . in introducing me to strangers he always did it as the inventor of that great, beautiful & wonderful power press on exhibition at the fair in the American department. . .

I dined by invitation on Monday at the Great London Coffee house. The dinner was given by a Mr Peabody, an American Gentleman long resident in London, a private Banker. . . There were about 120 persons at the dinner about half English, the rest Americans. Several Speeches were made occasioned by Toasts. Mr Lawrence spoke first, Lord Granville & Sir H. Lytton Bulwer each spoke twice, R. I. Walker, Mr Davis, Mr Thompson among the Americans, several others. What was called the loving cup was passed around but a good many of the Americans myself among the rest passed it without drinking.

We were determined not to drink the health of R. I. Walker & free trade. Quite a revolution in the sentiments of many that came here free trade men has taken place. They will go home strong tarrif men & no mistake. I could write much on this subject to elucidate the importance of tarrif to us. The English have been trying their best to cajole us into free trade notions for they certainly now most clearly see that under a good protective system we must & will so outstrip them that we instead of them must become the manufacturers of the World.

Our part in the fair has brought out a great many compliments to Americans . . . in articles of originality, importance & usefulness, but in awarding medals they have done us great injustice. This I cannot say for myself because they have given me the highest award. . .

Having received the Council Medal at the Great Fair in London, the highest award which was seldom bestowed, David Dick's Anti-Friction Press also won recognition and praise from the press in America. This and other inventions earned honors in his own country—silver medals at the Metropolitan Mechanics Institute and the American Institute, New York, 1848; a gold medal from the American Institute in 1849; and a bronze medal at the Exhibition of the Industry of All Nations, New York, 1853.

Man makes his own equipment for growth and accomplishment in life, and of this truth David Dick was a remarkable example.

CHAPTER XXIII

TURNPIKES AND TOLL GATES

More often than not the motive prompting men to leave familiar surroundings to seek their fortune in a new and unknown place is not clear, even to themselves. The urge to seek change comes from their innermost being and few probe deeply enough to know the source. The visible manifestation of this is frequently attributed to personal ambition for gain.

For this reason men usually surge forward blindly, working for the solution of each problem as it arises. Man finds living easier and more pleasant in association with others of his kind. The important thing to the settlers and settlements of French Creek Valley as they became established was means of communication, especially for transportation of all sorts of material goods. Transportation by water was hampered by difficulties and uncertainties, and by land it was almost as hard before there were roads. Overland travel presented obstacles more easily overcome. Realization of this prompted the settlers to expend their energies and resources in developing roads. Roads as a solution of communication became a governing factor in building this new country and continue so down to the present.

The portage or "carrying place" from Presque Isle

to Lac Le Boeuf was fourteen miles of delay, discouragement, and exasperation. To transport troops and supplies the French cut a strip of underbrush and trees in 1753 wide enough for a wagon to pass, and called it a road. The English in 1761 found it "full of bushes grown since." In 1795 it was cleared again but soon became impassable, so new tracks were made by its travelers until in width it ranged from one to four miles.

In 1796 Andrew Ellicott made a survey for a road to connect with the old portage road at Fort LeBoeuf and run through Meadville and Franklin to Curwensville in Clearfield County as part of a road from Erie to Philadelphia. Construction of the Susquehanna and Waterford Turnpike was delayed.

It was much quicker and less expensive to bring New York State salt to the French Creek settlements by the old portage than to have it transported over the mountains. The condition of the portage road was a serious obstacle in this trade. Agitation over the difficulties so arising resulted in the incorporation of the Erie and Waterford Turnpike Road to facilitate commerce and incidentally earn money for the stockholders.

Subscription books were opened in Pittsburgh in December, 1804, for the Erie and Waterford Turnpike. . . . the whole expense[1] of the road cannot possibly exceed twenty thousand dollars. The price of each share is fifty dol-

---

[1] *Crawford Weekly Messenger*, January 2, 1805.

lars, payable in instalments; no money will be demanded till three hundred shares are subscribed and the company incorporated. Nearly one hundred shares are now subscribed.

JOHN WILKINS, junr.
HENRY BALDWIN,
WILLIAM GAZZAM.

In this and succeeding issues of the *Messenger* appeared this cordial invitation:

WATERFORD AND ERIE
Turnpike-road

For the accomodation of persons residing in Meadville and its vicinity, who may be desirous to become stockholders in the Erie and Waterford turnpike-road are informed that the books are now opened at the store of colonel Joseph Hackney in Meadville, where they may subscribe for any number of shares which remain unscribed for.

TH. R. KENNEDY, R. ALDEN,
J. COLT, D. MEAD.
J. HACKNEY,

This year passed and the subscription books were still open, although the project had the endorsement of many prominent men living in the district between Erie and Pittsburgh, which would be greatly benefited by more rapid transportation of merchandise. Pittsburgh was a market for quantities of the salt manufactured in New York and hauled to Lake Erie to be stored at Erie until the road was in a condition permitting it to be moved to Waterford. This growing industry was seriously hampered by delay between these points.

Appeals were published.

We[1] cannot but regret that so much backwardness should exist on the part of citizens of this place and neighborhoods in coming forward with their exertions . . . to such . . . by combining the accomplishment of all these objects with private emolument—the subscribers address themselves. . . From the books of the collectors at Erie it appears that the quantity of sale imported in

1800 was	714	barrels.
1801	362	
1802	854	
1803	2784	
1804	3600	
1805	6659	

Total number of bar. 14967

The average price of transportation for each barrel has been 2 dol. 50 cents; and with the road in its present state, and the quantity on hand at Erie so considerable as now (exceeding 3000 barrels) the price will not be less. . .

Will not the citizens of the western country, be willing to subscribe the sum of 20,000 dollars; for which they will receive an annual interest of 8 1-4 per cent, and save annually, to the country 38,125 dollars, . . .

Persistent effort finally caught up with accomplishment. At a meeting

held at the house[2] of Hannah Pym, in the town of Waterford, the following gentlemen were elected officers—

---

[1] *Crawford Weekly Messenger*, March 20, 1806.
[2] Ibid., June 26, 1806.

TURNPIKES AND TOLL GATES

President—Thomas Forster.
Treasurer—Judah Colt.

Managers.

Henry Baldwin,	John Vincent,
William Miles,	James E. Herron,
James Brotherton,	Ralph Marlin,
John C. Wallace,	Joseph Hackney.

Having the organization completed and the stock subscribed, collecting the money was another thing. Reminders like the following appeared in the *Messenger*.

NOTICE
IS HEREBY GIVEN.

THAT suits will be commenced against all stockholders in Erie and Waterford turnpike road company, who shall have not made the first payment of six dollars on each share before the first day of November next—and further that orders drawn by any of the persons who have contracted or shall contract with the President and Managers of said company to make any part of said road in favor of any of the stockholders, payable by the President and Managers, will be received in payment of the shares of such stockholders.

By order of the President and Managers.

JUDAH COLT, *Treasurer.*

Erie, October 2nd, 1806.

This "improved road" had a dirt surface. Eventually it was graded, bridges built and opened to the public.

ERIE AND WATERFORD [1]
Turnpike Road.

A meeting of the President and Managers of the Erie and Waterford Turnpike Road.

October 29, 1807.

Resolved, That all wagons, the wheels whereof shall be more than seven inches in breadth, shall pass over the said road, free from toll for one year from the time that the company shall commence receiving toll thereon.

That the above resolution be published three times in the papers printed in Pittsburgh and in the Crawford Messenger.

THO. FORSTER,
Attest. *President.*
Wm. Wallace, *Sec'ry.*

It was 1809 before the Erie and Waterford Turnpike Road was completed. For a few years it earned money for the stockholders, then as expenses increased and repair costs grew larger the tolls collected ceased to be sufficient to meet the expenditures. Many of those who used the road objected to paying toll and found ways to detour around the toll houses to avoid doing so. As the condition of the road grew worse from lack of repair, waggoners refused to pay and there were many arguments and fisticuffs. On account of non-compliance with the stipulations the Charter was revoked, and about 1845 an outraged public organized and tore down the toll gates after which the company abandoned all pretense to ownership and control.

---

[1] *Crawford Weekly Messenger.*

TURNPIKES AND TOLL GATES

In the winter of 1806-7 the legislature granted money for the improvement of roads: Pittsburgh to Butler, $400; Butler to Meadville, $600; Meadville to Erie, $450; Meadville to Franklin, $400.

These funds were barely sufficient to make roads passable for heavy wagons by cutting out the wood, without ditching or the removal of stumps. Only the smaller streams were bridged as the larger creeks and rivers were crossed by ferries.

It was not until February, 1812, that an act was passed for the construction of the Susquehanna & Waterford Turnpike Road, sixteen years after the Andrew Ellicott survey. The state agreed to furnish $125,000 provided that 2000 shares of stock were subscribed within three years. The subscriptions came slowly during the years of the war—450 in Crawford County, 80 in Erie County, 300 in Mercer County, and 300 in Venango—when a meeting was held on the fifth of August, 1815, in Meadville. Another meeting was held on the nineteenth at which a committee was appointed—R. Alden, John Reynolds, H. J. Huidekoper, T. T. Cummings, S. B. Magaw, Thomas Atkinson, Samuel Torbett, Patrick Farrelly, E. Betts, J. Foster, Henry Hurst, Wm. Clark, John Brooks, with others were present. The three-year limit was up and something must be done to secure this turnpike and the $125,000 appropriation. It seemed impossible to secure the additional subscriptions to make the 2000 required. John G. Brown, a tailor, without means or responsibility, was passing the house of William Dick where the meeting was in session. Some one had a bright idea. Brown was called in, summarily persuaded to subscribe for the balance of the shares—and the turnpike was assured.

It was toward the end of 1818 before the work of construction was started, and two years more before its completion in the western part of the state, and 1824 saw it finished to Philadelphia from Erie. When the toll receipts no longer paid for the upkeep of the road the stockholders turned it over to the townships through which it passed for maintenance.

The stock for which John G. Brown[1] had subscribed was the cause of much future litigation, as it continued to pass into the possession of other persons with resultant disputes of title.

1817 saw the incorporation of another road, the Mercer and Meadville Turnpike Company, which at Mercer connected with another turnpike which ran to Pittsburgh. It was completed in 1821, but proved to be no better as an investment than the other two, so after a few years it also became a free road.

This same year the state appropriated $3000 for a road 50 feet wide to start at the New York State line in Warren County to run to Meadville in practically a straight line. Of the three commissioners in charge, one

---

[1] Not the John Brown who lived in and had a tannery at Blooming Valley many years prior to his famous raid.

View of Meadville, Klecknerville, and Edinboro Plank Road, Water Street, Meadville, between Walnut and Center Streets. Note white oak plank. This was the second pavement on this block.

was interested in lands to the north and another in lands south of the line of the road. This had its influence in laying out the road, for when it was suggested that the line run around a hill on the north side one man objected, and the positions were reversed at mention of the south side. The result was a road up hill and down dale.

Another period of road building came to this Valley with what was known as the "plank road mania" which spread over western Pennsylvania in the years of 1848 and 1849. John Stuart Riddle impressed the community with the idea that here was a solution for the problem of poor roads throughout this district, especially those men who owned large tracts of land between Meadville and Warren. With the building of the Meadville, Allegheny, and Brokenstraw Plank Road it was hoped that people could be induced to settle on these lands. With a charter obtained the company was organized, and J. S. Riddle was elected President. The Managers were John Dick, Alfred Huidekoper, William Thorp, John M. Osborne, and William Reynolds. The road was started at the arsenal in Meadville. White oak planks made from trees cut in the Gill woods were used to surface it. By December, 1851, five miles had been completed and opened to the public, and this had exhausted the money raised by subscription. The Managers personally borrowed $4000 and finished the road to Guys Mills. Construction was never resumed and in 1857 the toll gates were removed.

Connecting with the Erie and Edinboro Plank Road at Edinboro, the Meadville, Klecknerville, and Edinboro Plank Road was opened to public traffic in 1852. Although mail stages were transferred to this route and the grades were easy, the tolls collected were insufficient to pay the upkeep and repairs and this road, following its predecessors after a few years of struggle, ceased to be a private institution and the public was free to travel over it without let or hindrance.

These were a part of the 220 Turnpike Roads of which Pennsylvania boasted in 1832, at which time it was a leader among the states in the matter of road networks. But with all the expense these roads had been to those who invested in them, they had their place in the building and growth of French Creek Valley.

CHAPTER XXIV

CANAL DAYS

A possibility of increased and better communication than could be obtained over roads was presented by the construction of canals. Enthusiasm for this idea was manifested by the people at large and reached its height soon after work was started on the Erie Canal in New York State. A State Association for Internal Improvements and county organizations after numerous enthusiastic meetings succeeded in impressing the Pennsylvania Assemblymen with the importance of a canal which would connect the Ohio River and its tributary waters with Lake Erie. Always alert for public betterment, Crawford County had members on both the State and the County organizations working with untiring energy to secure this canal.

Differences of opinion and controversies arose over the best course for the canal to follow. The inhabitants of each section presented their arguments with feeling and force. State and Federal engineers surveyed several routes and finally recommended one following up the valley of Beaver Creek across Crawford County west of Conneaut Lake up over the watershed and down connecting with Lake Erie at the town of Erie. This plan would necessitate raising the level of the water in Conneaut Lake ten or eleven feet to provide sufficient water in the canal at the summit. To accomplish this, water

Course of the French Creek Feeder Canal through Meadville.

must be diverted from French Creek. Over this route the Beaver and Erie Canal was eventually constructed.

The French Creek Feeder starting at Conneaut Lake followed an easterly course on the north side of the outlet crossing over French Creek by an aqueduct, up the east bank through Meadville and two miles north of the town to Bemustown Dam. When word was received that the Feeder would be built there was real and enthusiastic rejoicing in the community. This tremendous public improvement meant the stimulation of business and new communication with the outside world. Citizens of the town and countryside met at the Court House and elected Colonel James Cochran, Chairman; and R. L. Potter, Secretary, Tuesday, August 21, 1827. It was resolved that John Brooks, Arthur Cullum, Jared Shattuck, Daniel Shryock, and David Dick be appointed a Committee of Arrangements for the purpose of adopting such order as they deemed necessary on the occasion of "breaking ground." Work on the Feeder was to begin in Meadville before the construction of the main line of the canal was started, the contract for building the section through the town having been given to Arthur Cullum. On Friday evening the twenty-fourth, at another large meeting held in the same place with George Hunt in the chair and John Gibson, Secretary, William Foster, Ebenezer Betts, Colonel William Magaw, Richard Patch, and Samuel Derickson were designated to arrange for the ceremony of breaking ground for the French Creek Feeder.

This period was announced[1] by a gun from Capt. *J. D. Torbet's* company of Artillery; and amidst the music of the ringing of bells, several hundred citizens were formed in procession by the Marshalls of the day, in the following order:

Marshal on horseback—Col. John Dick
Captain Torbet's company of Artillery; and
Captain Berlin's company of Light Infantery.
Band of Music
President, Jas. Harrington, Esq.—Orator, Henry Baldwin, Jr.
Secretaries, S. Miles Green and Cyrus T. Smith, Esq.
Superintendent, Gen. J. Phillips—Engineer, J. Ferguson, Esq.
Reverend Clergy.
Committee of Arrangement.
Persons appointed to break the ground—Robert Fitz
Randolph and Cornelius Vanhorn.
A team of seven yoke of oxen, with a plough—James Fitz
Randolph to hold the plough—Samuel Lord, Esq., John
Wentworth, John Ellis, Esq. and Edward Fitz
Randolph to drive the oxen.
Eight laborers—Levi Cox, James Throop, Jas. Porter, Robert
M'Curdy, Thomas Stockton, James M'Math, William
Johnston and R. Neal, dressed in proper costume, with impliments for excavation.
Contractors.
Two Vice-Presidents—Jas. Burchfield and John Reynolds, Esqs.
Town Council.
Judiciary.
Gentlemen of the Bar.
Sheriff and Coroner.
Citizens two and two.
Two Vice-Presidents—Eliphalet Betts and Samuel Torbet.
Marshal on horseback—Col. Joseph Douglas.

---

[1] *Crawford Messenger*, August 30, 1827.

CANAL DAYS

The procession moved to South street, thence to Water street, thence to section No. 29, on the Eastern bank of French Creek, opposite to the dwelling house of Mr. James White,[1] where the whole was formed into a hollow-square around a rostrum erected for the occasion, when the Rev. Alden offered up an elegant, impressive and appropriate prayer to the throne of Deity — then succeeded the Oration — next "breaking ground." This was in the highest degree interesting—Robert Fitz Randolph and Cornelius Vanhorn, the one nearly 90, the other 80 years of age, performed this duty with as much alacrity as if the light of but 20 summers only had shone, upon their heads. The hearty cheers, that made the "welkinring" testified the feelings of the assembly at this moment—next came the team and plough—Huzza! let it in beam deep!! echoed from side to side, from shore to shore—when the glittering iron, was lost beneath the sward; next the labourers with their wheel-barrows and shovels, carried off several loads of clay, amidst the repeated cheers of the people, and thirteen rounds of cannon from the Artillery company.

The procession was then again formed and proceeded to the spring of Samuel Lord, Esq. where they partook of a cold collation prepared by the committee, and the head of a barrel of fine old Whiskey was staved in—merriment and glee was the order—after refreshing, the procession marched down Water Street to Walnut, thence to the public square, where they separated in good order and high *spirits*—after receiving the thanks of the Marshals and committee for their orderly deportment.

This was a great day to the people of Western Pennsylvania; a day for jubilee to the citizens of Crawford county. Every individual seemed to take a deep and anxious interest in this,

---

[1] Later called "Lord's basin."

to them, and the country, important work. It appeared as if but one soul, and desire animated the whole community, an ardent wish for its progression and completion. It was truly gratifying, and the heart thrilled with its finest emotions, at beholding many of the earliest settlers of the country convened upon the ground, to witness and take an active part in this, to them, novel and unlooked for event. They, who in their youth, actually skirmished, with a cruel and savage foe, armed with a rifle and tommahawk, on the very ground they now weilded the spade and grubbing hoe—men, who traversed the country when it was but a howling wilderness, to behold it now, decked with flourishing towns, an intelligent and enterprising population—a work, which none but refined society dare commence, in rapid progression, would indeed fancy, that it was magic, that they lived in a fairy land!! and yet these pioneers, these veterans of Indian wars, may in a few months be hailed by their admiring fellow citizens, triumphantly floating in canal boats along the bargin of that stream, where they had beheld no other vessel, than the Indian canoe.

In a few years we may now expect to see our country densely populated—certainly no other possessed superior advantages—with a fertile soil, salubrious atmosphere and the best of water—what more can we desire? The Lakes and New York are open to us on the north—Pittsburg and the Ohio on the South—and, we hope soon to see, Philadelphia on the East. Produce may be taken to market with but very little expense—to a choice of markets—and all kinds of produce may be raised with ordinary care—nothing is required but a moderate degree of industry and attention, with a knowledge of husbandry—the luxuries of life we have in abundance—Let those who wish to migrate, call and view for themselves.

(The Oration will be published in our next.)

CANAL DAYS 277

Of the problems encountered in the construction of the French Creek Feeder, the most troublesome seems to have been the question of what should be done with Mill Run. It was not always an orderly stream and had many times left its usual course to spread over a portion of the town—which always caused discontent and grumbling by those so invaded. So it was proposed to divert the channel at the old dam above Liberty Street and send it down the course of the mill race made by General Mead, crossing under the canal south of the intersection of The Terrace and Water Street. An arched culvert of stone was built for this purpose. In a February freshet Mill Run made a tour of inspection and washed out the culvert. Nothing further was done about changing the course of the stream.

During its construction, several breaks occurred in the bank of the Feeder in and near the village, causing delay in its completion. The opening, another memorable occasion, was aptly described in the *Messenger*.[1]

FRENCH CREEK FEEDER NAVIGABLE.

The completion of the first letting was celebrated on Saturday the 28th ult. by citizens of Meadville and its vicinity. It had been doubtful until within a few days previous whether the water would be let in this season, in consequence of some heavy slips from the upper bank. A boat of large size was

---

[1] December 3, 1829.

procured by Messrs. R. L. Potter, Nathan F. Randolph and Jno. Masters, and launched upon the waters of the canal at Lord's basin, just above town, which they fitted up with great dispatch, for the accomodation of passengers. But it was foreseen that one boat could not accomodate all who were anxious to participate, and several of our enterprising citizens determined to build a boat and provide more extensive accomodations—and such was the unparalleled perserverance of our expert boat builder, J. H. Mattox, assisted by Messrs. Patterson, Patch, Sexton and others, that within *less than two days* from the time the timber was growing in its native forest a fine boat, 50 feet in length, was launched at the Chestnut street Basin, and within *four hours* afterwards fitted up for the accomodation of passengers.

Messrs. Jos. Douglas, Jno. Dick, W. A. V. Magaw, B. B. Vincent, J. M'Farland and R. L. Potter having been appointed a committee of arrangement, a *nine pounder* from the Arsenal was put in requisition, under the charge of Lieut. Mattox. The national colors were waving from a mast erected on Chestnut street bridge—and at 11 o'clock the town was enlivened by the ringing of the bells, when a large concourse of citizens assembled at the Basin and on the several bridges. The firing of the cannon and the cheering of the multitude announced the approach of the boat from Lord's Basin.

The boats were then severally named by Wm. Dickson, Esq. Superintendent, who had been appointed Marshal of the day. That of Messrs. Potter, Randolph and Masters, was called the "*Enterprise,*" and the other at the request of the gentlemen who has so patriotically called her into existence, became the "*Wm. Lehman,*" in honor of him to whom Pennsylvania is more indebted for her system of internal improvement than any other individual.

The name of each boat was seconded by cheering and the

discharge of cannon. At 12 the "Enterprise" drawn by five fine horses, followed by the "William Lehman," propelled by three beautiful bays, elegantly comparisoned, rode by three lads appropriately and fancifully dressed, left the Basin in fine style, while the enthusiastic rejoicing of the crowd of spectators was overpowered by the thunder of cannon, and proceeded down the canal about four miles, where the boats were halted, and the party consisting of from 2 to 300—among whom were the venerable Robert F. Randolph, Vanhorn, and Lord and others the pioneers and first emigrants to French Creek,—partook of a collation, prepared by the committee of arrangement, when they returned—the "Lehman" first, followed by the "Enterprise," and proceeded some distance above the town, and returned to the Basin at Chestnut street, where the Rev. Mr. Alden, Pres't. of All. College from on board the Enterprise delivered an eloquent and highly appropriate address to the assembled multitude; a national salute was then fired, and the following toasts delivered:—

1. *The day we celebrated*—The grand era in the happy destinies of west Pennsylvania.—May each revolving year witness the rapid march of an enlightened legislature in completing the great work now in extensive progress.

2. *The President and Constituted authorities of the United States.*

3. *Governor Shulze*—Alike respected for his private virtues and the fidelity with which he has discharged the important duties of the executive department of the commonwealth.

4. *George Wolf, Governor elect*—May an ardent devotion to the interests of the state, be the great landmark of his administration.

5. *The State Legislature*—Justice—good faith—and the public interest,—call for a speedy requisition on the ample resources of the commonwealth.

6. *Pennsylvania*—May her public works prove an exhaustless store of perminent blessings to the present and future generations.

7. *The Board of Canal Commissioners*—Enlightened and patriotic.—May their decision of the all-important question of routes, prove their wisdom and disinterestedness.

8. *The French creek Feeder*—May its completion be a stimulus to an immediate extention of the canal in western Pennsylvania.

9. *The Allegheny Steam Boat*—May the most sanguin expectations of its friends be realized.

10. *The Harbor of Presque-Isle*—May it soon receive the waters of French creek.

11. *Clinton and Lehman*—Their names and their public services will find a sure passage to future ages on the floor of time.

12. *The Treasurer of the Internal Improvement fund*—May he ever be prepared to honor all drafts presented.

13. The fair sex—The zealous patrons of every noble work.

This list was followed by ten "Volunteer" toasts proposed by prominent citizens, among which were these:

By J. S. Riddle, Esq. *The French creek Feeder*—May the present board of Commissioners speedily convince us that it was not intended merely as a tub to amuse the whale.

By Wm. Sarber. *The Watermen of French creek*—No more going ahead backwards—We can now overcome the strongest rapids without the setting pole, and with our arms folded.

The Engineer and the Superintendents were also remembered, and after them, the State Officials.

By Robert Adrain. *Daniel O'Connell*—the champion of liberty.

CANAL DAYS

The committee of arrangements tendered their unfeigned thanks to the Rev. President of Allegheny College for honoring the celebration with his presence, and for his appropriate and eloquent address on the occasion. They also acknowledged their indebtedness to the Marshal of the day—to Lt. Mattox for the many and important services which he rendered, and to all those citizens who so promptly and cheerfully volunteered their assistance.

Canal and slack water navigation became popular with the people of the middle west. Shortly after the completion of the Feeder the Pennsylvania Assembly undertook to make slackwater navigation possible between Meadville and Franklin. A connection with the Feeder was made at the point where the Aqueduct crossed French Creek. By a series of locks boats were lowered from the Feeder to the Creek and floated down to Franklin. Dams and locks were built at shallow rapids which divided the slackwaters.

Early in December five boats loaded with freight left Meadville for Franklin via the French Creek Feeder and the Slackwater canal to proceed on down the Allegheny River to Pittsburgh. The honor of conducting the first boat through this improvement devolved upon Hon. John Dick. The French Creek Pioneer was launched on April 29, 1834, the first and probably the only passenger canal boat between these points. Scarcity of water at certain seasons of the year hampered this enterprise from the start. The larger boats from upper French

Creek had great difficulty in passing through the locks and around the dams. During high water the locks did not have capacity to pass any large number of boats and rafts; this occasioned great loss to the boatmen and lumbermen. Ten years after the opening, in an effort to get their boats through, the boatmen attempted to destroy the dam at Franklin, precipitating a riot. Floods changed the channel by washing it out in some places and filling in others. After high water had broken out some of the dams, the project was abandoned, to the great disappointment of the promoters.

In building the Beaver and Erie Canal, the problem was to have water at the summit of the divide south of Lake Erie. To do this Conneaut Lake was turned into a supply reservoir by raising it eleven feet. To fill this extra eleven feet the French Creek Feeder was constructed, twenty-seven miles in length. The reservoir when full was 510 feet above Lake Erie and there were 72 locks between them—40 miles.

The hope for more rapid transportation in sending the products of farm and factory to market and for an easier means of travel was quickened when construction of the Canal was actually begun. The people in French Creek Valley had visions of greater prosperity and increased activities. Waiting years for its completion, they realized more keenly the advantages to be developed in the future. It was a day long to be remembered when the

Locks where boats were lowered to Slackwater Navigation from Feeder of Beaver and Erie Canal, showing Canal Aqueduct over French Creek. Broad guage tracks of the Atlantic and Great Western Railway, Franklin Branch. 1864.

North Street Bridge over Canal.

Canal became an actuality with boats arriving to discharge cargoes and load others for distant cities.

THE CANAL OPENED TO MEADVILLE![1]—It is at least fifteen years since ground was broken on the Erie Extension. The hopes and wishes of our citizens, after this wearisome anxiety and suspense, was finally realized by the gladsome notes of a canalboat horn on Wednesday night last, announcing the safe arrival in our town of the packets HUDSON and PILOT from Beaver laden with freight for some of our citizens. The event sent a thrill of pleasure to the hearts of the whole population... The arrival of the boats, unexpected as they were, was an event too important to be passed over quietly... An arrangement was made for an excursion on the canal Thursday... No opportunity for a celebration was to be passed over lightly. The Boats proceeded to the Dam[2] at the head of the Feeder, turned about, and returned... Their approach to the town was greeted with the roar of cannon and the inspiring strains of the Band, (who never performed better) and the novelty of the scene, drew immense crowds upon the different bridges through the town, who lustily cheered the boats as they passed onward. After a pleasant trip of about five miles down the canal, the boats landed again at Chestnut st. at twilight.

"The State[3] had expended somewhat over *$4,000,000. in construction of the canal and only $211,000.* was required to complete the work on the main line to Erie— yet the State made a transfer of the entire property to the Erie Canal Company in 1843."

---

[1] Meadville *Crawford Democrat*, May 30, 1843.
[2] Bemus town on French Creek.
[3] William Reynolds, Reminiscences of the Old Canal, May 1904 (Reynolds Collection)

Work of construction was completed by the Company the following year, but it was the middle of October before the water was let in. Toward the end of the next month, the first boat left Erie. Cold weather interfered and this boat was frozen in before reaching its destination. On the twenty-second of April, 1845, the first packet arrived at Meadville enroute to Erie from Beaver.

The Beaver and Erie Canal by furnishing rapid and cheap transportation did much to build up commerce and prosperity in the French Creek Valley over a long period of time. In the forties and fifties this means of transportation grew to such an extent that canals were over-crowded and it was often difficult to move freight and passengers. This continued until better facilities were established by the Erie and Pittsburgh Railroad. By 1870 it could no longer compete with the railroad and, having served its purpose in the march of progress, the Canal which started so auspiciously with "a concourse of sweet sounds" by the Meadville Band, the cheers of the citizens, and the roar of "deep mouthed cannon," was abandoned.

Canal Measurements

10'   40'   5'
Towing path   Water surface   Berm bank
28'

Canal Basin, Market Street, Meadville. David Dick house, northeast corner of Market Square, the present site of the Kepler Hotel.

CHAPTER XXV

THE FIRST STERN-WHEELER

Before the Beaver and Erie Canal was completed another agent of commerce, the steamboat, appeared on the Allegheny River. The *William B. Duncan*, a steamboat of eighty tons with paddle wheels at the sides, was the first of the river steamboats to ascend the river as far as Franklin. Arriving on January 28, 1828, with 150 passengers and thirty tons of freight on board, this steamboat created great enthusiasm for the new mode of commerce and travel.

The following year, August 13, Robert L. Potter read an account in an eastern paper of the "successful experiment of a steam boat on the Connecticut river by a Mr. Blanchard." Realizing that the Connecticut River presented more difficulties to navigation than the Allegheny, he published his ideas on this subject, together with the notice he had read, in the *Crawford Messenger*. After consulting "Mr. Atkinson, Mr. Shattuck, and Dr. Bemus," he wrote to "Mr. Blanchard who built the steam boat, *Vermont*—Springfield, Mass.," requesting the Postmaster to forward the letter if Mr. Blanchard had left that place. Five or six weeks elapsed and there was no reply when one morning Blanchard came to his office announcing that he "had come to examine the Allegheny river, should he receive any encouragement."

Squire Potter introduced Blanchard to David Dick and other gentlemen. The river was examined and, the report being satisfactory, a contract was entered into between Blanchard and David Dick and others.

In due time the following announcements appeared:

Blanchard's Steam-boat,[1] building at Pittsburgh, has been launched—and is expected to ascend the Allegheny, to Franklin, Warren, &c. about the 10th or 12th inst.

The *Blanchard* Steam-boat[2] was expected to leave Pittsburgh yesterday, for Franklin and Warren. Her performance, on trial, we are assured, has been found to meet every expectation.

For navigation shallow rivers required boats of light draft. Up to this time all steamboats had been built with the paddle wheels at the sides, but Blanchard moved them to the stern of the vessel. The success of the *Allegheny* revolutionized the building of steamboats for navigating inland rivers, especially the Mississippi and its tributary waters.

David Dick's account of the *Allegheny's* sail up the river is self-explanatory.

The Steam Boat Allegheny[3]—The following hasty sketch of the passage of this vessel from Pittsburgh to Franklin, was politely handed to us by our enterprising townsman, Mr.

---
[1] *Crawford Messenger*, April 1, 1830.
[2] Ibid., April 15, 1830.
[3] Ibid., April 22, 1830.

THE FIRST STERN-WHEELER 287

DAVID DICK. We congratulate the public on the result of this experiment. It has established the important fact that steam may be advantageously applied to the navigation of the Allegheny river when the water is at an ordinary stage, and with a modest expenditure in its Improvement, at its lowest state. By this conveyance, notwithstanding the many interposing difficulties, goods have been brought from the wharves at Pittsburgh and offered for sale in our village on the *fifth day*. This is an interesting fact. By no other means of transit have they ever been delivered in so short a time.

Mr. Atkinson—At your request I hand you a few particulars, hastily put on paper, touching the passage of the Steamboat ALLEGHENY, up that river.

We left Pittsburgh on Tuesday at 11 o'clock A. M. in rather an unprepared state, being desirous to try the boat before the water got too low, and arrived at Freeport, a distance of 30 miles, that evening. Started next morning—met with a little trouble at the Kiskiminitas aqueduct. Unaware of meeting with an extra current, occasioned by the piers of the aqueduct, we were passing rather carelessly and had got two thirds through when the current struck the bow in a quarterly direction and turned her about. On second trial she passed through without difficulty. Patterson's falls was the first that presented any difficulty to her progress. Here the water, at a low stage, is confined to a very narrow channel—It is considered the most formidable rapids in the Allegheny. She assended the falls about two thirds their distance, and became stationary. This was entirely owing to the bad quality of wood—by which the steam could not be raised beyond two thirds of the common working pressure—By application of machinery she was warped a distance of about 30 feet, which carried her over the pinch.— We arrived at Franklin at 2 o'clock P. M. on Sunday and on the same day the Allegheny proceeded on her course to Warren. Making all proper deductions for stoppages to take in and put out passengers, and to obtain supplies of wood, &c. and the loss of an afternoon at Patterson's falls, we may state the time in making the trip at about 36 hours. From the result of this experiment, we may fairly assume, that the passage from Pittsburg to Franklin can be made by this boat in two days, and to Warren in three, running only in day-light, the river being in the same state it was when we assended, the engine in good order, and driven by wood of suitable quality.

This being the first and altogether a trip of experiment, it may be naturally supposed that many difficulties would present themselves, equally as we regard her machinery and the tact necessary to her navigation—This was anticipated. Several matters have been found defective, and will be promptly remedied.

No serious problems present themselves to the navigation of the Allegheny river, by steam boats, from Pittsburgh until you arrive within about 40 miles of Franklin. Catfish Falls is a strong rapid. Parkers, Patterson's and Montgomery's falls, followed in pretty quick succession, all being embraced within no less than 20 miles distance. Should these places be improved by dams of 4 or 5 feet high, and the channels deepened elsewhere where the river spreads over much surface, the Allegheny could be rendered navigable, it is my deliberate opinion, for Steam boats as the Ohio now is, and both rivers could, by a comparative small expenditure be rendered navigable, for boats of 100 tons in the lowest stage of water.

New possibilities in passenger and freight transportation opened up by the performance of the *Allegheny* awakened a lively interest at all of her ports of call. This forward step for building commerce in northwestern Pennsylvania was noted at length in the press with each succeeding trip up and down the river.

The local newspaper hailed the first entry of the *Allegheny* at the "Port of Franklin" with this paragraph.

STEAM BOAT ALLEGHENY.[1]

This welcome guest arrived at this place on Sunday evening last, about three o'clock. The water in the river was uncommonly low for the season, taking into consideration all the circumstances, was easily, indeed beyond the expectations of the most sanguine... The expense of connecting the Allegheny river, at the mouth of French creek, and Erie, either by slack water or canal, is so inconsiderate, that the great objects to be obtained by it, will certainly not be lost sight of by the legislature. We consider the success of the steam boat as fixed beyond all question, the route of communication to Erie, by French creek, where nature has determined.—VENANGO DEMOCRAT, April 20.

The second visit of the *Allegheny* also created excitement so a more extended account of it was published in the Franklin paper.

THE STEAM BOAT "ALLEGHENY." [2]

This valuable steamer made her second trip up the Allegheny river last week. She arrived at Warren on Friday morning about 8 o'clock, having been detained a day or two in her passage by the accidental breaking of her rudder. She had on board about 35 tons of freight and a number of passengers. It being court week in Warren, at the general solicitation of

---
[1] *Crawford Messenger*, May 6, 1830.
[2] Ibid., May 20, 1830.

the citizens, jurors, commissioners and members of the bar, the court adjourned at 12 o'clock until four P. M. for the purpose of affording an opportunity to the public of deciding on the practical advantages of the new and great improvement of the navigation, and expressing their gratulations upon the occasion. About 130 or 40 persons, among whom were more than twenty ladies, several strangers from New York state, and the members of the Court and Bar, took an excursion up to Kinzua, about fourteen miles above the town of Warren. She passed over Hook's dam, and several rapids on the river with a facility, far exceeding the expectations of any one, even the most sanguine. She went up at the rate of nearly four miles per hour and returned in one hour and ten minutes. Upwards of twenty genteel females and a number of gentlemen taking tea in a comfortable room moving at the rate of four miles an hour up the wild rapids of the Allegheny more than 200 miles above that point which has heretofore been considered as the head of steam boat navigation, afforded a delightful, cheering scene to the contemplative lover of improvement, and furnished a striking manifestation of the powers of genius and the efforts of enterprise in man. This boat's having stemmed with so much ease, the current of the Allegheny river *above* Warren, where it is well known to be much more rough and rapid than *below*, and where it wants the waters of the Conewango, which it receives at that handsomely situated village, satisfactorily proves to the most scrupulous the complete success of the undertaking, the trifling expenditure of money necessary to render her passage easy between that point and Pittsburg, at the lowest stages of water.* * * *Venango Democrat.*

A keel boat would have required at least *eighteen* days to make the trip, which the Allegheny has performed in *six* deducting the time spent at Warren and Franklin. This of itself is a great gain in the facility of transportation; but this is not all the gain which the boat will make. The experiment is novel; pilots are not skilful in navigating this river with steam boats; the wood is bad, unseasoned, and difficult to procure. These difficulties will all gradually be overcome, and then, we have no doubt, the same boat will be able to perform the trip to Warren and back in five or six days. *Pittsburgh Gazette.*

In the same issues of the *Crawford Messenger* which contained these successful records of the *Allegheny* other columns contained detailed accounts of steamboat disasters which had occurred on the river below Pittsburgh.

It will be seen by the following communication,[1] copied from the Pittsburg Gazette, that the steamboat ALLEGHENY has successfully and triumphantly extended her navigation to Olean, in the state of New York.

The New Steamboat Allegheny, built on an improved plan, by Mr. Blanchard, of Connecticut, 90 feet long and 13 wide, cabin on deck, separated lengthwise, giving each 30 feet, worked by a distict double engine principally made of *wrought iron*, two stern wheels, extending 12 feet behind the boat, drawing, with wood and water, about 12 inches; left Pittsburgh on the 14th of May, on her third trip up the Allegheny with 64 passengers and 25 to 30 tons of freight, stemming the current of this noble and most valuable river (affording lumber in the greatest quantities,) at the rate of three miles per hour. . .

Franklin is situated at the out let of French creek, (which is navigable for keel boats to Le Boeuf, above Meadville, 40.6 miles; this is an old village, and surrounded by iron furnaces,

---

[1] *Crawford Messenger,* June 3, 1830.

where also is now made good quality bar iron, one hundred and twenty five miles up. Oil creek is seven miles above. On this stream there are quantities of Seneca Oil gathered; its smell is very perceptible at its outlet; here there is a valuable furnace.

We arrived in Warren, a beautiful village, situate at the outlet of Connewango creek, at 9 o'clock, on the 19th May, near two hundred miles above Pittsburgh, in three and a half days running time. . . It requires from eighteen to twenty-five days for canoes and keel boats, manned in the best manner, to perform this trip. This is the highest point on the river that ever had been made by a steam boat, and to this point only by this boat. However, the usual enterprise of its owners prompted them to explore further this valuable river, and on the evening of the 20th May she departed from Warren, for *Olean in the state of New York*, seventy-five miles above (by water,) with freight and passengers from Pittsburgh. At nine o'clock the next day, she arrived opposite the Indian village of *Cornplanter*, seventeen miles up. Here a deputation of gentlemen waited on this ancient and well known Indian King, or Chief, and invited him on board this new, and to him wonderful visitor, a steam boat. We found him in all his native simplicity of dress & manner of living, lying on his couch, made of rough pine boards, and covered with deer skins and blankets. . . This venerable old chief was a lad in the first French war in 1744, and is now nearly one hundred years of age. He is a smart, active man, seemingly possessed of all his strength of mind, and in perfect health, and retains, among his nation, all that uncontrolled influence he has ever done. Cornplanter's wife and her mother, one hundred and fifteen years of age, are in good health. . .

We found many rapids and generally very strong water, until within twenty miles of our destination, at the Great Valley. Here the mountains began to decrease fast, and the current became easy, until gradually, we seemed to have reached the top of the mountain which we had been so long assending; at 11 o'clock, A. M. on Friday, the 21st May, we landed safely at *Olean point,* nearly three hundred miles from Pittsburgh, amidst the loud and constant rejoicing of hospitable citizens of the village. The first person landed was Mr. D. Dick of Meadville, the principal & enterprising owner of this boat. . .

The boat left Warren on the morning of the 23rd; and landed at Pittsburgh at 4 o'clock, P. M. on the 24th, with a number of passengers, 18 tons of pig metal, and 9 tons bar iron, in perfect safety. The time employed in running, during the trip, was 7 days, (running by daylight only,) exclusive of delays at Franklin, Warren, and Olean, but including stoppage for wood, &c.

THE STEAM BOAT ALLEGHENY.[1]—During the passage, on board this boat, to and from the place of Celebration, on the 5th instant, we were gratified to perceive that Mr. Blanchard's plan of a boat for shallow water was highly approved by some of the most experienced steam boat captains and engineers belonging to the society of *Snag Marines.* We ourselves have had considerable experience in steam boat travelling, both on the eastern and western waters, and we do not hesitate to say; that this boat is, beyond comparison, more completely noiseless, and less agitated, while running, than any other steam boat we have ever travelled in. A very old and experienced steam boat captain concurs entirely with us in this opinion. . . Pitts. Gaz.

---

[1] *Crawford Messenger,* June 15, 1830.

Meadville citizens voiced their appreciation of the *Allegheny* and her accomplishments at the 4th of July celebration in Meadville that year.

> The 54th anneversary of our National Independence celebrated by a large number of citizens, who assembled at the tavern of Mr. Sexton, and marched in procession to the spring of Samuel Lord, Esq. immediately north of the town, where they sat down to an excellent dinner provided by Mr. Sexton, at only a few hours notice—The Hon. STEPHEN BARLOW was President, and Col. JOSEPH DOUGLAS, Vice President of the day... The weather was unusually pleasant, and nothing occured to interrupt the harmony and festivity of the occasion... toasts were drank, accompanied by the discharge of musketry.[1]

Thirteen toasts were followed by twenty-three by Volunteers, including this: "R. Hurst. The Steam-boat Allegheny—may her worthy proprietor of this place receive a full reward for his labor."[2]

In appreciation of their achievement, the citizens of Franklin held a celebration in honor of those who made it possible—

> ... three[3] of the worthy proprietors of the Steam Boat *"Allegheny,"* to wit: DAVID DICK and JOSEPH DOUGLASS, *Esqrs.* of Meadville, and PHILIP MECHLING, *Esq.* of Kittanning, attending on special invitation, sat down to an elegant dinner ... the following toasts were drank, accompanied with

---

[1] *Crawford Messenger*, July 15, 1830.
[2] Ibid.
[3] *Venango Democrat*, August 10, 1830.

appropriate music and grateful and hearty cheers, and occasionally an animated song by a gentleman of this company.

TOASTS.

The Steam-boat "Allegheny."
Thomas Blanchard.
The enlightened and enterprising proprietors of the "Allegheny."
The Allegheny River.
French Creek.
The immortal De Witt Clinton.
Dr. Wm. Lehman.
Robert Fulton.
The President of the United States.
The Governor of Pennsylvania.
Our National and State Legislature.
Agriculture, Commerce and Manufactures.
The American Fair.

After the above toasts were drank, the President, Mr. CRARY, rose and in a feeling and impressive manner addressed Mr. DICK, and his associates present. . .

Sir—Your active exertions and liberal expenditures for the purpose of building and getting into operation the Steam Boat *Allegheny;* . . . have been observed and highly approved by your fellow citizens throughout the country . . . the inhabitants of this borough and vicinity, . . . desirous of giving the most public testimony of their respect and grateful acknowledgements—have invited you and your associates to meet us. . .

Mr. DICK then arose, and after expressing in a neat and forcible manner his warm and grateful feelings . . . observed that there was a gentleman present (R. L. Potter, Esq. of Meadville) to whom we were, perhaps, more indebted than to any other person, for originating the idea of constructing a steam boat to do an advantageous and useful business on the Allegheny river. . .

Following R. L. Potter's recital of his writing to Thomas Blanchard and the results it produced, there were 35 Volunteer toasts, and,

"The company separated at a seasonable hour, and good order, and a strong manifestation of social feeling, and a free exchange of friendly sentiment prevailed throughout."

At the "Conniautt lake" celebration[1] of July 4th "a sumptuous dinner" was followed by the drinking of toasts "accompanied by the discharge of cannon," the first Volunteer being "By the President of the day . . . *Mr. David Dick, the Fulton of the West* . . . His fame is carried on the bosom of the 'Allegheny.' "

---

[1] *Crawford Messenger*, July 8, 1830.

CHAPTER XXVI

A RAILROAD AT LAST

The Indian Trail, the first means of communication between settlements for trade, was developed into a Wagon Road. This mode of transportation was supplanted by a Canal. As a carrier of commerce the Canal passed into the land of the forgotten with the construction of the Railroad.

At this period steam railroad building in the western United States was in its infancy, although for years they had been in operation in the large cities of the east. In this growing country increasing business created a demand for better transportation, so it was natural to seek in the steam railroad a solution of this problem. A letter[1] received by John Reynolds in 1851 was the suggestion needed to start action.

Mr. Jno. Reynolds Esq
Dear Sir—
 Permit me to intrude upon Your time for a moment—
 Mr. F. Kinsman of Warren, O—wishes me to write to some Gentleman in Your place on the Subject of a Rail Road from near Jamestown N. Y—through Your place & west to Warren, Ackron: a route ORIGINALLY PROJECTED *by Mr. Clinton of N. Y.* I will mention a few arguments in favor of the route:

---

[1] Atlantic and Great Western Railway, Papers. (Reynolds Collection)

It is said that the N. & & Erie Co are not satisfied with their Terminis at Dunkirk.

Also that the Lake Shore track west of D— is only 4 feet wide. Now the N. Yorkers wish to get as far west as possible. This Route is a very desirable One in many Respects. Your place Warren, Revenna, Ackron, are important points:—at the *two last,* connections would be formed with important Roads, now commenced.

Again, it is said that Pittsburgh wishes to reach Olean, on the Allegheny;—and that it is as near, & a better route than any other to come down to Beaver, thence up near Mercer, a little south of Your place & so to Warren. Now if this is so, a Road west to Ohio & south to Pittsburgh, might be obtained through Meadville. The road west would be *the road.*

Now do You wish such a road in M? If You wish the Road west, You will have to obtain it by a ruse of Penn—the State will not give such a Route directly to the New Yorkers. But under the plan of a Road to Pittsburgh, You can now obtain a Charter.

The subject is now discussed in Ohio & N. Y.—& if such a Charter is obtained it ought to be this winter, before the plan becomes public.

If You can obtain a Charter, I believe that the N. Yorkers will build the road in 5 years—

If the plan seems visionary to You, then please excuse me. If not, by all means act upon the subject this winter, and obtain a charter.

Being a Stranger in Meadville, my Father suggested Yourself as a very suitable person to address—

Yours,

Kinsman O— Very Respectfully
  Feby 17 1851— D. Allen M. D.

The interest inspired in the town by Dr. Allen's letter grew rapidly and resulted in the formation of a company, The Meadville Railroad.

The energy and enthusiasm put into this project by its backers overcame all obstacles so that on August 19, 1853, the citizens of the community assembled for another celebration. On the bank of French Creek near the intersection of Water and Linden Streets ground was broken and construction started for the Pittsburgh and Erie Railroad. It was done with ceremony, John McFarland being marshal with Horace Cullum and Major Samuel Torbett as aids. The Honorable Gaylord Church delivered the address. One of the oldest settlers, David Compton, broke ground with a shovel, then Taylor Randolph ran the first furrow, his brother Edward driving four yoke of oxen. Other addresses were made by William H. Davis, David M. Farrelly, and Hiram L. Richmond. In this manner it was announced that Meadville was to have a railroad.

New difficulties prevented the completion of the Pittsburgh and Erie Railroad and a new charter was granted on May 20, 1857, for The Meadville Railroad. A reorganization was effected on July 3 of the same year, at which William Reynolds was elected president, and John Dick, Gaylord Church, D. A. Finney, J. J. Shryock, J. E. McFarland, O. Hastings, A. W. Mumford, and H. Cullum, directors. This organization was soon afterward superseded by The Atlantic and Great

Western Railway Companies of New York, Pennsylvania, and Ohio, whose purpose was to start at Salamanca, New York, at a connection with the road coming from New York and build west to Marion, Ohio, to connect with the road continuing to Chicago.

Unforeseen contingencies prevented progress, plans were abandoned and reformed, so that it was not until after the services of James McHenry, London, England, were secured that construction advanced. William Reynolds, the president, wrote on September 6, 1861, to the Chief Contractor McHenry:

We have secured the oil sent to the eastern market by rail from Union (City) and other points on the Sunbury & Erie Railroad, but as stated in my last letter, a very large quantity is waggoned to and shipped from a point on the Canal[1] five miles South of Meadville (two and one-half miles from our line). This averages from 300 to 500 barrels per day, although on Monday reaching 1800. Our line if completed to Meadville would secure that now taken by the Canal and a large proportion of that sent by River. The quantity now sent daily from the wells exceeds 2000 barrels, and I am assured this does not exceed one-fourth part of the quantity actually yealded by the wells, the other three-fourths being stored in tanks in the ground awaiting better prices. Some wells have from 40 to 60 tanks full, averaging from 200 to 500 barrels. Owing to present low prices, few of the pumping wells are in operation. You can therefore estimate the present capacity of the oil region if stimulated by advanced prices on those now ranging at from four to five cents per gallon at the well. It

---

[1] Shaws' Landing.

may from eighteen months' experience be safely assumed that this business is perminent and may enter into future estimates of the profits of the road. Each month has produced wells surpassing those previously drilled until many of those a year since considered a fortune are now regarded as small affairs. The yield of some of the late wells is truly wonderful, forcing from a depth of 600 feet from 200 to 800 barrels per day with such power as to throw the oil and water like a vast fountain to a greater height than the surrounding forest trees.

With the Civil War started in the spring, money to build railroads became increasingly difficult to obtain, and William Reynolds with a committee of officers of the Atlantic and Great Western went to Europe for the purpose of interesting capital in that enterprise. His diary[1] tells of meeting Don Jose de Salamanca:

Paris, Nov. 5, 1861, Tuesday. Salamanca arrived this morning and Mr. Kennard and I called to see him. We were much disapointed in not seeing Mr. McHenry, as Salamanca leaves in the evening. By appointment, Mr. Kennard, Mr. Kent and myself met him (Salamanca) at three o'clock and had an interview of half an hour. Mr. Levita acted as interpreter. Salamanca is dissatisfied with the progress of the road and says that under Mr. McHenry's agreements with him the work should have been completed to Akron, McHenry furnishing the rest of the funds and that he (Salamanca) was then to provide funds to complete to Dayton. A misunderstanding of such importance renders the failure of meeting very unfortunate. Salamanca stated that if McHenry could not comply with his agreements to complete to Akron that he would agree to take the whole line, furnish all the money and complete at once—but only with the understanding that he was himself to be the managing contractor. We left with his agent authority to make settlement of account from McHenry and report the same to him.

Salamanca is a fine looking man with ease of manner and pleasing address. He is said to be the greatest railway builder of the age. That the profits on his present contracts in Italy will reach five millions of dollars. I am informed by those who pretend to know that he has 40,000 men on his many works.

The committee went to Spain arriving on the nineteenth of November. They met Salamanca and were entertained at his house in Madrid and his country place in the suburbs on the twenty-third and twenty-fourth. Through his influence Queen Isabella and other Spanish dignitaries became interested in the railway.

The station at the junction of the New York and Dunkirk Railway and the Atlantic and Great Western was named in his honor Salamanca. This was the eastern terminus of the road. After seven years of delays, difficulties in raising money, and a seemingly unusual amount of trials and vicissitudes in organizing and constructing the railroad, items like the following spurred the imagination and deferred hopes of that section of French Creek Valley through which it was proposed to run the line.

---

[1] William Reynolds, Diary. (Reynolds Collection)

A RAILROAD AT LAST 303

JAMESTOWN JOURNAL — — — EXTRA[1]

RAILROAD EDITION

Jamestown, N. Y., Saturday, Aug. 25, 1860.

* * * * *

As anticipated in our regular edition of Thursday evening, the work reached this place at an early hour this afternoon. At twenty-five minutes past twelve o'clock the first rail lapped on the Main St. Bridge, and at two o'clock the workmen had finished the work of track-laying up to the Depot Grounds.

At 4 o'clock the whistle announced in the distance the approach of the train from New York, and in a few minutes the first iron horse that ever neighed in our town strode with majestic tread across the Main St. Bridge. The train was a small one, being only for the accommodation of the few invited guests. The Jamestown Cornet Band, which had been taken onto the train at Kennedyville, added to the occasion the lively strains of the appropriate air "Ain't I glad to get out of the wilderness?" The occasion, although to be merely private and complimentary to Mr. KENNARD, was marked by the presence of an eager multitude who thronged the avenues, vacant places, windows and house tops, to witness the first throb of this great artery of civilization in Southern Chautauqua.

On board the train were Messrs. KENNARD and HILL, Chief Engineers, Messrs. MINOT and MARSH, officers of the New York & Erie Rail Road, and SIG. DEOSDADO, Agent for DON JOSE DE SALAMANCA, and SIG. NAVARRO, Agent for the DUKE DE RIENZARES, and other representatives of the Spanish interests in this country, JOHN GODDARD, ESQ., of London, ROBERT THALLOW, ESQ., of New York.

---

[1] William Reynolds, My Connection with the Atlantic and Great Western Railway, 1851 to September 30, 1864. (Reynolds Collection)

It was October 28, 1862, when an editorial[1] appeared in the local press of Meadville:

The Atlantic & Great Western Railway Company has at last been completed to this point. The track layers reached here on Tuesday last and the construction train passed through the depot grounds at the lower part of the town heralded by the ringing of bells, bands of music, and the liveliest demonstrations of gratitude on the part of our citizens. The long talked of and much abused road has at length been finished to Meadville and the shrill whistle of the locomotive daily wakes up the echoes of old Cussewago and is already becoming a familiar sound.

On Wednesday morning the fine new locomotive "William Reynolds" left the depot at half past eight o'clock with Messrs. Kennard, chief engineer; William Reynolds, president; Gaylord Church, J. J. Shryock and James E. McFarland, directors; and a few attaches of the road on a business trip. . . .

We arrived at Correy, 40 miles distant, about half past one o'clock. . . Correy is one of the wonders of the age in which we live—the creation of the combined efforts of oil and steel. . . . Some half dozen locomotives puffing and screaming, long trains of cars laden with oil barrels standing along the tracks —one of the largest brick oil refineries, a large and handsome hotel, and many dwelling houses, &c., gave unmistakable evidence of a prosperous village, where, but a few months since, stood the primeval forest. Aladin, with his wonderful lamp, could scarsely have worked a more magical change! . . . We reached Meadville about nine o'clock in the evening, highly delighted with our trip on the first locomotive that ever left the Borough, and satisfied that a new era of prosperity is about to dawn upon us, maugre the croakings of old fogies

---

[1] *The Crawford Democrat.*

who have imagined our town was finished and should be fenced in! All honor, we say, to the men who have battled long and bravely to secure this consummation—who have stood up in the dark days of the enterprise and pressed onward, through the most discouraging difficulties, until their efforts have been finally crowned with glorious success.

Horace Greeley's story of the A. & G. W. which appeared in the *New York Tribune*, January 19, 1864, included this paragraph:

At Meadville is the great Hotel and Dining-Hall[1] of the road—the Dining-Hall among the best in America. Here also are the machine shops, etc., for the eastern division of the road. Meadville, formerly one of the most secluded and out-of-the-way county seats in the West, is henceforth as accessible and eligibly located as any town in Pennsylvania west of Pittsburg. It was always a beautiful spot, situated in a fertile and delightful region. Henceforth, its trade must be large, and its growth rapid and sure.

The railway was built largely by English capital and British ideas dominated its construction and management. The track was standard English gauge, which was known in this country as "broad gauge," wider than that used by most American railroads.

The New York *Tribune*[2] understands that arrangements have been made to lay a third rail upon the track of the Pittsburgh, Ft. Wayne & Chicago Railway, from the junction of the Atlantic & Great Western Railway to Chicago, to make the gauge

---

[1] The McHenry House.
[2] *The Crawford Journal*, April 28, 1863.

correspond with that of the Atlantic & Great Western and Erie roads—thus forming an unbroken line of the six foot gauge from New York to Chicago. . . .

The last spike on the main line was driven June 20, 1864, making a record for McHenry—the completion of 200 miles of railroad in 200 days.

The Atlantic and Great Western Railway Depot, Meadville. Between Chestnut and Center Streets.

One of the largest in the country, the Meadville station was built over and along both sides of the tracks. Entering it passengers on trains got the effect of going into a tunnel. The *Crawford Democrat*[1] called it "A Magnificent Depot."

. . . The whole building, at least the main part of it will be 327 feet in length by 127 feet in width—embracing an area of forty-one thousand and five hundred and twenty square feet.

Again a local paper[2] expressed its approbation:

This great road, one of the most wonderful and successful enterprises of modern times is of course the great feature of Meadville. To it Meadville owes its recent life and bustle, its influx of population, business and riches. Its big depot, its

---
[1] December 16, 1862.
[2] William Reynolds, Scrap Book. (Reynolds Collection)

A RAILROAD AT LAST

huge machine shops, its numberless tenement houses for its employees, and last but not least, its magnificent hotel, the McHenry House, are the most prominent and important buildings in the city. The railroad, which seen anywhere, impresses one at once with the energy and ability which characterizes its Managers, is nowhere seen to such advantage as at Meadville, where its big depot, its handsome, well lighted, orderly offices, and above all its unequalled hotel, which has brought to this little city of the West the luxury and magnificence of New York living, all strike even the most casual spectator with admiration.

The McHenry House is of enough importance to claim separate mention, although owned by the A. & G. W. road. It is "run" by our well known and popular townsman, R. M. N. Taylor, Esq., who now superintends the entire dining department of the road. The Road has built the house in the best of style, with the finest dining-hall in the West, and has given Mr. Taylor instructions to make it in all respects a first class house, assuring him that they will foot all the bills. Of course, under such auspices it cannot fail being the pleasantest and most agreeable stopping-place for the (rail) way-worn traveler.

The McHenry House, west of the Depot.

Quoting one traveler:

In speaking[1] of the dining-hall of the already popular McHenry House, she says: "Arriving at Meadville you are conducted into the splendid dining-hall, which, but for the numerous tables loaded with good things, would remind you of some Gothic church, with the open roof and chancel in the centre. . . I comprehend why passengers are allowed fifteen minutes beyond the time for refreshments—there is a feast for the eyes, which are scarsely satisfied when the stomach is full."

Situated just west of the station, the McHenry House was more than a railway hotel, splendid in its appointments, while the excellence of its food soon won a wide reputation which attracted guests from near and far. At holiday time and on special occasions it was not unusual to find five or six different kinds of game included on the menu[2] served in the great dining-hall. This room was finished in the finest black walnut with windows of stained glass. The grounds surrounding the building were planted with evergreen and ornamental trees, shrubbery and flowers in beds between which were winding driveways and gravel paths circling pools where fountains played.

This was the scene of elaborate entertainments. Balls and receptions were given in honor of the distinguished Europeans and Americans who were interested in the railroad, surpassing anything hitherto known in this part

---

[1] *The Crawford Democrat*, February 9, 1864.
[2] See Appendix, 338.

The McHenry House Dining Room.

of the country. For these affairs the townspeople sent east to the centers of fashion for evening apparel both smart and chic befitting the occasion. At such times the beautiful grounds were illuminated and for special events there were fireworks.

CHAPTER XXVII

AN HISTORIC LETTER

Early in 1800 the road from Philadelphia over the mountains to Pittsburgh was rough and hazardous, and with inclement weather the hardships increased, taking a heavy toll of strength and health from those who traveled it. The journey from Pittsburgh to Meadville was equally difficult for all but the most robust, as much of the traveling was done in open wagons or keelboats. About 1816 a young man from Philadelphia made this journey, arriving in Meadville somewhat discouraged and ill from the experiences which he had encountered. He was alone and knew no one in the village; his search for a place in which to start the practice of law was fruitless. It was obvious that this young man was a gentleman of culture and education. He gave his name as Samuel Mifflin, a son of the Thomas Mifflin who had once been a governor of Pennsylvania in residence at Lancaster and a general in the army under Washington's command during the Revolutionary days.

With the hardships of his own early life still fresh in his memory, John Reynolds had great sympathy for this young man whose money was exhausted and offered him room for his desk in the Reynolds office on Water Street. Sam Mifflin gratefully accepted this offer and moved in, bringing with him a small haircloth trunk which contained papers, books, etc. It was generally understood that Sam had come west in the interests of an eastern land company.

As the days passed, young Mifflin's illness grew worse rapidly, and it was only a short time after his arrival in Meadville that his death occurred. Thus, far from home, alone, Samuel Mifflin died, a young man in his twenties who had seen much sorrow before coming to this part of the country. It is very probable that he was laid to rest in the old Grave Yard on Randolph Street, but that is not certain because some of the graves there were unmarked and no records of burials were kept. Then, too, most of those graves were removed by 1874 or 1875, and, later, the property sold.

John Reynolds probably knew more about young Sam Mifflin than anyone in the village, and that was not much. However, after his death, John Reynolds had his few possessions, papers, etc., packed in the little haircloth trunk to await claiming by relatives or friends. The trunk was placed in the loft over the Reynolds office. Years afterward, when the office building was to be remodeled for a dwelling house, the trunk was put in the barn, which stood near the east bank of French Creek.

The old haircloth trunk was forgotten and remained in the barn until the early 1870's when the property was sold. It was then that William Reynolds, son of John Reynolds, remembered it and had it sent up to his residence on The Terrace where, with the assistance of his nephew, T. R. Kennedy, the contents of the little trunk were taken out and sorted. Papers and documents of Thomas Mifflin were found, maps, letters and deeds of Colonel George Croghan, and a general order in the handwriting of General George Washington which mentioned Generals Wadsworth, Green, and Mifflin, Colonel Putnam and Captain Johnson, who were engaged in the defense of New York in the early part of the Revolutionary War. Originally there must have been a second sheet of this order containing the signature, but this was not found. The most important papers were placed in William Reynolds' collection and the others kept in the drawers of a desk in his office at his residence.

For many years after the death of William Reynolds the files in his office were undisturbed. In the summer of 1937 these files were looked over for the purpose of deciding what disposition should be made of them. There were quantities of papers, letters, and records dating from the time of John Reynolds, and to these many more had been added by William Reynolds—interesting deeds, documents, maps, and old account books. In going over the last, one was found on the cover of which was the name of John Mifflin. The old ragged brown paper cover showed signs of hard usage, and on the first page was written in large letters

JOHN MIFFLINS DAY BOOK
June 3   1767

Most of the pages which followed were filled with entries of business transactions and personal accounts covering the period from 1767 to 1787. It was evident from the writing that several persons had made the entries, which covered a miscellaneous assortment of subjects from personal accounts with his tailor and wigmaker, and the lending of money, to supplies for ships, which ran into large amounts for that day. There was also record of the collection of rents from various properties, including his bake house, cooper shop, and dwelling houses. Notations and comments sometimes followed the latter; for instance: "went off with the British his wife stade behind." Elsewhere appeared this item: "15 Nov 1780   Robt Morris cred by cash in part for the green wood now standing on the piece of Land he Bog^t of Mr Hamilton   5000 dollars." In still another place were long, complicated, and very detailed directions for making wine.

Where the accounts stopped, blank pages began, and then—a three-page letter! Not just an ordinary letter, but one bearing the signature of George Washington! The letter obviously never reached the man to whom it was written, Brigadier General Ewing. Why? No one knows. The most painstaking research has not yet been able to answer that question.

314   IN FRENCH CREEK VALLEY

The 161-year-old letter is reproduced on the following pages.

(AUTHOR'S NOTE: A remarkable coincidence occurred only ten days after the Washington letter was discovered, a tale told by a Mifflin County hunter which in some of its details fits with astonishing accuracy into the story just related. It is not authentic enough, however, to explain the presence of the letter in Meadville. The tale does make interesting reading in spite of its many romantic inaccuracies and for that reason alone is included in the Appendix.)

Head Quarters at Keith's December 14th 1776

Dear Sir,
    Lest the enemy should in some degree avail themselves of the knowledge (for I do not doubt but that they are well informed of every thing we do) I did not care to be so particular in the general orders of this day, as I mean to be in this letter to you. —

As much Time then would be lost (in case the enemy should attempt crossing the River at any pass within your guard of it) in first sending you notice, and the Troops to wait for orders what to do, I would advise you to examine the whole River from the upper to the lower guard of your district, and after forming an opinion of the most probable crossing places, have those well watched, and direct the Regiments or Companies most convenient to repair as they can be formed, immediately to the point of attack, and give the enemy all the opposition they possibly can. Every thing in a manner depends upon the defence at the waters edge. In like manner one Brigade is to support another without loss of time, or waiting orders from me. — I would also have you fix upon some central Spot convenient to your Brigade, but in the rear a little, and on some road leading to Philadelphia for your unnecessary Baggage,

Waggons & Stores, that in case your opposition should prove ineffectual, these things may not fall, but be got off & proceed over Neshaminy Ferry, or Bridge, towards Germantown, agreeable to the determination of the Board of Officers this day. — Let me intreat you to cast about to find out some person who can be engaged to cross the River as a Spy, that we may if possible, obtain some knowledge of the Enemy's situation, movements, & intention; particular inquiry to be made by the person sent, if any preparations are making to cross the River, whether any boats are building, & where; Whether any are coming across land from Brunswick? Whether any great collection of Horses are made, & for what purposes. Expence must not be spared in procuring such intelligence, and will readily be paid by me.

We are in a neighbourhood of very disaffected people; equal care should therefore be taken that one of these persons do not undertake the business in order to betray us.———

As your numbers are rather small, endeavour to show them, now & then, to the best advantage. An appearance might be made with those you have, as if fresh troops were coming in and if you stop all intercourse, but such as is

Carried on

carried on to the other side by your own friends.
It will take a little time to discover the deception
and every hour gain'd is of service in our present
situation. —

If possible get some person into Trenton — and
let him be satisfied if any Boats are Building
at that place and on Crosswicks Creek. —

I am with respect Sir,
Y.r most ob.t Serv.t
G. Washington

To
Brigad.r Gen.l Ewing
Trenton Falls.

A PLAN ALL BUT FULFILLED

Destiny's hand guiding the discovery and settlement of North America is discernible also in the events which built the United States into a great nation. Nor is it by chance that many changes have come to French Creek Valley since hardy pioneers braved the wilderness to start the chain of significant events. With increasing rapidity the changes have come, as year succeeded year, on down to the present, affecting the growth of the little Valley as surely as of the whole nation.

The character of Washington on his military mission was the character of those early settlers who brought to the life of French Creek Valley the homely virtues and sterling qualities which were the sure foundation upon which this nation was builded. The men and women who lived in the Valley were no ordinary adventurers—their works show that. Deep spiritual feeling gave them vision and guided their undertakings. Their innate culture sought expression in making beautiful the useful things which they created, striving always for that which was better. As soon as homes were established and while industries were being built to supply their needs, these people made sure that religion and education would continue as paramount forces in their community. In a very short time, too, they turned to science, literature, and the arts for expression of their desires. They lived their beliefs.

Out of the structure which these sturdy people built developed a stability which pervaded the entire Valley. A second generation carried on the traditions of their fathers, welcoming the improved conditions which came with peaceful times. The spiritual quality of their progenitors continued in succeeding generations and developed the institutions begun by their forefathers. Imagination and invention brought better modes of living, commerce and manufacturing grew, and prosperity increased. Fortune has smiled on the wooded hills and fertile lowlands in French Creek Valley.

APPENDIX

THREE OF THE LETTERS WRITTEN BY HENRY BOUQUET TO BRIGADIER GENERAL MONCKTON

CAMP AT THE SECOND CROSSING OF BEAVER[1]
CREEK 9th July Evening 1760.

Sir,

The day the Detachment left Pittsburgh, we encamped about four miles, having followed a wrong Path we marched at least six.

The 8th everything being put in order, we marched six miles without obstruction, but having afterwards six miles and a half of Barren Hills without Water, the Men and Horses suffered much, and several tired.

We encamped at Camp Pleasant, good Ground, and Water, supposed 18 miles from Pittsburgh.

This day we marched about 12 miles to this Camp, through a very hilly, swampy, and Barren ground, great scarcity of Water, several Horses have tired. I have met here Mr. Hutchins, who will give you an account of his Journey. I am sorry Major Gladwyn has so much the start of us, and you may depend that I will lose no time in reaching Presqu' Isle, where (accidents excepted) I hope to be the 16th.

I will not trouble you with all the difficulties attending our march. No Body without exception knows any thing of the Country, or distances, except the Indians, who have been constantly drunken.

The Path is very narrow, full of fallen Trees, and requires many repairs to make it passable.

---

[1] *Massachusetts Historical Society*, Fourth Series, IX, 264-6.

The Pack Horses, having no saddles, and some no saggings their loads are continually tumbling down, and tho' we march from morning to night, halting only at noon, we make very little Way, as we must keep together. . .

The Suttlers have not joined us yet, your orders shall be obeyed, & their Rum lodged in the stores.

       I have the honour to be
        Sir,
         Your most obedient &
          most Humble servant
           HENRY BOUQUET.

Brigadier General MONCKTON.

Paterson informs me that Levy's Horses have almost all given up.

        CAMP AT VENANGO 13th. July 1760.[1]

Sir,

We arrived here late Yesterday, and it was dark when the Rear entered in the Camp. . .

We find this Place at least 80 miles distant from Pittsburgh, and Mr Huchins says that he committed that mistake in his Report in following Evan's Computation, and not his own Judgment. He was 26 hours on Horseback to join us, and as he rode a little better than three miles an hour our Calculation does not differ much. . .

The stockadoe Fort here is burnt to the ground, and the few Huts around it pulled down. No Iron to be seen but a few trifles.

The saw mill is hardly worth repairing. The two saws are gone, and the Dam fallen down. None of our Artificers under-

---

[1] *Massachusetts Historical Society*, Fourth Series, IX, 267-8.

APPENDIX 319

stand saw mills, but they imagine that in a Week's time, it could be repaired so as to have one saw going.

The Allegheny is very shallow here, and scarce navigable for Canoes. Stoddert who left Pittsburgh the 4th is not yet arrived...

We have already left 13 Horses behind, dead, tired, or lost, and two Bags of flour which Col. Mercer brings up; since my last Return, We miss one man of the Virginians, Thos Warner supposed to have lost himself in the Woods the 11th.

We have a few men *really* Sick to carry on horseback. Capt. Croghan goes to day to Custologa's Town with some Presents... I have the honour to be
    Sir,
      Your most obedient and
        Humble servant
General MONCKTON.   HENRY BOUQUET

   CAMP NEAR THE MINGO TOWN ON BEEF RIVER [1]
Sir,   14th July Even^g

.... We marched 104 miles and are yet 39 from Presqu' Isle The Indians have lent us some Horses, without which we would have been obliged to leave loads behind...

We shall want some Locks for the stores, and garden seeds, chiefly Turnips.

Croghan is obliged to stay to morrow at Custologas all the Indians being drunk *with their own Rum;* he can do no Business with them at present. I am
    Sir,
      Your most obed^t Hble ser^t
        H. BOUQUET.

---

[1] *Massachusetts Historical Society*, Fourth Series, IX, 269.

CAPT. CROGHAN'S JOURNAL TO PRESQUE ISLE AND INTELLIGENCE RECEIVED LATELY.

A Journal Commenced at Fort Pitt.[1]

August 1st 1760.

The 7th of July 1760, I set out for Presque Isle in company with Colonel Bouquet and a Number of the Royal American and Virginia Troops to take Post there and send a Detachment to Niagara. I was accompanied by Custologa and several other Indians. Marched this day about five Miles, two Miles of which through a fine Bottom & the other three Miles up a small Run to the head of it, where we encamped on the side of a Hill, where several fine Springs take their rise, which makes the Run we Marched up.

The 8th Decamped early in the morning and Marched six Miles along a fine Ridge well Timbered and good Soil to the partings of the Road that off to the Kuskuske, from thence we Marched seven Miles across several Hills, some of which were Barren to a Run that emptys itself into Beaver Creek and there we Encamped in a Barren Savanna.

The 9th Decamped Early and Marched Seven Miles through Pleasant Woods, well Timbered and good Soil, to a small Draught of Beaver Creek which Runs through barren low ground at the Foot of a steep hill, where we made a halt for three Hours, then Marched four Miles to the first Crossing of Beaver Creek, over some Hills well Timbered and good Soil where we Encamped about 4 o'clock, this Creek abounds with Plenty of Fish.

The 10th Decamped early and Marched through a very Pleasant, level Country, well timbered and Rich Fertile Soil, but ill Watered, to a small draught of the second Crossing of Beaver Creek, where we encamped about Thirteen Miles. This Run passes through very Pleasant Barrens of good Food.

---

[1] *Massachusetts Historical Society*, Fourth Series, IX, 283-5.

The 11th Decamped and Marched to the Second Branch of Beaver Creek two Miles, the Bottom of which is one entire Rock all across, and below the Ford Twenty Yards is a Fall from Rock to Rock about 10 Yards, from thence we Marched through level pleasant Woods Six Miles to a Spring, where we made a Halt, then Marched four Miles to a Run and Encamped.

The 12th Decamped Early and Marched Six Miles through level Woods, then entered amongst a Number of Fallen Trees, blown down by a Hurricane across the Path for Six Miles in length, level Country with Timber and good Soil to Sandy Creek, the going down to which is very steep and long, after crossing the Creek, passed through a fine level Bottom about half a Mile long, then ascended a hill which continued Stony near four Miles where we had a steep descent to Venango. Venango is situate in a large fine Bottom, on the bank of the Ohio, the food all Clover & Wild Timothy, the works are all destroyed except the Saw mill which is standing, but that appears as if it would be attended with as much trouble to repair it as to build a new one.

The 13th I set off before the Troops with Custologa and the Indians to his Town, in Order to Collect the Indians that live near that place to hold a Conference with them, soon after we set out Crossed French Creek a little above the Mouth, and Marched through a pleasant country, of good Land, well Timbered and Watered, Sixteen Miles to Custologa's Town, which is situate near French Creek in a Pleasant Savanna, fine Land all about it, well Timbered and Watered. The Indians with me fired off their Guns, upon which we were immediately saluted from the Town with the Firing of their Guns three several times. In this Town is about 40 Houses, and when all are at home, there is about 120 fighting Men. . .

        GEO. CROGHAN
          Deputy Agent.

The following papers, undoubtedly written by Timothy Alden using the pen name "OLAPH," appeared in successive issues of the *Alleghany Magazine*.

ABORIGINAL NUM. I.

IN ammassing American historical documents,[1] the aboriginal department has, within a few years, obtained a greater share of attention, than at any former period. This, to the no small regret of the antiquary, was much neglected at the time when it was practicable to have ascertained various interesting facts, at present unknown, and to have collected all those philological minutiae, which are now become a matter of difficult investigation....

The American Indians furnished names for their rivers, mountains, plains, vallies, and settlements, which, while they distinguished one from another, had an appropriate descriptive meaning.

A translation of all aboriginal names, were it possible to obtain it, would probably afford a lucid view of the topography of our country, as it existed for ages before the discovery of Columbus.

In subsequent numbers of the Alleghany Magazine, an enlargement on some of the ideas, and an elucidation of some others, suggested in this introductory paper, may be expected,

OLAPH.

NUM. III.

... *Ohio*,[2] as universally pronounced, affords another instance of similar corruption. If it were written *Ho—hee-yu*, and the drawling accent placed on the middle syllable, a tolerable idea

---

[1] Alden, *Alleghany Magazine* (Meadville, 1816-17), 18-19.
[2] Alden, *Alleghany*, 71.

would be formed of the aboriginal method of pronouncing it. This name, in a different dialect, appears to have the same appropriate import with Wauh-hauh-pee-yuh, (*beautiful water.*) . . .

OLAPH.

NUM. VI.

Alleghany[1] is the name, in the language of the Delaware Indians, given to one of those nearly parallel mountainous ridges, which stretch through our southern and middle states. The late Benjamin Smith Barton, M. D. who had a more extensive general knowledge of the numerous aboriginal dialects of this continent, than any other person has ever attained, informed the writer, not long before his death, that this word signifies *the great war path*. This sublime rampart of nature, reaching to the clouds, was, as may be supposed, like the wall of China to the inhabitants of that empire in reference to the Tartar hordes, an important barrier between the warlike natives of the atlantick and those of the western region. . .

Alleghany is the name, which has likewise been applied, by the people of the United States, to one of our navigable rivers, probably, in consequence of some of its contributory streams taking their rise in the Alleghany mountains. This noble river, decending from the north east, cutting its channel through lofty mountains, forms a confluence with the Monongahela at the city of Pittsburgh. The junction of these is now considered as the commencement of the Ohio. Though we retain this corruption of the aboriginal name, for an extent of eleven hundred miles; yet our Ohio is several hundred miles less, than the Ho-He-Yu, or Oh-he-yu, of our tawny predecessors. The fact is, the Alleghany river, now so called, was always known

---

[1] Alden, *Alleghany*, 146-148.

by the name of Hoheyu, in ancient times, and the Senecas are still tenacious of this appellation. It is a *handsome* or *beautiful river*, according to the original import, as well as the modern Ohio. If any one were to ask a Seneca the length of the Ohio, or rather Hoheyu, his calculation would be made from its entrance into the Mississippi, at least, to Olean. . . .

OLAPH.

NUM. VII.

EIGHT miles,[1] in a southwesterly direction, from Meadville, is a beautiful lake, somewhat of an oval form, three or four miles in length and perhaps over one in breadth. The orthography of its name seems to be unsettled, as it is written variously. It is commonly pronounced, as if spelled, *Con-ne-ot*, with a slight accent on the last syllable, but the principal on the first. The intermediate syllable is short, according to invariable usage; but no one would conjecture the right aboriginal pronunciation of this word, either, from any of the ways, in which it is written, or, from the manner, in which it is, at present, spoken. To convey an idea of its true Seneca pronunciation, it might be expressed in these letters, *Kon-ne-yaut*. The first syllable is to be pronounced distinctly, but is short. The second has the Indian characteristick drawling accent. The last is long and commences with the liquid sound of the letter, *y*. The radix, from which the word is formed, is *ne*, signifying *snow*. The *e*, in this monsyllable, as in Kon-ne-yaut, has that sound, which we find in the English word, *knee*, but is not to be prolonged as in the derivative. The reason for giving this name to the lake is, that, being frozen, the snow was frequently noticed to remain on the ice, a considerable time,

---

[1] Alden, *Alleghany*, 170.

after it had disappeared in its vicinity. It, therefore, means *something about snow*, or, *the snow place*.

Con-ne-aut-te, a name given to a very small lake, some miles northerly from the former, is not the Indian name, but has been derived, by the successors of the aborigines, from Konneyaut, and is used as a diminutive. It is, therefore, the same as *Little Konneyaut*. This anglicised aboriginal word has an accent on the last, the only long syllable in it.

OLAPH.

NUM. VIII.

Cussewago,[1] as the word is usually written, is the name of a navigable creek, of considerable length, in the vicinity of which is an extensive body of excellent land, and which, meandering from the north, empties into the west side of French-creek opposite to the lower, or southwestern corner of Meadville.

Following the pronunciation of the venerable Cornplanter, the writer of this paper, to give a correct idea of the sound of this word, would spell it, in this manner; *Kos-se-waug-ga*. The first two syllables and the last are short; the third is long, and is to be a little protracted.

The aboriginal tradition states, that, when the wandering inhabitants of the wilderness first came to this creek, their curiosity was excited by discovering a large black snake, with a white ring round his neck, in an elevated situation, among the limbs of a tree; but, what most arrested their attention was a wonderful protuberance, which the snake exhibited, as if he had swallowed some animal as large as a rabbit. From this circumstance, they called the creek *Kossewauga*, which, literally interpreted, means *the big belly*.

OLAPH.

---

[1] Alden, *Alleghany*, 194-195.

NUM. VIIII.

... *Venango*[1] is the name, by which, among the settlers of European extract, French Creek has been formerly known. This is the name, which the French gave to their establishment at the mouth of the creek. It is the name of a county, of which Franklin is the seat of justice. It is also the name of a township in the county of Crawford. It is, however, a gross corruption of the aboriginal appellation of French Creek, which perhaps, can scarsely be better expressed in the letters of our alphabet, than in this manner; *In-nun-ga-ch*. The mode of pronouncing this word it is difficult to explain, except viva voce. The two first syllables are short and are to be uttered as spelled; but the *a* of the next is flat, as in the word, *make*, and is to be prolonged, in the Indian characteristick way, with an accent, and an aspirate designated by the German *ch*, and forming a very short syllable, not unlike, in sound, though shorter, to the German pronoun, *ich*. This name was given to the creek, by the Senecas, in consequence of a certain figure, carved on the bark of a tree near its bank, noticed at an early period after they came to this region, and expressive of the representation made by the rude sculpture, but an explanation of which delicacy forbids to record.

OLAPH.

In a manuscript of John Reynolds, "Reminiscences of the Olden Time," there is a delightful description of a turkey hunt.

1753.

Presqu'Isle abounds in game of different kinds, deer, roebuck, venison, bear, swans, bustards, ducks, turkey, herron, red partridges and doves.

The most courious and frequent sport that I had in this

---
[1] Alden, *Alleghany*, 220.

APPENDIX 327

place was turkey hunting. Turkies are as plentiful as they are amusing. This hunt takes place on moonlight nights by at least two or three persons; these birds habitually go in droves always to the heights from where they can take their flight and perhaps in case of surprise; they only come down to the low ground at night to drink. They choose the tops of trees with the most branches on which to perch with as many on each branch as it will support, sometimes as many as 150 will be found in the same tree. When the district they frequent has been discovered the hunters creep as silently and as near as possible to the tree where they are perched, without speaking or scarsely moving one of the hunters will fire his gun bringing down at least four or five turkies. The remainder awake at the noise screech and squak a while, if they hear nothing more they go back to sleep. The same performance is repeated until the hunters decide they have had enough.

If any of the turkies fall and are only wounded and they try to escape the hunters take a chance on loosing them, otherwise those left in the tree would be frightened and more would be lost. At last when they have enough they gather up those that have been killed and carry them to the canoe which has been brought up as near as possible to the hunting place, otherwise, it would be impossible to take many as some of them weigh as much as 35 pounds. It is only by surprising them that these birds can be killed by daylight; if they are surprised and overtaken from the ground where they cannot fly because of their weight and lack of sufficient air they use their feet to climb to the heights where they go so swiftly that a dog can hardly follow them. When they are high enough they take their flight towards the hollows to find more air and fly on their way.

April the 16th we left Toronto in boats and canoes we took the route to the south of Lake Erie said to be 300 leagues long. . . .

Fishing and hunting is plentiful in this lake. There are swans, bustards, ducks, herrons and wild geese.

The woods about it abound with deer, roebuck, bear and turkies. (Turkies originated in the eastern and western parts of America. The first sent to France were served at the wedding of Charles the 9th in 1760.)

A letter in the Reynolds Collection, one written by John Reynolds to L. McKnight, tells of the very early appearance of oil in the Oil Creek region.

Meadville Jany 9 1860

/ L McKnight Esqr
Dr Sir

In reply to yours of 3^d ins^t the discovery of oil is not of recent date, it has been gathered in small quantities on surface springs 8 or 10 barrels during a summer season, the last 60 y^{rs} or coeval with the settlement of the oil creek region limited however to a mile or two on the bottom land near the mouth of the creek. a few years ago attention was directed to ancient diggings near Titusville on an extensive piece of bottom land at the forks of Oil creek, upon examination, it was found that vats had been made of hewed plank over a surface of 15 or 20 acres—5 or 6 feet deep in some of which the plank were still tolerably sound and it was evident the design had been to collect oil, with which the earth appeared saturated, these digg^s probably the work of the French when in poss-&c an Eastern Comp (in con^t) took a lease of this location and commenced operations, by boring, and after passing through strata of gravel & rock 69 feet, they struck a vein of oil, from which they have been pumping by steam power from 12 to 15 bar-

APPENDIX 329

rels per day during the last 4 or 5 months, the excitement produced by this success, hurried men into insane speculations and hundreds of claims (so called) have been sold or leased embracing the whole valley from the said forks to the mouth of the creek, a number of borings have been commenced, and two or three have been reported successful, near the mouth, on or near the site of the surface springs where they had previously gathered the oil. about 18 or 20 miles is the distance from Titusville to the mouth. the creek runs in a deep ravine, the hill on each side abrupt & 4 or 500 feet high, the bottom narrow, & shifting from side to side as the current is varied by the direction of the banks, and to this bottom (principally) the attention has been confined.

For the purpose of increasing the population of the Settlement and stimulating its business, the following elaborate advertisement was distributed widely in the East by a Committee of Correspondence.

TO ALL THOSE WHO MAY BE DESIROUS OF EMIGRATING TO THE WESTERN COUNTRY:

A number of the inhabitants of western Pennsylvania, many of them formerly from different parts of Europe, the New England states, the states of New York and New Jersey, and the eastern counties of this state, having taken into consideration the embarrassments and difficulties to which emigrants are too often exposed, for want of proper advice and assistance, have formed themselves into an association, under the name of the *"Western Pennsylvania Emigrant Society."*

The object of the society is to furnish to emigrants all the information and assistance in its power, in procuring employment for them, locating them to the best advantage, according to their different situations, trades, or occupations; in aiding them to make a judicious choice of the lands they may wish to purchase; in procuring these for them on the most advantageous terms;—and in rendering them all such services in establishing themselves, that they may need. Believing that the inducements this country holds out to emigrants, only require to be known, to be duly appreciated, the society have appointed a committee of correspondence, to make you acquainted with this portion of the United States and its advantages, natural and artificial, and to point out a few of the errors into which emigrants, particularly those from Europe, are liable to fall, on their arrival in this country.

The United States of America possess advantages which are not to be found in Europe, nor in any other quarter of the globe. Enjoying an almost total exemption from taxation, the whole earnings of the inhabitants enure to their own use, & every emigrant who settles here, can by industry and economy not only provide amply for the wants and comforts of himself and family, but render himself independent, provided he is careful in the first instance in choosing a proper situation.

It is an error into which emigrants too frequently fall, to settle in the large cities on the coast, or in the thickly settled country in their vicinity, where property is high and competition great, instead of moving directly to the west, where an excess of lands and a less abundant population create a greater demand for labor; and where in the course of a few years industry, he may become the independent proprietor of property sufficient for the wants and comfort of himself and family.

In the western country, not only the labors of the field but those also pertaining to the mechanic arts, are in great demand. The emigrant therefore, immediately on his arrival, should move thither; but in so doing, he should avoid another error into which many have fallen, by moving too far to the south and west down the Ohio and Mississippi and their tributary streams, not only because in that case the length of the journey tends to exhaust too much the means of the emigrant; means which are essential to his welfare in procuring him cattle, implements of husbandry and subsistence for his family, while making his improvements; but because this southern portion of the United States is subject to other and more serious objections. It has but one market and that a very distant one, viz: New Orleans; and which, situated as it is, in a very hot and moist climate, is calculated to destroy almost every description of produce which may be stored there for any length of time; and neither the consumption, the trade, nor the capital of that city, will bear comparison with those of the great commercial emporiums of the middle states. Hence the produce raised to the south-west will always go to a bad market, and the cultivator will never be able to dispose of it to the same advantage as those whose export trade is to Quebec, New York, Philadelphia and Baltimore. But the last objection to a settlement in the south-west part of the United States, is the most formidable. The climate of that country is inimical to men from more northern countries, subjecting them to agues, fevers, and bilious disorders, which, though they do not always prove immediately fatal, yet tend to undermine the constitution and bring on premature old age; and as these seize on the emigrant during the first years of his residence, they deprive him and his family of the power of exerting themselves in the commencement of their settlement, when all their efforts are needed to clear their farm and provide for their support—Hence many are plunged into a state of poverty and want, from which it requires years to recover.

The principal requisites for which the emigrant should look, in determining the place of his future residence, are a healthy climate, good water, a large extent of fertile land, not too thickly settled, and a good market. Now, an experience of more than twenty-five years enables us to assert with confidence, that no portion of the United States possesses these advantages in a higher degree than the western parts of Penn'a. The counties of Crawford, Mercer, Erie, Venango and Warren, bounded on the north by New York and Lake Erie, on the west by Ohio, and having the beautiful Allegheny river on the east, contain a body of uninterrupted good land, equalled by few, and perhaps surpassed by no district of the same extent, in the United States. Situated between the 41st and 42d degree of north latitude, the climate is delightful and perfectly healthy. It requires no seasoning to habituate the emigrant to it; and those agues and fevers and other bilious disorders to which the southern and even some of the more northern settlements have always been subject, have been totally unknown since the first settlement of this country. This country too, is better watered than any part of the United States we are acquainted with. Besides the Allegheny, the French creek, the Shenango and their tributaries, the small rivulets, and springs are so numerous that few farms of one hundred acres can be found which are not provided with a spring or rivulet of the best and most wholesome water during the whole year. The emigrant can here cultivate, with success, those fruits, grains and grasses to which he has been accustomed in his own county, while the climate is warm enough to bring to perfection many productions to which that of Europe is not congenial—such as the Indian corn, the peach in open-field culture, melons, apples, pumpkins, &c. of the finest kinds, and in the greatest abundance. As a grazing country for raising cattle, this portion of Pennsylvania is perhaps unrivalled in the world.

Our local advantages are also great. By means of our connection with Lake Erie, we have an easy water communication with the vast extent of country on the upper lakes, and with

APPENDIX 333

the Montreal, Quebec and New-York markets. Our communication with this last city has been immensely facilitated by the completion of the great western canal, which has now for upwards of two years been in successful operation throughout its whole extent. We are enabled by means of it to carry the most bulky of our products to an advantageous market, at a cheap and easy rate. To the east we are connected with the cities of Philadelphia and Baltimore, by excellent turnpike roads, and to the south, we have an easy water communication with Pittsburg, N. Orleans & the intermediate cities, by the French creek and the Allegheny, Ohio and Mississippi rivers. The grand Pennsylvania canal which is intended to unite the waters of the Delaware and the Susquehanna with the Ohio and Lake Erie, is now vigorously progressing, both on the eastern and western side of the Allegheny. That part of the line which passes through this country, has been placed under contract. Already has the ground been broken, and the work commenced. There now is and will continue to be an immediate demand for laborers of every description, who will meet with constant employment and liberal wages.

The government of the United States have it also in contemplation to unite the Chesapeake and Potomac with the Ohio at Pittsburg—When these great works shall be completed which there is every reason to believe they will be at no distant day, this section of country will stand upon enviable ground. Situated in the centre of trade and navigation, we can carry our produce to the east, or to the west, to the north, or to the south, according to the fluctuations of the market, while at the same time we can procure the articles we need, whether for comfort or luxury, in the shortest time and at the most reasonable prices.

Nor will the emigrant here find himself transplanted to a dreary wilderness secluded from intercourse with mankind.

Already are these five counties inhabited by a population of from fifty to sixty thousand souls.—Many flourishing villages, such as Erie, Meadville, Mercer, Franklin, Waterford and Warren, have been founded; roads of communication through every part of the country have been opened; churches for the different denominations of christians have been built; schools organized for the instruction of youth: in short he will find every thing requisite to supply the real wants, or that can minister to the real comforts of civilized life.

With all these advantages unimproved land of the best quality can yet be had at very moderate prices, say at from two to four dollars per acre, & on such a liberal credit, that an industrious man can pay for his land by the produce of it, while to the person whose means enable him to pay cash, a generous deduction is made for prompt payment.

Such are the inducements, which this country presents to emigrants in general. To Irishmen it holds out an additional one, which must be dear to them on their arrival in a strange land. This country is already in part settled by emigrants from Ireland, and the Irishman on his arrival here, will find countrymen from every county of his native land, who with their characteristic hospitality, stand ready to welcome him, and to use their best endeavours to promote his views and secure his interests, in this happy country.

To emigrants from other parts of Europe and the different sections of the United States, it may be remarked, that they too will meet friends and acquaintances, who will not be behind hand in the offices of kindness and hospitality. The Germans in particular, are informed that there is a large and respectable body of their countrymen already settled in this county, which is receiving almost daily accessions.

To those who intend emigrating to the western country, this is the most favorable time. The projected improvements have given a spur to the industry and enterprise of the inhabitants—

APPENDIX

and the money they will distribute among us, will furnish a brisk circulating medium, and add considerably to the wealth of the country. With these additions to the manifold advantages this country already possesses, it *must flourish*. Those who come first will have it most in their power to profit by the opportunities it offers.

It now only remains to point out the most eligible routes for reaching this country. By the way of Quebec, the route is as follows:

From Quebec to Montreal,	190 *miles*.
Montreal to Lachine,	15
Lachine to Prescot,	150
Prescot to Fort George,	300
Fort George to Buffalo,	35
Buffalo to Erie,	80
Erie to Meadville,	37

The whole of the above route is by water carriage, except about 40 miles.

By the way of New York.

From New-York to Albany, by water,	160 *miles*.
Albany to Buffalo by canal,	300
Buffalo to Erie by water,	80
Erie to Meadville by Turnpike,	37

By the way of Philadelphia.

From Philadelphia to Meadville by the way of Bellefonte, is about 350 miles by land, by a good turnpike road.

Emigrants on their arrival will apply to John Brooks, Esquire, one of the judges of the court of common pleas—formerly from the county of Donegal, in Ireland, and president of the society, or to any of the persons referred to below.

JOHN BROOKS,
ROBERT L. POTTER,
DAVID DERICKSON,
J. STUART RIDDLE,
} *Committee of correspondence.*

Meadville, Crawford county, Aug. 31, 1827.

REFERENCE.

J. B. Wallace, Esq. from Burlington, N. J.
William Wikoff, "
Hon. Henry Shippen, " Lancaster, Pa.
Andrew Wilson, " Bucks co. Pa.
C. Meredith, Esq. " Doylestown, "
Dr. A. N. M'Dowell, " Franklin co. "
J. Stuart Riddle, Esq. " " "
J. N. Conrod, from Northumberland Co. "
David Derickson, Esq. " "
Thos. Atkinson, Esq. Dauphin " "
Daniel Saeger, Esq. Lehigh county, "
Christian Blystone, " " "
Daniel Shryock, Franklin " "
Frederick Brown, Berks, " "
Jacob Shantz, Lancaster " "
James Hamilton, Esq. Lycoming co. "
William Foster, Esq. Chester co, "
John Lupher, Cumberland " "
H. J. Huidekoper, esq. Amsterdam, Hol'd.

Harris' *Business Directory of Pittsburgh and Environs*, published in 1837, included a description of Meadville.

Meadville, Pa.
The Capital of Crawford County.

Meadville is situated on one of the principal tributaries of the Allegheny, on a stream called by the aboriginees Venango River, but now known by the name of French Creek, latitude 41 31, thirty-seven miles south from the town of Erie, 99 miles north from Pittsburgh, and 25 miles from the confluence of the Venango and Allegheny Rivers; and is surrounded with a beautiful and fertile agricultural country, Pittsburgh and

APPENDIX

many of the towns below, are supplied from Meadville with the principal part of the cherry, poplar, ash and oak sawed lumber consumed by them; and also considerable pine lumber generally descends the Venango, in arks or flat boats of about 40 tons. There is at present slack water navigation, and canal from Allegheny as high as Meadville, which will doubtless be extended to Erie in the course of three or four years.

Meadville and its environs contains about 1700 inhabitants, 11 stores, 6 blacksmith shops, 1 edge tool manufactory, 3 hat factories, 2 grist mills, 2 carding and fulling mills, 3 paper mills, 1 oil mill, 1 furnace and plough manufactory, 4 furniture manufactories, 6 boot and shoe manufactories, 2 wagon and coach manufactories, 1 chair manufactory, 1 tin plate manufactory, 2 saddle and harness manufactories, 4 tanneries, 3 drug stores, 5 tailor shops, 3 printing offices, 1 book store, 7 hotels.

The principal public edifices are:

One Presbyterian church, 1 Cumberland Presbyterian, 1 Episcopal, 1 Methodist, 1 Baptist, 1 Congregational, erected at the expense of about $19,000.

One courthouse, 1 academy.

Allegheny College, now in a flourishing condition, number generally from 110 to 140 students. Rev. Dr. Rutter, president; Rev. Homer J. Clarke, A.M.; Rev. Wm. M. Burton, Rev. Matthew Simpson, A.M.; Rev. George W. Clarke, Preparatory Department.

Seminary for ladies, under the superintendence of Mrs. G. Purson and Mrs. Jenkins.

One postoffice—Daniel Andrews, postmaster.

Manufacturers—Wm. Magaw, W. A. V. Magaw, Silas Townsend.

Merchants—J. & D. Dick, J. M. McFarland & Co., Hastings & Smith, Douglass & Herr, Shryock & Boileau, Gill & Derickson, E. Betts, Andrew Smith, J. Shattuck, Reynolds & Kennedy.

338   IN FRENCH CREEK VALLEY

The *Crawford Democrat* of December 1, 1863, gave a glowing account of the celebration arranged by jubilant Meadville citizens upon the completion of the Railway.

AN OVATION BY THE CITIZENS OF MEADVILLE TO THE ATLANTIC AND GREAT WESTERN RAILWAY COMPANY.

. . . On Saturday evening some two hundred of our citizens repaired to the McHenry House to close the week, principally devoted as a tribute to the Railway, by a dinner. At eight o'clock the doors of the dining hall were thrown open and the guests permitted to enter and take their seats. We will not attempt a description of the brilliancy of that immense hall, not of the taste and order indicated in all things. Had Taylor's skill and genius been called into service in making provision for a royal banquet, he could not have done himself more credit than he did in getting up the "Citizen's Dinner." We append the following as some "extracts" of the

BILL OF FARE.

Soup.—Oyster, St. Julien.

FISH.

Cold Dishes.—Ham, Tongue, Roast Chicken, Pressed Corned Beef.

Boiled.—Leg of Mutton,—Caper Sauce, Turkey, Oyster Sauce, Chicken and Pork, Parsley Sauce, Ham, Tongue.

Game.—Venison, with Jelly, Pheasants,[1] Larded, Roast Quail, stuffed with Oysters, Mallard Duck, Game Sauce, Wild Turkey, Cranberry Jelly, Fricasseed Squirrel.

Entrees.—Small Oyster Pattie, Chicken Salad, Pinions of Turkey, Larded, Parsley Sauce, Beef a la mode, Wine Sauce, Tenderloin Pork, Smothered, Apple Sauce.

---

[1] Grouse.

Roasts.—Ribs of Beef, Brown Sauce, Spareribs of Pork, Apple Sauce, Fillet of Veal, Turkey, Cranberry Sauce, Chicken, Giblet Sauce.

Relishes.—Cold Slaw, Worcestershire Sauce, Cranberry Sauce, Mixed Pickles, Pickled Beets, Sardines with Lemon, Spanish Olives, Chaw Chaw, Celery.

Vegetables.—Boiled and Mashed Potatoes, Mashed Turnips, Stewed Tomatoes, Boiled Onions.

Pastry.—Boiled English Plum Pudding, Brandy Sauce, Baked Tapioca Pudding, Butter Sauce, Apple Pie, Mince Pie, Cranberry Tarts.

Desert.—Wine Jelly, Whips in Glasses, Jelly Cake, Vanilla Ice Cream, Apples, Almonds, Layer Raisins, Kelly Island Grapes, Delicate Cakes.

TEA — COFFEE.

A HUNTER'S TALE

The following story came out of the Mifflin County hills shortly after the discovery of the Washington letter which is included in Chapter XXVII. The tale contains many obvious inaccuracies, and the author has not been able to find verification for any of its details. It is given here solely as an amazing coincidence.

Harold Nageotte of Crawford County, while talking of his hunting experiences in Mifflin County, Pennsylvania, told the author's brother-in-law the story of a lost letter. Nageotte knew nothing of the discovery of the Washington letter, yet the events in the tale he told fitted with astonishing accuracy into what was already known of the lost letter.

In New Lancaster Valley, some miles from Milroy, there lived in a lonely shack at the end of the road an old recluse known by the name of George Grimble, or the Hermit. He seldom spoke of his past, and few knew his real name or why he had come to this remote valley. A rare mention of Philadelphia only accented the mystery surrounding him and piqued the curiosity of his few acquaintances. Hunters who stopped at his door to rest were sometimes offered good wine of his own making. In 1933, the year before the Hermit disappeared, a party of hunters was passing his cabin, and on learning that one of them, Nageotte, lived near Meadville, the old man remarked that Meadville reminded him of a story which he might tell—sometime. On the next hunting trip, Nageotte, who was curious and liked a good story, left his companions to go up the mountain and rest at the shack—with the hope of hearing the tale. He was not disappointed, and this is the story he heard.

Eight miles up the Delaware River from Philadelphia, in colonial times, Keith's Tavern was well known, as was its owner and landlord, George Keith. He often had business with his friend John Mifflin, of Philadelphia. The 14th of December, 1776, was a cold, damp day, but that did not keep John Mifflin from riding up to Keith's Tavern on horseback to check over accounts with the landlord. To refresh his memory, John took his Day Book with him. The business was amicably disposed of, and George set out some mellow wine for his friend. John consumed quite a liberal amount of wine to fortify himself against the cold ride back to Philadelphia—and this might have accounted for the fact that when he departed he forgot his Day Book and left it at the Tavern.

Early that same evening another friend of the host arrived at the Tavern, General George Washington, who brought with him Captain Hansen and an aid. At this vital time in the American Revolution, when the British were driving the Continental Army before them with Philadelphia as their objective, and the famous Crossing of the Delaware was only a plan, Washington was sorely in need of information concerning the enemy. He came to the Tavern to write a letter to General James Ewing. Writing paper in that day was not plentiful, and while searching for some, William Keith, who kept his brother George's books, remembered the book which John Mifflin had left behind. Using the blank pages at the back of this book, William wrote what Washington dictated. The letter finished, it was arranged that when daylight came an old negro who worked for George Keith should tear out the pages on which the letter had been written and go on foot to take them to General Ewing at Trenton Falls. Washington knew that the negro could be trusted because the old man had been freed by him for a boyhood service.

Having written his letter, so the story goes, Washington left immediately to join his troops, counting on his friends to carry out his plan. But as sometimes happens, plans went awry. As daylight was breaking on December 15, a platoon of British soldiers raided the Tavern. As they believed George Keith to be a spy, they took him prisoner and burned the Tavern and its contents. In the excitement, George Keith's wife, his brother William, and the old negro made their escape. There was only time to snatch up a few clothes, but Mrs. Keith gathered up also a tablecloth which was one of her prize possessions. In her agitation, however, she did not realize that within the folds of the cloth she also had Washington's letter in the Day Book which John Mifflin had left at the Tavern the afternoon before. The three who escaped made their way to Philadelphia, and there Mrs. Keith found shelter at the house of her cousin, a man named Cutchall.

It was at this time, the old Hermit went on to say, that

Cutchall, a carpenter by trade, finished the work he had contracted to do on a wharf for John Mifflin. When he went to John to collect for his labor, John refused to settle with him because his Day Book had disappeared. Cutchall had a temper, and a fiery dispute followed. It was by mere chance that more than a year later Cutchall found John Mifflin's Day Book in his own house! Then, armed with the book, and with blood in his eye, he went back to collect his money long overdue, and incidentally to restore the Day Book to its rightful owner.

One of the rich men of Philadelphia, John Mifflin had reason to be relieved at having his Day Book in his possession once again. During the years of the War he had sold supplies to both the Continental and the British armies; and it was currently rumored that he and Benedict Arnold had had friendly negotiations. This Day Book was supposed to contain notations of these transactions. John also had sold supplies to his brother Thomas, the trusted friend of Washington. As Arnold was also Thomas Mifflin's friend, it was not surprising that rumor connected both John and Thomas with the Arnold scandal. Benjamin Franklin, according to the narrator of this tale, was the man who finally cleared Thomas Mifflin of any connection with the scandal.

During the time that the British were in the Philadelphia area, John Mifflin lost the larger part of his business and most of his fortune. It was not until the War was over that he went to live with his brother Thomas and continued to carry on his business in a small way. Where John went, his account books went also; he never gave up trying to collect money due him!

Thomas Mifflin's only son Samuel, the old Hermit continued, was born outside of Philadelphia at the time when rumor was rife concerning the Mifflins and Arnold. As he was the favorite child of his father, every precaution was taken to shield Sam from scandalous report. After the death of his father in 1800, Sam went to live in Philadelphia, and there he met Miss Betty Gooch and fell deeply in love with the beautiful girl. Returning to the Gooch home from church one Sunday evening, the lovers were met in the hall by Betty's father, in whose heart there was no kindly feeling for the son of a Mifflin. This he made clear as, leaning on his cane, he shook his fist in Sam's face and said, "No traitor's son can enter my home!" Knowing nothing of the still current gossip, Sam, of course, did not understand what Betty's father meant. Poor Betty, being a very loyal daughter, was forced to tell Sam of the stories about his family and the notations of the Arnold transactions supposed to be in his Uncle John's books. Amazed at the revelation, Sam vowed never to darken the Gooch doorway again until his family name had been cleared. Betty, as much in love as Sam, knew that this scandal could make no difference in her feeling toward him and declared she would wait for him.

Sam Mifflin, having heard that a man named Bart Cole, who had worked for John Mifflin years before, had gone to live in the Dutch settlement at Albany, New York, sent him a letter. Many months passed; then finally an answer came. It told him to come to Albany where he could make money as a lawyer. The letter also told him that a man by the name of M'Gill who had been with John Mifflin at the time of his dealings with Arnold, was living in the vicinity of Meadville, Pennsylvania, and that Sam should see M'Gill and get the truth from him. Albany was north and Meadville was west, and long journeys were hazardous. Sam, nevertheless, determined to clear his family name of all scandal, collected all of John Mifflin's books and papers which he could find and started west. He had learned that it was possible to go north from Meadville to Lake Erie, and from there to follow a road to Albany. Leaving Philadelphia by coach, Sam started his difficult journey over the rough mountain road, finally riding most of the distance in a wagon. Arriving at last in Pittsburgh, he had little money left for the passage up the Allegheny River to Meadville.

And here the Hermit's tale to Harold Nageotte ended. The reader should take it for what it is worth—no more.

BIBLIOGRAPHY

BOOKS, PAMPHLETS, PERIODICALS, AND DOCUMENTS

Timothy Alden—The Alleghany Magazine, or Repository of Useful Knowledge. From the Press of Thomas Atkinson, Meadville, Pennsylvania, 1816.

Samuel P. Bates—History of Crawford County. Chicago, Illinois, 1885.

John Romeyn Broadhead—Documents Relating to the Colonial History of the State of New York. (Volume VI) Albany, New York, 1855.

DeWitt Clinton—Discourse delivered before the New York Historical Society at their Anniversary Meeting 6th December, 1811, by the Honorable DeWitt Clinton, one of the Vice Presidents of the Society. New York, 1812.

Ebenezer Denny—Memoirs of the Historical Society of Pennsylvania—A Military Journal kept by Major Ebenezer Denny, 1781 to 1795. (Volume VII) Philadelphia, Pennsylvania, 1860.

William H. Egle—History of Pennsylvania. Harrisburg, Pennsylvania, 1796.

Paul Demund Evans—The Holland Land Company. Buffalo, New York, 1924.

C. B. Galbreath—Expedition of Celoron to the Ohio Country in 1749. Columbus, Ohio, 1921.

Don Marshall Larrabee—The Journals of George Washington and his Guide, Christopher Gist, on the Mission to the French at Fort LeBoeuf in 1753. Including Excerpts from the Writings of Historians and Statesmen as to the Importance of the Mission, its Results and Effect on the World's History.

Edited and Compiled by Don Marshall Larrabee, of the Williamsport Bar, 1929.

John B. Linn and William H. Egle, Editors—Pennsylvania Archives, Second Series, Volume IV. Harrisburg, Pennsylvania, 1890.

Catharine Van Cortlandt Mathews—Andrew Ellicott, His Life and Letters. New York, New York, 1908.

Andrew White McCollough—An Address: Historic and Reminiscent. Greenville, Pennsylvania, 1905.

Captain A. McGill—The McGills. St. Paul, Minnesota, 1910.

T. L. Montgomery, Editor—Pennsylvania Archives, Sixth Series, Volume V. Harrisburg, Pennsylvania, 1907.

William Reynolds—Fifty Years of the Bench and Bar of Crawford County. Meadville, Pennsylvania, 1904.

Charles T. Rogers—American Superiority at the World's Fair. (Report of Commissioner) Philadelphia, Pennsylvania, 1852.

Ernest A. Smith—Allegheny, a Century of Education. Meadville, Pennsylvania, 1916.

Albert T. Volwiler—George Croghan and the Westward Movement, 1741-1782. Cleveland, Ohio, 1926.

MANUSCRIPTS

*In the John John E. Reynolds Collection,
Meadville, Pennsylvania.*

J. B. C. (Probably by M. Bonnefons, who served under Captain Pouchot)—Voyage to Canada.

George Croghan, Papers.
Alfred Huidekoper—Holland Land Company. 1876.
John Reynolds—A letter to L. McKnight, January 9, 1860.
William Reynolds—Pits and Mounds.
        Early History of the Petroleum Industry. 1905.
        The Old Town. 1906.
        Reminiscences of Early Citizens. 1900.
        Public Enterprises of Early Citizens.
        Home Life—Lifetime Memories.
        Water Street and the Residents of Olden Times. 1907.
        Deed for Pew. 1826.
        David Dick, Papers.
        Reminiscences of the Old Canal. 1904.
        Atlantic and Great Western Railway, Papers.
        Diary.
        My Connection with the Atlantic and Great Western Railway, 1851-1864.
        Scrap Book.

Others

Thomas Mifflin—To William Irvine and Andrew Ellicott, April, 1793. Irvine Papers. In the Library of the Historical Society of Pennsylvania, Philadelphia.

Newspapers

The Crawford Democrat—Meadville, Pennsylvania.
The Crawford Weekly Messenger—Published at Meadville, 1805-1831.
The Crawford Journal—Meadville, Pennsylvania.
    All the above papers are in the files of the Meadville Public Library, Art and Historical Association.

The Daily Tribune-Republican—Meadville, Pennsylvania. Centennial Edition, May 12, 1888.

Meadville Daily Republican, June and July, 1867—Reminiscences of the Olden Times, by John Reynolds, Esq. In the files of the Tribune-Republican, Meadville, Pennsylvania.

The New York Tribune—New York, clipping, January 19, 1864.

Pittsburgh Gazette—quoted in the Crawford Messenger, June 3, 1830.

Venango Democrat—quoted in the Crawford Messenger, May 6, 1830.

A clipping quoting Harris' Business Directory of Pittsburgh and Environs, 1837.

INDEX

Adams, James, 101.
Adrain, Robert, 136, 180
Advertisements, 97-102.
Afton, Owen, 229.
Alden, Robert, 239.
Alden, Roger, agent for Holland Land Co., 108-112; 118; mills, 120; member American Antiquarian Society, 125; North Western Bank director, 126; Bible Society director, 132; cousin of Timothy, 140; 144, 189, 267.
Alden, Timothy, member of American Antiquarian Society, 125; Bible Society director, 132; arrives in Meadville, 139; biography, 139-141; founder of Allegheny College, 144-146; leaves for east, 147; publishes *Alleghany Magazine*, 156-166; date of death, 166; address on "Enterprise," 279.
Alden, Timothy J. Fox, 239
Aldenia, 142.
Alden's Mills, 120.
Alleghany Magazine, 156-166; quotations: 133, 157, 158, 159, 160, 244, Appendix.
Allegheny College, founding, 144-146; first commencement, 153; contract with David Dick, 252.
"Allegheny" Steamboat, 286.
Allen, D., letter, 298.
Allen, Hugh, 229.
American Antiquarian Society, members of, 125; 143.
Anderson, William, 234.
Andrews, Joseph, 96.
"Ann Eliza," 94, 95.
Anti-Friction Press, 253-260.
Arsenal, 216.
Atkinson, Thomas, 122, 126, 144, 267.
Atlantic & Great Western Railway, 299, 304.
Audubon, John James, 97.

Baldwin, Henry, Jr., 173.
Baldwin, Jesse, 218.
Bank, North Western of Pennsylvania, 126-128; of Pittsburgh, 128.
Barlow, Stephen, 149.
Barton House Tavern, 182.
Barton, Livi, 136, 182.
Bemus, Daniel, 132, 173.
Benedict's School, Miss, 149, 179.
Bennett, John, 172.
Bentley Hall, 147-153.

Bentley, William, 141, 143, 147.
Betts, Ebenezer, 99, 176, 267, 273.
Betts, Eliphalet, 126, 176.
Bible Society, 132.
Birth, John, 103, 153.
Blanchard, Mr., 285.
Bliss, John, 205.
Block House, 38, 40, 171.
Boats, "Ann Eliza," 94, 95; Patch's keelboat trip, 119; "Enterprise," "William Lehman," 278; 281; first sternwheeler, 285.
Bonaparte, Joseph, 196.
Boquet, Colonel, 55.
Bosler, Henry C., 177.
Brawley, Hugh, 149.
Brendle, W., 122.
Brick Church, The, 237.
Bridges, 96.
Brooks, John, 102, 118, 126, 144, 267, 273.
Brotherton, James, 265.
Brown, John G., 267.
Buchanan, Alexander, 118.
Buchanan, James, 136, 207.
Burr, Aaron, 225.

Canals, 271-284.
Carver, John, 118.
Cazenove, Theophile, 104, 108.
Celoron, Bienville de, 20.
Chappotin, Sebastian, 136, 203.
Charles II, 91.
Chase, Amos, 239.
Church, Gaylord, 205, 299.
Churches, Brick, 238; M. E., 240; Lutheran, 240; Congregational, 241; Christ Protestant Episcopal, 241; Baptist, 242.
Clark, Conner, 173.
Clark, John, 136.
Clark, Samuel, 126.
Clark(e), William, 118, 126, 144, 216, 267.
Cochran, James, 273
Coffen, Stephen, 22.
Colson, Augustus, 177, 200.
Colson, Charles William, 164, 240.
Colt, Jabez, 228.
Colt, Judah, 265.
Compton, David, 118, 129, 299.
Compton, Mrs. Elizabeth, 134.
Connelly, William, 81, 127.
Contrecour, General, 27, 209.
Cornplanter, 61, 213, 292.
Cotton, Hugh, 132, 236.
Cotton, Mrs. Margaret, 134.
Cotton, Mrs. Mary, 135.
Couer, Jean, 7, 8.

INDEX

Courtney, Bailey, 182.
Crawford County, 1848 map, 2; No. of Inhabitants in 1810, 96; Sabbath School Union, 131.
Crawford Democrat, 206, 283, 304, 308.
Crawford House (tavern), 220.
Crawford Weekly Messenger, first issue, 122; quotations from: 97, 100-102, 121-125, 129, 135, 142, 144, 145, 147, 154, 156, 159, 185, 188, 191, 201, 203, 213, 214, 215, 227, 228, 229, 230, 236, 262, 264, 266, 274, 277, 286, 289, 291, 293, 294, 296.
Croghan, George, 195.
Crossed Keyes Tavern, 175.
Cullum, Arthur, 178, 273.
Cullum, Horace, 299.
Cummings, Mrs. Sarah, 135.
Cummings, T. T., 267.
Cunningham, C., 185.
Currin, Barnaby, 14.
Cussewago Rifles, 219.

Davis, Mrs. Elizabeth, 135.
Davis, George, 132, 237.
Davis, John, 118.
Davis, Patrick, 118, 182.
Davis, Robert, 188.
Davis, Samuel, 189.
Davis, William (H.), 71, 229, 299.
Denny, Ebenezer, 56.
Derickson, David, 137, 239.
Derickson, Samuel, 273.
Dick, David, 136, 137, 251-260 (biography); 273, 286, 294.
Dick, John, 144, 177, 205, 216, 260, 281, 299.
Dick, William, 117, 168, 176, 236
Dick, Wilson, 136.
Dickson, James, 144.
Dickson, Joseph, 96.
Dining hall of A. & G. W. Ry., 305.
Doud, Samuel, 222.
Douglas, Joseph, 294.
Dumars Hotel, 206
Duquesne, Fort, 27

Early promotion, 83-90.
Ellicott, Andrew, 58, 61-66 (letters); 262.
"Enterprise" named, 278.
Evans, Paul Demund, footnotes, 104, 108.

Famous visitors, 195-207.
Farm life, 76-82.
Farrelly, David M , 299.
Farrelly, J. W., 204, 212.
Farrelly, Patrick, 126, 144, 171, 216, 226, 267.
Federalists, 225.
Female Cent Society, 133
Finney, D. A , 299.

Finney, Jannet, 118.
Fitz Randolph, James, 40, 91.
Forster, Thomas, 232, 265.
Foster, J., 267.
Foster, William, 144, 201, 273.
Franklin, Fort, 31, 34, 73.
Frazier, John, 8, 26
French Creek, early description of, 3; as La Riviere aux Boeufs, 6; source, 54; 20.
French Creek Feeder, 273-277.
"French Creek Pioneer" launched, 281.

Gehr's Tavern (The Bear), 240.
Gibson, James, 118, 178.
Gibson, John, 211, 273.
Gibson Tavern, 178.
Gill, William, 118
Gist, Christopher, 8, 10, 13.
Goodrich, Brasilla, 181.
Grant, Thomas, 40, 91.
Greenwood Rifles, 222.
Griffith, Judge, 112, 113.
Guilded Lion Tavern, 181.
Gurnfay, David, 102.

Hackney, Joseph, 118, 173, 212, 265.
Hains, Albert, 101.
Hamilton, James, 132, 144.
Hammond, William, 132.
Harrington, James, 118.
Hastings, O , 299
Hatton, Robert C , 240
Haymaker, Frederick, 130, 171.
Herriott, James, 118, 126, 173.
Herron, James E., 265.
Hill, Luke, 130.
Holland Land Company, purchase, 104-106; sale, 112; office, 113.
Home furnishings and life, 184-194.
Hopkins, John Henry, 241.
Huidekoper, Alfred, 68; footnotes, 104, 105; 137, 269.
Huidekoper, Arthur C , 68.
Huidekoper, Frederic, 241
Huidekoper, Harm Jan, 111-113, 144, 182, 193, 241, 267.
Huidekoper, Jan, 195
Hull, Jacob, 151.
Hunt, George, 273
Hurst, Henry, 118, 126, 144, 175, 267.
Hurst Tavern, 135.

Indian Trails, 53, 297.
Indians, 14, 32
Inns (see Taverns)

Jennings, Mr , 148.
Johnson, Wm F., 206.
Johnston, Mrs Eleanor, 134.
Johnston, Robert, 125, 132, 146, 236.

INDEX 351

Joncaire, Captain, 26.
Kennedy, Joseph C G., 122
Kennedy, T R., 68, 96, 118, 173
Ketch, Jack, 226.
King, George, 136
Kirkpatrick, Samuel, 242.

Lafayette, General, 201.
Lane, Harriet, 207.
LeBoeuf, Fort, 10, 15.
Leffingwell, Mr., 148.
Lewis, Enoch, 58.
Liberty Guards, 222
Library, first in Meadville, 130.
Locks, 281.
Long, Captain C, 148.
Lord, Samuel, 144, 148, 150, 153, 168, 215, 234.
Lovitt, Anne, 131.
Luper, John, 240.

Machault, Fort, 26, 28.
Magaw, Samuel, 102, 126, 144, 175, 267.
Magaw, William, 174, 273.
Magaw, William A. V., 175, 202.
Magill, Samuel W., 180.
Marley, Henry, 118, 182
Marlin, Ralph, 144, 265.
Martin, Thomas, 40, 91.
Mattox, J. H., 278
McArthur, William, 118, 144
McCullough, Andrew White, footnote, 196.
McCurdy, Elisha, 235.
McDowell, Thomas, 192.
McFadden, George, 182.
McFarland, John (E), 170, 173, 299.
McHenry House, 307
McHenry, James, 300.
McGill, Arthur and Patrick, 115.
M'Intire, Alexander, 188.
M'Mannany, Steel & Dempsey, 99
Mead, David, founder of Meadville, 32; acquires land title from Penn, 91; plants corn, 93; "first citizen," 97; makes survey, 118, 182; 167, 209, 212, 214, 216; obituary, 244-248
Mead, Mrs Jannet (see Jannet Finney), 134
Mead, John, 91.
Mead, Joseph, 40, 91.
Mead, Mrs. Sarah, 134.
Mead's Settlement, 31.
Meadville, population, 96, 119; early residents, 118; Academy, 120; early enterprises, 115-128; Singing School, 129; Library, 130; Bible Society, 132; Female Cent Society, 135; Thespian Society, 135; first fire engines, 136; *Alleghany Magazine* description of town, 160; incorporated, 167; Water Street, 167-183; Arsenal, 216; Diamond, 222; churches, 238-242; roads, 261; railroads, 299-309.
Meadville Artillery, 222
Meadville Grays, 218.
Meadville Light Dragoons, 220
Meadville Society for the Encouragement of Domestic Manufacturers and the Useful Arts, 83-90.
Meadville Theological School, 241.
Mechling, Philip, 294.
Medal of David Dick, 259.
Merrick, John M, 241.
Mifflin, Sam, 310
Mifflin's Daybook, 313.
Miles, William, 265
Military activities, 208-224
Mill Run, 277
Molthrop, David, 149.
Moore, Jesse, 125, 132, 144
Moore, Samuel, 97.
Morris, William, 109, 127
Morrison, Joseph, 144.
Mounds, and pits, 68-72
Mumford, A W, 299.
Music in Meadville, 129.

Neville, General Presley, 208
North Western Bank, 126, 172.

Oil, 72, 73, 75, 300.
Olean, 293.
Osborne, John M., 269.

Patch, Richard, 118, 119, 135, 273.
Peck, Gad, 112.
Perkins, Daniel, 144.
Perkins, Mrs. Sarah, 135
Pews, sale of church, 238.
Pickett, Anne, 131.
Pits, and mounds, 68-72
Plank roads, 269.
Politics, 225-234.
Pomona Hall, 113, 182
Potter, Robert L, 176, 273, 286
Presque Isle, 24, 58.

Radle, John, 182.
Railroads, 297-309.
Randell, Maxon, 198, footnote.
Randolph, Taylor, 299.
Rasor, Jacob, 118
Reed, Rufus, 174.
Reichard, Henry, 118, 172.
Religious building, 235-243.
Reynolds, John, comes to western Pennsylvania, 42; writes of farm life, 76-82; early settlers, 107; North Western Bank director, 126; receiver, 128; Bible Society director, 132; Lyceum president, 137; secretary of Allegheny College, 144; house,

INDEX

174; 193; political parties, 225; mobilization and politics, 231-234; religious meetings, 242; David Mead, 249; David Dick, 251; road committee member, 267; letter from D. Allen, 297; and Sam Mifflin, 310.
Reynolds, William, brief biography, 69; pits & excavations, 70; oil springs, 74; first oil exported, 75; trades in Meadville, 100; work of John Birth, 103; Sabbath School Union, 131; about P. Farrelly, footnote, 171; Miss Benedict's School, 179; Brasilla Goodrich, 181; his mother, 189; kissed by Lafayette, 203; Cornplanter, 213; road Manager, 269; Old Canal, 283; president of Meadville R. R., 299; writes to McHenry, 300; goes to Europe, 301; connection with A & G. W. Ry., 303; files, 312.
Richmond, A. B, 216.
Richmond, Hiram L., 299
Riddle, John Stuart, 137, 269.
Riviere aux Boeufs, La, 6, 20; "Beef River," 56.
Roads, 53-67, 260-270.
Roberts, Robert R., 240.
Robertson, John, 98.
Rogers, Robert, 195.
Ruter, A. W, 137.

Saegertown Company, 217.
Salamanca, Don Jose de, 301
Schools, Meadville Academy, 120, 121; Allegheny College, 144-146; Miss Benedict's, 179.
Sexton Tavern, 191.
Shattuck, Jared, 112, 170, 273.
Shattuck, W. P, 136.
Shaw, Peter, 132.
Sherwood Hotel, 206
Shryock, Daniel, 130, 180, 273.
Shryock, Jacob, 126.
Shryock, J J., 299
Sign of the Golden Eagle, 172.
Sign of the Stag, 137.
Slackwater navigation, 281.
Smith, Mrs Agnes, 135.
Smith, Andrew, 181.
Smith, Charles, 242.
Smith, J. E, 172, 181
Smith, Wilson, 126.
Snyder, Christopher, 40, 91.
Stewart, Archibald, 136.
Stockton, Joseph, 118, 121, 129, 235.
Stockton, Robert, 132, 236
Survilliers, Count de, 196

Tallyrand, Prince, 195.
Tannehill, Adamson, 231

Taverns (Inns), Sign of the Stag, 137, 178; Reichard's, 172; Traveler's Rest, 172; Sign of the Golden Eagle, 172; Crossed Keyes, 175; Hurst's, 175; White's, 175; Gibson, 177; Sexton, 181; Guilded Lion, 181; Barton House, 182; Crawford House, 220; Gehr's, 240.
Taylor, R. M. N., 307.
Taylor, Zachary, 206.
Temple, Mr., 148.
Terrace, The, 167.
Thespian Society, 135
Thickston, Lewis, 242.
Thomas, Isaiah, 143, 153.
Thorp, William, 269.
Thumb, Tom, 207.
Thurston, David and Deborah, 191.
Titus, Johnathan, 239.
Titusville, 71.
Toasts, 279, 280, 294.
Tollgates, 266.
Torbett, Mrs Catharine, 134.
Torbett, Samuel, 100, 118, 126, 144, 178, 267, 299.
Training Days, 217.
Traveler's Rest, 172.
Turnpikes, 262, 267, 268.
Tyler, Comfort, 229.

Van Horn(e), Cornelius, 40, 91, 93, 209, 211.
Venango, Fort, 26, 29.
Venango Trail, 167.
Village life, 184-194.
Vincent, John, 265.
Volunteers, 209.

Wallace, John B, 113, 241.
Wallace, John C., 265.
War of 1812, 212, 230.
Washington, George, journey to Fort LeBoeuf, 5-16; diary excerpts, 6, 8, 9, 12; advance against Fort Duquesne, 27; letter, 314
Washington Guards, 221.
Water Street, 167-183.
Watson, John, 40, 91.
Western Star Lodge, 150, 164, 178
White, Bartholomew, 175, 225.
White, James, 102, 168.
Wilkins, John, Jr 210
"William B. Duncan," 285.
"Wm Lehman" named, 278
Wilson, Hon. James, 104.
Wilson, William, 73.
Winthrop, James, 143.
Winthrop, William, 153.
Wurtz, ———, 113.

Yates, C. M., 180; Mrs, 207.

www.ingramcontent.com/pod-product-compliance
Lightning Source LLC
Chambersburg PA
CBHW050326230426
43663CB00010B/1753